The Sacred Cause of Union

IOWA AND THE MIDWEST EXPERIENCE

Series editor, William B. Friedricks, Iowa History Center at Simpson College

The Sacred Cause of Union

IOWA IN THE CIVIL WAR

THOMAS R. BAKER

UNIVERSITY OF IOWA PRESS, IOWA CITY

UNIVERSITY OF IOWA PRESS, IOWA CITY 52242

Copyright © 2016 by the University of Iowa Press
www.uiowapress.org
Printed in the United States of America

DESIGN BY TERESA W. WINGFIELD

The University of Iowa Press is a member of Green Press Initiative and is committed to preserving natural resources.

Printed on acid-free paper

LIBRARY OF CONGRESS CATALOGING-IN-PUBLICATION DATA

Names: Baker, Thomas R. (Thomas Robert), 1959– author.
Title: The sacred cause of union : Iowa in the Civil War / Thomas R.
   Baker.
Description: Iowa City : University of Iowa Press, 2016. | Series: Iowa
   and the midwest experience | Includes bibliographical references.
Identifiers: LCCN 2016007489| ISBN 978-1-60938-435-7 (pbk) |
   ISBN 978-1-60938-436-4 (ebk)
Subjects: LCSH: Iowa—History—Civil War, 1861–1865. | Iowa—Politics
   and government—19th century. | United States—History—Civil War,
   1861–1865.
Classification: LCC E507 .B35 2016 | DDC 977.7/02—dc23
LC record available at https://lccn.loc.gov/2016007489

CONTENTS

The Sacred Cause of Union

Introduction

A Civil War history of Iowa is long overdue. A comprehensive analysis has never been published despite the state's prominent role in the conflict. A series of journal articles has covered topics in Iowa's Civil War history, but no researcher has attempted to weave together these threads of information. Nor have researchers fully explored the reams of documents and data produced by nineteenth-century administrators. In synthesizing the material contained in the scattered sources, new technology, particularly the internet, facilitates a fresh analysis of the economic, political, military, and demographic data in provocative ways. Culturally oriented research is relatively new, and the many American history books published over the last twenty-five years reveal a multitude of unresolved research issues. Even the most fundamental issues related to the conflict—such as the war's causes—are hotly debated still.

I chose a single state as a research topic for several reasons. State and county officials during the Civil War enjoyed considerable latitude in administering military affairs, quite unlike the situation in the modern age. With no centralized Federal system, each state pursued its own path during the four-year conflict. A state-based approach allows us to consider in depth how one jurisdiction enlisted citizens, trained them, fed them, nursed them, equipped them, appointed their officers, and grouped the volunteers into companies and regiments.

The one-state approach also facilitates a culturally sensitive analysis. The experiences of different communities can be compared with respect to demographic background, local enlistment trends, battlefield participation, gender conflict, election results, and the politics of dissent, among other critical topics. One-state studies are relatively rare in the field of Civil War research, but more will follow in the years ahead as researchers continue to narrow their focus and examine the day-to-day experiences of individual citizens and communities.

The choice of a Union state west of the Mississippi River allows us to examine the meaning of unionism in the Louisiana Purchase (referred to here as the "New West"). The New West in 1860 included Missouri, Arkansas, Louisiana, Iowa, Kansas, Minnesota, and the territories of Oklahoma and Nebraska. Iowa was the first jurisdiction in the New West to achieve statehood with slavery prohibited.

During and after the war, Iowans preserved several types of vital records—voting results, enlistment documents, and regimental histories, for instance—that constitute an invaluable resource for twenty-first-century scholars. Letters sent home from Washington by senators and representatives chronicled the motives of Iowa's leading politicians during the long winter of 1861. Hundreds of Hawkeye soldiers kept diaries during the conflict, some of which have been published. Several collections include letters written by wives as well as husbands, enabling us to understand women's experiences during the war. The title of this book is taken from a letter written by an Iowa wife to her army captain husband. The role of Iowa's African Americans is also accessible through contemporary and postwar accounts.

To assess enlistment motivation and enrollment patterns, this study follows six families involved in the war effort. The families represent different regions of Iowa as well as different cultural backgrounds. Five are Caucasian and include families headed by an Oskaloosa carpenter originally from Ohio, a farmer in Delaware County with New York roots, a Keokuk merchant's wife with roots in Virginia, a farmboy living near Council Bluffs, and a land surveyor from Pennsylvania who represented Fort Dodge in the state legislature. The sixth family is African American and headed by Alexander Clark, a black businessman in Muscatine who was one of thousands of middle-aged married men anxious to serve in the military conflict. The list of young bachelors who did serve included Benjamin "Ben" Stevens (Oskaloosa), Abner Dunham (Delaware County), Charles Musser (Council Bluffs), and Cyrus Carpenter (Fort Dodge). A few miles west of Keokuk, four bachelor brothers of Annie Wittenmyer helped their parents run the family farm when the war began.

This study examines Iowa's war against secession from a social history

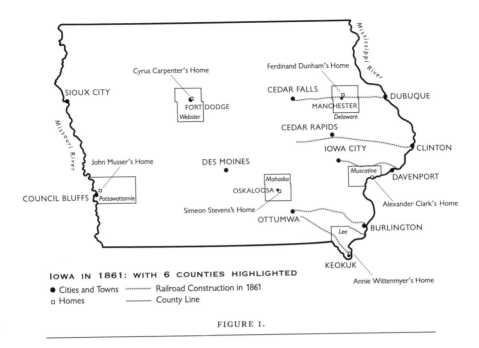

IOWA IN 1861: WITH 6 COUNTIES HIGHLIGHTED
● Cities and Towns ········ Railroad Construction in 1861
□ Homes ———— County Line

FIGURE I.

perspective, interweaving local history with state and national developments. The narrative follows the military progress of the several army units recruited in the six counties—Mahaska, Lee, Muscatine, Delaware, Webster, and Pottawattamie (fig. 1). A large body of research produced by military historians allows us to evaluate the combat performance of Iowa's various regiments.

Iowa's Unique Geographic Position

At the start of the war, Federal authorities in Washington relied heavily upon Iowans to stem the secession movement in Missouri, the slave state immediately to its south. Missouri experienced more counter-insurgency warfare than any other state, and more Iowans were assigned to police its rural backwaters than soldiers from any other Union state. With so many Hawkeye soldiers deployed in the New West, not a single Iowa unit marched in the Army of the Potomac or deployed with the Army of the Cumberland in eastern Tennessee. Soldiers' diaries and correspondence contain substantial evidence about the Civil War in the New West, a strategically critical theater of military operations.

Iowa, admitted to the Union in 1846, was still a frontier state when the war began. Kansas, Nebraska, and Minnesota had only recently opened to white settlement, and as a result slave states dominated the New West demographically. The white population of Texas, Louisiana, Arkansas, and Missouri outnumbered that of the free states in the New West by three to one. If slaves are included in the calculation, the ratio grows to four to one. The Union cause did benefit from the contributions of Missouri unionists who enlisted in the Federal army, but Confederate enrollment figures in the New West still exceeded free state enlistment totals.

With or without superior numbers, Union military success in Missouri was hardly inevitable. More than 30,000 Missourians fought in the Confederate Army, and thousands more operated as irregular guerrillas. Missouri's Rebels enjoyed an advantage in resources compared to unionists in the state, and at the start of the war slaveowners controlled much of the state's wealth and political power. Missouri's slave population exceeded 114,000 in 1860, and more than $3 million from Missouri banks helped feed and equip local Rebel units. Although the state never formally seceded, Confederate forces refused to abandon their plans to capture St. Louis, which had become the Federal army's chief transportation center due to its location near the confluence of the Missouri and Mississippi rivers.

Confederate armies operating in Arkansas invaded Missouri in 1861, 1862, and again in 1864. Each time, Union forces found themselves outnumbered on the battlefield. To offset the Rebel advantage in numbers, unionists recruited thousands of non–English-speaking immigrants who opposed the power of Missouri's slavemasters. In Kansas, former slaves and Native Americans trained to fight as early as 1862. White unionists from Arkansas established a Federal cavalry regiment, and Union soldiers from states like Iowa recruited and trained Arkansas slaves to march in unison and maintain unit cohesion in battle. As a result of these efforts, outnumbered Federal armies managed to prevent Confederate forces from moving directly on St. Louis.

Each time Rebel forces in Arkansas threatened Missouri, the U.S. War Department looked to Iowans to bear the brunt of the work. For Iowans, the problem was not manpower but resources. In 1860, few residents owned substantial liquid assets. Transportation difficulties complicated the task of recruiting men and collecting agricultural produce. Miles and miles of landscape remained vacant, particularly in the northwestern quadrant of the state. A majority of Iowa's 675,000 inhabitants resided in the eastern third of the state. Without modern iron foundries, Iowa's Mississippi River towns could not manufacture guns and ammunition. State officials struggled just to clothe and shoe army recruits. Wool, cotton, and leather were in short supply, and few industrial looms operated in Iowa in 1860. Cavalry and artillery units were difficult to equip, and as a result more than 90 percent of the state's recruits of 1862 marched in an infantry regiment.

Examining Iowans' role in preserving Missouri enables us to consider the irregular, backwoods nature of warfare in that state. Just as they do today, military police during the Civil War had to track down guerrillas without antagonizing civilians. The guerrilla war lasted four years and ultimately killed 27,000 Missourians, yet few researchers have examined how the ill-equipped and ill-trained Union Army recruits managed to cope with the day-to-day terror of flushing out hidden cadres of guerrillas. In an era when the fictional glory of Sir Walter Scott defined military honor, counter-insurgency warfare held little appeal for citizen-soldiers. Yet few other tasks performed by Union soldiers became more critical to the war effort.

Union soldiers stationed in Missouri faced severe logistical challenges. No region between Kansas and Virginia received less Federal military resources than the New West. Only a few railroad lines operated west of the Mississippi River before the war. Dozens of steamboats moored along the Mississippi, but low water frequently inhibited boat traffic into the interior regions. Without direct rail and steamboat access, soldiers marched on foot and hauled supplies in wagons pulled by animals. In this underdeveloped region, rocky trails and deep-cut ravines obstructed the movement of infantry and cavalry. Potable water was often scarce, and continental weather patterns challenged the hardiest soldiers. Many of the New West's most significant battles took place during the hottest or coldest months of the year.

Inadequate prewar planning by state officials exacerbated the shortage of trained men and equipment. Lacking proper military firearms, Iowa volunteers trained with wooden sticks. Camp facilities were primitive at best, and in many cases a lack of tents forced New West soldiers to build their own shelters.

As soldiers, Hawkeye frontiersmen proved very resourceful, which served the Union cause well in the New West. They survived long marches through the most difficult terrain. They marched in terribly hot and miserably cold conditions, over primitive dirt roads and rocky landscapes devoid of human inhabitants, without adequate equipment, food, shelter, or potable water. In between forced marches, supreme boredom gripped the citizen-soldiers. Yet relatively few Iowa soldiers deserted, even when thousands of them became sick and died in makeshift hospitals under appalling conditions.

Iowans' success on the battlefield was remarkable. Once the shooting began, Iowa's citizen-soldiers displayed a firm resiliency in combat. During 1862 and 1863, Iowa troops contributed directly to the capture of Nashville, Vicksburg, and Little Rock. In early 1864, Federal military authorities transferred as many Iowa generals and units as possible to General William T. Sherman's army in Georgia. By the end of the conflict, Iowans had taken part in the capture of Montgomery, Atlanta, Savannah, Columbia, and Raleigh.

Why were Iowans so successful? The soldiers' prewar experience had endowed them with many of the physical skills necessary to survive long marches through semi-wilderness. Frontier farmwork, in particular, served as ideal physical training for many recruits. Psychologically, the arbitrary nature of frontier life enabled citizen-soldiers to weather the storm of a four-year struggle. Surviving droughts, famines, floods, and prairie fires provided them with critical coping skills. Experience defending their farm livestock from bears, wolves, and rattlesnakes prepared them for the task of rooting out insurgents in hostile territory. Surviving the tumultuous economy of the late 1850s also steeled them to sustain their commitment to military success.

The War's Impact on Women

Once the conflict began, the absence of military-age men imposed considerable hardships on women. Of course, this was by no means unique to Iowa. Women in other states performed traditionally male tasks, but in Iowa the frontier environment and lack of a railroad system imposed greater burdens on them, particularly in the sparsely settled interior districts of the state. In addition to planting, plowing, and harvesting crops, they had to haul grain to mills for processing. Goods had to be purchased in distant markets. Firewood was the only source of fuel, and obtaining wood was particularly difficult in the tallgrass prairie districts.

These were all tasks that men performed before the war. In their absence, women had to do them in addition to their own work. Among many other chores, family gardens required an enormous amount of work, but they enabled farm families to survive year in and year out. Yet the women who shouldered this double burden found the time to go from house to house seeking food, clothing, and other donations to support local soldiers. Some ventured south to nurse critically ill soldiers in army hospitals.

Historians have come to different conclusions regarding women's impact on the war and the war's impact on women.[1] Iowa's experience suggests that women leaders acted independently and contributed directly to the Union victory. Frontier soldiers desperately needed clothing, pillows, blankets, dried fruit, baked goods, and medical supplies, and to meet their needs Iowa women arranged to transport the donated goods in addition to collecting them.

As was the case in other states, female charity workers questioned the competency of the male civilians who supervised what was called "sanitary" work. On their own initiative, Iowa's assertive women leaders maintained a separate network for collecting donated goods. When the all-male Iowa sanitary commission attempted to force the local ladies' aid societies to submit to their authority, female civic leaders organized a state convention of their own.

The Political Revolution in Iowa

Iowa's African American community experienced an emotional roller coaster during the long war. After a long period of blatant discrimination, black men and women in Iowa saw their desire for civil rights realized when a majority of white Iowans chose to define patriotism by supporting color-blind laws. The recognition of African Americans' civil rights gave postwar Iowa a radical reputation.

In terms of progress on black civil rights, no other nonslave state witnessed a more radical swing than Iowa. When the war began, violent antiblack attitudes pervaded every community in the state. In the southern border counties, white families with roots in Kentucky and Virginia had taken up residence. Many Iowans supported forcibly deporting freed blacks to Africa or Central America in what was called "colonization." Compared to their numbers in other free states, antislavery radicals made up a very small proportion of voters in Iowa. Although an active network of white sympathizers operated to assist escaping slaves,[2] Missouri fugitives who reached the Iowa-Missouri boundary line usually left Iowa as soon as possible by crossing into northern Illinois.

Despite a long tradition of racism, Iowa's white leaders adopted a new perspective near the end of the Civil War. Military success achieved through interracial cooperation transformed conservative white Iowans' attitudes toward black civil rights and compelled the state's political leaders to embrace equality legislation in the late 1860s.

Unionism

Researchers today struggle to explain why so many men risked their lives for the sake of national unity. The short answer is that unionism in 1860 represented something much more complex than simple patriotism.[3] Iowans' devotion to self-governance and geographic unity had its roots in global affairs. As most residents understood world politics, the United States represented the only successful democracy in a world plagued by tyranny. In their minds, democracy had operated for more than eighty years because the nation remained unified.

As a result of Iowa's location in the New West, historical events contributed to forge an intense devotion to unionism. At mid-century, Iowa's first generation of political leaders celebrated the 1848 U.S. military victory over Mexico and the annexation of Texas. They rejoiced despite the congressional implications of Southern expansion: more senators and representatives supporting slavery. While voters in other free states opposed the Mexican War and Texas annexation, frontiersmen in Iowa saw their dream of a continental nation realized with the addition of California. Others were not so sanguine.

Slavery had always been prohibited in Iowa, at least officially. Migrants came to the state precisely because slavery was banned north of Missouri.

Yet only a small percentage of residents demanded that Congress abolish slavery. Putting up with slavery was a price they were willing to pay to avoid permanent political disintegration. If secession occurred, it would introduce, they expected, a period of tyranny and catastrophic economic collapse, including political chaos on the Great Plains. When the national furor over the outcome of the Mexican War forced Congress to enact another grand intersectional agreement to follow on the Missouri Compromise of 1820, Iowans' zeal for unionism drove them to endorse this so-called 1850 Compromise, which included five measures intended to keep free and slave states on par with each other.

Iowans worshiped at the altar of the 1850 agreement to such an extent that they continued to honor all five bills in the package during the 1850s, including the most controversial, the Fugitive Slave Act. This measure compelled all U.S. citizens to help capture fugitive slaves and return them to their owners. Strongly condemned in most free states, this law remained an object of reverence for many Iowa residents, particularly those who settled near the border with Missouri.

Unionism represented progress to Iowans. In 1850, no state stood to benefit more from white settlement of the lands west of the Missouri River. Secession by Southeasterners or Northeasterners would immediately halt westward migration, they expected. In hopes of hastening white settlement of the Great Plains, Iowans welcomed California and Oregon to statehood status and demanded Federal funding to build a transcontinental railroad.

The reverence for national unity became so fixed among a majority of Iowans that they terrorized the small number of state residents who condoned disunification because of their opposition to slavery. Dissident neighbors were subjected to violent intimidation, particularly those who violated the Fugitive Slave Act and those who favored the immediate abolition of slavery regardless of its impact on national unity.

Growing Opposition to the Extension of Slavery

Unionism also induced most Iowans to reject the nascent Free Soil Party in 1848. The Free Soil platform was not truly radical—it did not demand that slavery be abolished in the states where it currently operated—yet

Iowans in 1848 publicly opposed anti-extensionism as defined by the Free Soil Party as disunionist. They did so because they feared the passage of a ban on the extension of slavery into new territories would induce slave states to secede from the Union.

The prospect of secession in 1848 was real. Unionists in slave states cautioned that a prohibition on slavery expansion would be seen in the Deep South as the first step toward total abolition. Parity in the U.S. Senate was necessary, Southerners argued, to block a constitutional amendment prohibiting slavery. When Southerners proposed extending the Missouri Compromise Line west to the Pacific Ocean, the Free Soil Party demanded a prohibition on slavery west of Missouri and Texas. A congressional law barring the extension of slavery would not only prevent Southern parity in the Senate but it would also repeal the Missouri Compromise Line. This "Old Line," the east-to-west geographic boundary between slavery and nonslavery, dated back to 1820 and served to unite free-state Whigs and slave-state Whigs on a common platform.

Whigs in Iowa in 1848 opposed repeal of the Missouri Compromise Line. Iowa Democrats also opposed the Free Soil platform, but for different reasons. Rather than Congress deciding the issue, they preferred local determination. Hailed by supporters as "popular sovereignty," the Democrats' argument in favor of local control presumed that Congress had no authority to predetermine the status of slavery in any territory; that decision, they insisted, should be left to each territory. Under this arrangement, each territory might enter the Union as a slave state or free state according to how its residents voted on the issue.

Support for local determination in the Western territories resonated across Iowa in the 1840s and 1850s. In the Compromise of 1850, Congress empowered residents in New Mexico Territory to determine whether to allow slavery within its borders. The 1850 Compromise stopped short, however, of applying local control to Kansas Territory. Because New Mexico was south of the Missouri Compromise Line and Kansas Territory north of it, the 1820 agreement—if it still applied—prohibited slavery in Kansas but not in New Mexico.

Congress in 1850 chose not to open the Great Plains to white settlement, knowing any proposal to do so would add fuel to the secession fires burning in the Deep South. Many assumed that when Congress did open up Kansas to white settlement, the 1820 Missouri Compromise would preclude slavery there. If Kansas entered the Union with slavery prohibited, another pair of free-state senators would appear in Congress. Legal slavery in New Mexico, if it was realized, would counter the two Kansas senators, but the fate of slavery in New Mexico remained undecided. Mexican law had forbidden slavery there, and the arid landscape was not suited to cotton production.

In the early 1850s, the status of Kansas became the subject of fierce intersectional debates. Despite the Deep South's objection to inviting white settlement in Kansas, the residents of Missouri, Illinois, and Iowa pushed to open the Great Plains. Notwithstanding the tradition of the Missouri Compromise, Western free-state Democrats in 1854 proposed to replace the 1820 ban on slavery in Kansas with popular sovereignty. In so doing, they gained the favor of slave-state politicians who feared a free-state Kansas would undermine Senate parity in favor of free states. The Kansas-Nebraska Act of 1854 declared that Kansas settlers would decide for themselves whether to allow slavery, and proslavery Missourians boasted that it would become a slave state by hook or by crook. In the end, hesitant Deep South politicians largely supported the bill despite its principle of local control.

The Kansas-Nebraska Act opened the Great Plains to white settlement. It also divided the huge swath of Great Plains land into two separate territorial jurisdictions, Nebraska and Kansas. In Iowa, whose western border rested on the Missouri River, the prospect of slavery on the Great Plains alarmed residents who had assumed slavery would be prohibited there. Because the act nullified the Old Missouri Compromise Line, many Iowans feared the controversy over it would rekindle the sectionalist passions that had nearly launched a secession movement in 1849. Thousands of unionists turned out to protest the bill in 1854, including a multitude of Iowans.

No other free state experienced more stress and turmoil over the events in Kansas and Nebraska than Iowa. "Bleeding Kansas," as the ongoing conflict between proslavery and antislavery settlers became known, quickly transformed the state's partisan environment. The 1854 act polarized unionists in Iowa into two camps, one strongly in favor and one strongly against. Unionists who favored popular sovereignty celebrated passage of the Kansas-Nebraska Act. Even though slavery might become institution-alized in both Nebraska and Kansas, the act's supporters in Iowa remained optimistic. They expected the first wave of settlers to the Great Plains would vote to prohibit slavery for the same reason that they had chosen Iowa as their destination over slave-state Missouri.

As the violence continued in Kansas, the popular sovereignty experiment quickly lost favor in Iowa. Some Democrats deserted their party's popular sovereignty candidate for president in 1856. That year, nearly 60 percent of Iowa voters cast their vote for one of the two presidential candidates who opposed the Kansas-Nebraska Act.

Critics of the Kansas-Nebraska Act split into two very different camps. Some opponents insisted on restoring the 1820 Compromise Line, the traditional platform of the national Whig Party. Other critics rejected the Old Line and embraced the anti-extension platform proclaimed by the Free Soil Party in 1848. Although the Free Soil Party had all but disinte-grated after the Compromise of 1850, the party's single principle gained new life following protests over the Kansas-Nebraska Act. In most free states, a majority of opponents of the act rallied around the anti-exten-sion banner. The conflict ultimately resolved itself with the demise of the Northern Whig Party by 1860 and the establishment of the Republican Party, which opposed the extension of slavery into any territory.

In Iowa, several factors contributed to promote anti-extensionism as a solution to sectional discord. In this staunchly unionist jurisdiction, more and more people came to believe that postponing resolution of the slav-ery issue in the West actually increased the likelihood of disunion. While some opponents of the 1854 act argued in favor of reinstalling the Missouri Compromise Line, many Iowans wanted the question of slavery resolved once and for all—and against the expansion of slavery.

Migrants arriving in Iowa in the mid-1850s tended to be vocal anti-ex-tensionists. By a five-to-one ratio, opponents of the act picked the anti-ex-tensionist Republican candidate over the Old Line Whig nominee for president in 1856. By 1860, Iowa's Old Line Whig faction had dwindled to almost nothing. Between 1856 and 1860, some Old Line Whigs joined the national Democratic Party, while others attended Republican caucuses.[4]

As Republican candidates seized the reins of power in Iowa in the mid-1850s, unionist sentiment strengthened. At no time did the state party propose that slavery be abolished where it currently existed. Within Iowa's nascent Republican Party, unionists outnumbered abolitionists by a wide margin, with the result that unionism lessened the scale of the Republican political transformation. Rather than enact state laws designed to undermine the Federal Fugitive Slave Act, the moderate Republicans who controlled the Iowa legislature avoided the issue and concentrated on instituting new banking laws. Compared to those of Republican organizations in New England, Iowa's Republican platform remained conservative. Fearful that Old Line Whigs would flee en masse to the Democratic fold, moderates courted conservative unionists by opposing the human rights bills sponsored by the radical wing of the party.

As the 1860 presidential election approached, both Iowa Republicans and Iowa Democrats appealed to voters by calling for the preservation of the Union. Each party had its own recipe for preservation, but when Confederate gunners shelled Fort Sumter, members of both parties predicted doom if the nation could not be reunited. The prospect of military casualties did not discourage Iowans from demanding reunion. For many, maintaining unity in the face of internal turmoil would signal the continuing success of America's radical experiment in self-government.

As the semisacred notion of unionism fueled a militant zeal in Iowa, local governments treated military service as another form of participatory democracy. They relied on civic participation to recruit, equip, and train soldiers. Newly formed private organizations collected funds, produced food, and supplied deficiencies in army hospital care. African Americans as well as European Americans organized public meetings, resolved procedural questions, and published the resolutions in an effort to shape the direction of the war. Women used the same forms of structured advocacy and dialogue. So many Iowans volunteered for military service that state officials did not have to conscript soldiers until the fall of 1864.

This study testifies to the perseverance of all Iowans, men and women, white and black, and helps explain how and why they participated in the war effort.

CHAPTER ONE

The Storm before the Hurricane

———————✦———————

A series of disruptive events rocked the state of Iowa several years before the Deep South states seceded from the Union. Starting in 1854, proslavery thugs in Kansas Territory harassed free-state settlers on a scale that intimidated Iowans, living in the closest free-state jurisdiction to Kansas. The violence had not abated by 1857, the year the regional economy collapsed. Every state in the Union suffered in this financial panic, but none experienced as deep a depression as Iowa. The 1857 credit crisis struck just when Iowans feared proslavery forces would migrate north to Nebraska and Iowa.

Extremely high voter participation reflected the intense disenchantment. In 1860, 90 percent of the state's eligible voters cast a presidential ballot. Iowans blamed Eastern capitalists for the credit crisis and Southern slaveholders for terrorizing free-state Kansans, and the confluence of the two inflamed their passions. The sudden refusal of financiers to lend money affected everyone. More than half of the state's residents had arrived just a few years earlier with little capital. Individual families had borrowed heavily to purchase land and build homes, and many incorporated towns and counties had borrowed much larger sums to build local infrastructure. As thousands of Western debtors faced bankruptcy, the rate of in-migration dwindled to almost nothing. Rather than relocate to the New West, people stayed put in the Eastern United States.

The Origins of the Credit Crisis

The inflationary spiral began in February 1857, the month when East Coast bankers first downgraded the value of paper securities issued by twenty-two Illinois banks. With no Federal paper currency in circulation, Illinois banknotes served as the primary currency in Iowa. When indebted

Western merchants discounted the value of the banknotes paid to them by indebted Western farmers, the economy began to unravel. Orders for Eastern goods dropped precipitously as Western merchants scrambled to collect the money they had lent to farmers and shopkeepers. As inflation rose, Eastern lenders stopped lending money on credit. In October, the editor of the *Keokuk Gate City* noted that the "country merchants owe the city merchants, the farmers owe the country merchants, and neither at the western end, nor in the middle, nor in the east end of this linked chain of debt is there any money."[1]

Every county, town, and rural village in the state felt the harsh effects of the Panic of 1857. One desperate Delaware County farmwife in the spring of 1860 appealed to relatives in Rhode Island for cash. "Eastern money is good here but Western money won't go at the East." Property owners, unable to resolve their debts or collect on debts owed by others, stopped paying their county taxes. As a result, counties owed the state treasurer nearly $400,000 in back taxes, an amount exceeding the annual state government expenses. The state owed its creditors $300,000. Municipal and county governments owed much more, having borrowed more than $7 million before 1857. Governing boards in several towns and counties attempted to repudiate their debts by canceling the loans unilaterally.[2]

The 1857 credit crisis struck Iowa when relatively few miles of railroad track had been laid. Iron tracks that began near the Mississippi River ended abruptly in dirt paths. The railroad stopped eighty miles short of Des Moines, the state capital. On the banks of the Mississippi, unused steamboats moored quietly, and unfinished canal projects stood silent. "I am sick of this whole state and all its associations," Cyrus Carpenter confided to a friend in 1859. Without incoming migrants, the young bachelor found little work surveying land near Fort Dodge. He wondered if the boom years would ever return.[3]

The economic stagnation did prompt some residents to exit the Hawkeye state. Carpenter, a Pennsylvania native, was one of them. He left Fort Dodge for Pikes Peak, Colorado, in 1859. After promising his fiancée he would return with money filling his pockets, he joined the caravan of gold-seekers.

Most Iowans endured the credit crisis as best they could, staying put in part because of Iowa's status as a nonslave jurisdiction. Most of the state's residents had earlier chosen Iowa over Missouri because slavery existed in the latter state, and in looking ahead they expected future migrants would do the same. Convinced that slavery would forever burden Southern states, Iowans assumed the boom years of the early 1850s would eventually return to their adopted state, as long as the nation remained united and a majority of its citizens continued to control the destiny of the nation.

To stimulate the economy and migration, anxious Iowans demanded Federal railroad projects, navigation improvements, and other measures. Both parties endorsed the proposed Homestead Act, a bill that would eliminate the per-acre fee Federal officials charged for unsold land. Ninety-seven percent of all public land in Iowa had been sold already, but across the Missouri River sat millions of unsold acres. Once Nebraska Territory was occupied by white settlers, Iowans expected the land rush would boost their own state's economy and revive plummeting real estate prices.

Iowa's Primitive Economic Infrastructure

Frontier states were particularly vulnerable to the aftereffects of Eastern financial panics, and in Iowa the 1857 credit crisis struck before the first generation of settlers could establish a system of regional economic distribution. The state's population had grown to 674,000 souls, but only six towns in the entire state exceeded 5,000 inhabitants. The census-taker counted fewer than 4,000 residents in Des Moines. Dubuque, the oldest and most populous town due to the lead mining boom of the 1830s, had 13,000 residents. At the time Carpenter migrated to Colorado, only 2,500 whites inhabited his home of Webster County, situated eighty miles west of the nearest railhead, in Cedar Falls.

In Iowa's largest Mississippi River ports, buildings constructed in the boom years stood silent. Grandiose plans to complete a series of railroads from Chicago to the Missouri River gathered dust. Of Iowa's many Mississippi River ports, only Davenport enjoyed a direct railroad connection to Chicago by the start of the Civil War. Without railroads, most Iowa merchants relied on steamboats to export produce and import manufactured goods, a mode of transportation restricted by seasonal changes in the water level. Not only did low water and high water prevent navigation, but when the water reached a moderate level, two sets of natural rapids inhibited boat traffic. Boats steaming up from St. Louis usually docked in Keokuk rather than challenge the rapids between that port and Fort Madison. Travelers disembarked at Keokuk and hauled their goods by road thirteen miles upstream, then reembarked on smaller vessels for the journey upstream. Eighty miles upstream, near Davenport, steamboat captains encountered a second series of water obstacles.

The dilapidated state of Iowa's housing in 1860 would dismay modern-day travelers. River port residents built simple frame houses using local hardwood and shopped at Main Street storefronts adorned with crudely made bricks. Because few fences had been erected, farm animals frequently wandered off nearby farms and into the ports. Farther to the west, simple log cabins became more common. Without milled lumber, residents constructed shelters as best they could, stacking logs to form walls, then packing clay soil between the logs to keep out the wind and rain. For roofing, pioneers cut shakes four feet long from the trunks of large trees. Chimneys were made of field stones molded with clay soil. Lacking plank roads and bridges, Iowans in their animal-drawn wagons bounced along on ungraded dirt paths and forded creeks and rivers. Seasonal floods stopped traffic in both directions until the high water receded and the mud roads dried.

The 89,000 farm families in Iowa often found it difficult to produce enough food to sustain and nourish family members. Having only recently broken the turf, the vast majority of farmers could plant only a modest amount of grain. Most owned a small number of domesticated animals, and one-cow families were common. The weather patterns of the 1850s brought too much rain or too little. Insect plagues and prairie fires further reduced crop production. "Early frosts in the fall and late frosts in the spring, chinch bugs, wet weather, sore feet, sore hands, dead cattle, etc.," noted Sarah Kenyon, a Delaware County farmwife, in a letter to relatives in New England. She wrote that when she went out to work "something not very much akin to gratitude swells in my bosom for . . . it is hard to see everything laid waste."[4] Most farm families relied on wild game and berries and nuts to supplement a diet of homegrown cornmeal and vegetables.

To survive, rural Iowans turned to their neighbors for assistance. With food and currency both in short supply, cooperative resource sharing sustained many rural neighborhoods. Farmers traded produce for shoes and

cloth, and swapped one type of produce for another. Families close to
starving offered their labor in exchange for food. At the start of the war, a
typical farm family owed favors to a list of neighbors, while another list of
neighbors owed favors to them.

The frontiersmen's work ethic caught the attention of one Hungarian immigrant who farmed in south-central Iowa in the 1850s. In a letter
home, he observed that "the American . . . minds his own business, and
when he works at something he does not understand, he keeps at it until
he learns it. All men make their own luck here."[5]

The letters of the Hungarian transplant also testify to Iowans' pride in
self-governance. A university graduate forced to flee Europe for political
reasons, he found his English-speaking neighbors quite unlike European
peasants. Although poorly educated, rural Iowans regularly engaged in
political discussions. Despite all the talk and speculation, however, few
residents in 1860 could have imagined the enormity of events to come.

Annie Wittenmyer, Alexander Clark, Ben Stevens, Abner Dunham,
Cyrus Carpenter, and Charles Musser all were swept up in these most
challenging circumstances. The fact that their families struggled economically during the years before the war compounded the task of preparing
for war. Their experiences offer a window on how Iowans coped with the
burden of war.

Keokuk and the Wittenmyer Family

The prewar credit crisis hit Keokuk particularly hard. Lawyer Samuel F.
Miller, a Keokuk businessman who amassed $40,000 worth of paper assets
before 1857, saw his fortune disappear almost overnight. A plot of land
valued at $1,000 in 1856 could not be sold two years later, even at the cellar
price of $10. In hopes of building a rail line to Des Moines, the port's gov-
erning council sold bonds to Eastern investors in the early 1850s. When
railroad construction halted far short of its target following the Panic of
1857, the port owed $900,000 to Eastern lenders. In 1858, the value of tax-
able property in Keokuk dropped by $5.5 million, and many of those owing
taxes failed to pay. Civic employees did not receive their wages as a result
of the lack of tax revenue.[6]

Merchant William Wittenmyer, like Samuel Miller, feared he would
lose his business enterprise and real estate holdings to creditors. William

FIGURE 2. A Civil War–era photograph of the port of Keokuk showing residential homes in the foreground with the Mississippi River and the state of Illinois in the distance. Thanks to its strategic location at the confluence of the Des Moines River and the Mississippi, Keokuk numbered some 10,000 inhabitants when the war began. Only Dubuque and Davenport surpassed the "Gate City" in population. *Reprinted by permission of the Keokuk Public Library.*

and his wife Annie also feared losing their newly built home. The couple had dedicated themselves to improving Keokuk since their arrival in 1850, and the possibility of bankruptcy represented a severe threat. Prior to the credit collapse, William accumulated real estate in several towns near the Missouri-Iowa border, where he resold merchandise purchased in St. Louis, Louisville, and Cincinnati. He had located his chief retail outlet in Centerville, the Appanoose County seat eighty miles west of Keokuk. As the population of Appanoose County tripled in size between 1850 and 1856, merchants like Wittenmyer earned a handsome profit buying clothing and dry goods on credit in Missouri, Kentucky, and Ohio, and then routing the merchandise by steamboat upriver through Keokuk for transportation by wagon cart to Centerville. As the population of Keokuk climbed from 2,500 to 8,100 during the six-year period, William and Annie built their large colonial-style home near Main Street, valued at more than $10,000. In 1856, 700 new homes and business facilities were built in the Gate City, construction that generated work for a multitude of sawmill hands, brickmakers, and carpenters.[7]

The credit crunch put intermediaries like Wittenmyer in a tight situation. William owed money to businessmen in other states, but he could not pay off his debts until his customers in Centerville paid off their debts to him. He owned full title to Annie's dream house in Keokuk, yet he could not afford to pay his annual property taxes. Pressed by his creditors, William sued customers in Centerville, only to find his customers short of currency. In 1859, William signed a deed granting Annie a life interest in their new home, a tactic frequently used by American businessmen anxious to discourage creditors from seizing a debtor's personal assets. William and Annie Wittenmyer survived 1859 and 1860 without being evicted, but creditors, both private and public entities, would come calling if the economic malaise continued. Unless back taxes were paid in full, the Lee County treasurer intended to put their property on the public auction block.[8]

The appearance of Keokuk in 1860 reflected the scale of the economic depression. Home to 431 merchants in 1856, Keokuk's commercial district seemed nearly deserted two years later. Empty storefronts sat abandoned, unfinished construction projects stood silent, unrepaired sidewalks hindered shoppers, and the gas lampposts, the pride of the city, remained unlit. Nearly every mill and brickyard had closed, and saloons did a brisk business among the unemployed while few steamboats docked along the riverfront. With few police officers available to keep order, gangs of dockworkers fought to control the handful of freight-handling jobs still available.[9]

The persistent economic crisis compelled Annie Wittenmyer to rededicate herself to volunteer charity work. During the boom years, she had led charity drives for the local Methodist church, and as the need for food and clothing multiplied, she felt an obligation to expand the scale of her work. In the worst times during the 1850s, Annie looked to her church congregation and family for comfort and strength. Her parents, John G. and Elizabeth C. Turner, and her five siblings had followed Annie and William to Keokuk in 1853. On their 300-acre farm five miles west of the port, the Turner family harvested grain and raised livestock. They also maintained a large garden, which supplied friends and relatives with vegetables and fruit during the leanest years.[10]

Persistent economic stress took a toll on the Wittenmyers' marriage, which was fragmenting for a variety of reasons. By 1860, William and Annie spent much of their time apart. William's two daughters by his first wife had married and moved to the Centerville area, leaving Annie's four-year-old son as the only child at their manor in Keokuk. Four other children born to Annie died during the 1850s, tragic events that apparently aggravated the growing religious gulf between husband and wife. A dedicated spiritualist, William skipped Methodist church services and met instead with others interested in communicating with deceased relatives. William's practice of attending séances disturbed Annie, a devout Trinitarian Christian.

Filling the needs of impoverished Keokuk residents helped Annie cope with the loss of her children and the frequent absences of her husband. At this critical time, she found herself inundated with requests from poor families for food and clothing. While William tended to his business affairs, Annie focused her attention on the welfare of Keokuk's most vulnerable families. She joined with other Keokuk women charity workers to establish a system for securing local donations and distributing food and clothing locally. "She went from house to house among the poor," noted a minister, "carried baskets of food, bundles of clothing, ordered fuel, visited the sick, [and] attended their funerals . . . In herself was a whole committee of the Mercy and Help department."[11] In the case of severely ill women who were unable to afford hospital care, Annie invited them into her two-story home where she could provide personal nursing care. Convinced that men had little or no ability to nurture the downtrodden, she and her female colleagues in Keokuk's charity system resisted attempts by leading male citizens of the community to minimize their leadership.

Muscatine and the Clark Family

Sixty miles upstream from Keokuk, citizens in the port of Muscatine contemplated an uncertain future in 1860. The city government's debt to Eastern creditors exceeded the value of its total assets. As in other river towns, a lack of available credit continued to stall economic growth. Before 1857, hundreds of migrants settled on farmland in the county or came to the bustling port to find work as laborers. Now, few migrants passed through the area. Muscatine's sawmills cut relatively little lumber, and the port's iron foundry operated with a skeleton crew. Without much industry, the port's population seemed stuck at about 5,300. Local investors directed much of the blame at Davenport, the transportation center twenty-five miles upstream that had eclipsed Muscatine as the chief commercial point between Burlington and Dubuque. Although a rail line connected Muscatine to Davenport, the rival river port controlled the direct rail connection to Chicago. Muscatine's own railroad endeavor, a project designed to run west of Muscatine through Washington County to Oskaloosa, remained in the planning phases due to a lack of funds.[12]

Down-on-their-luck businessmen in Muscatine gathered at Alexander Clark's barbershop on Second Street and complained about falling real estate values. Clark was a free African American, the child of former slaves in Pennsylvania. He was also one of Muscatine's stalwart residents, having arrived in the port by steamboat in 1842 at the young age of seventeen. Over the next eighteen years, he successfully navigated two very different social worlds. While he and his wife Catharine devoted their family life to helping Muscatine's African American community, his business pursuits put him in contact with local white elites. Publicly serving white clients by day at his Second Street barbershop, in the evening Clark mingled with fellow members of the African Methodist Episcopal (AME) congregation and the black Masonic chapter. He raised three children with his wife, and in his spare time served as a trustee at his church and took charge of the AME Sunday school program.

Although small in numbers, Muscatine's black community had grown since Clark's arrival. The city's population had diversified in other ways as well during the 1850s, with a large number of German-speaking inhabitants and natives of Ireland in addition to Caucasians born in a variety of states. Whites had come to Muscatine (city and county) from the Northeastern states, the Old Northwest, and the northern tier of slave states. By 1860 the county's population surpassed the 16,000 mark. Farmers in the county included a substantial number of German-speaking families who cultivated the land alongside English-speaking farmers from Ohio and Indiana.[13]

Clark welcomed European migrants to his hometown and promoted community harmony and progress in many ways. He bought and sold real estate as a side business, and by 1860 the barber owned property on more than a dozen blocks in town.[14] Like the other businessmen in Muscatine, Clark encouraged locals to support railroad construction projects. In cooperation with local white abolitionists, Clark assisted slaves escaping from Missouri on their way to Canada and freedom. When slavecatchers threatened members of Muscatine's African American community, Clark relied on his white mentors for protection.

Progressive reform was foremost on Clark's political agenda. His black and white connections enabled him to pursue a lifelong commitment to equal rights. The Pennsylvania native attended hundreds of conventions during his lifetime, in his hometown, in his state, and in his nation. He frequently delivered the main address at progressive political events. Despite the violence and threats he suffered in his hometown, he continued to champion democratic governance and pushed the United States to show by example the benefits of social equality and diverse representation in government.

Although he could not vote, Muscatine's foremost black citizen did not wait until the Civil War to challenge white elites who declined to repeal local laws aimed at discouraging blacks from settling in Iowa. White racism dominated Iowa's political culture when Clark arrived in Muscatine in 1842, and the extreme racism had not dissipated by the mid-1850s. Inspired by the example of black leaders in the Northeastern states, Clark submitted to the state legislature in 1855 a petition signed by thirty-three "Colored citizens of Muscatine County," demanding equal rights. In 1857, he organized an Emancipation Day parade in Muscatine, an event also held in other free states to celebrate the dissolution of slavery in the British Empire.[15]

Unfortunately, Iowa's racist laws still remained a part of the state code in 1860. The few legislators who pushed to enact the reforms listed in the Muscatine petition in 1855 quickly abandoned the effort. Two years later, with the equal rights bills stalled in the state legislature, the 1857 constitutional convention refused to grant black Iowans equal rights. Although the convention delegates did agree to place the question on the referendum ballot, a majority of white voters soundly rejected equal rights. Rather than usher in a new age, the 1857 state constitution barred nonwhites from voting and serving on juries, among other things, and an 1851 state law remained in effect that prohibited African American migrants from relocating to Iowa.[16]

The exclusion statute did not compel Clark and other blacks to leave the state, but the law did discourage them from leaving their home base and traveling to districts where local law enforcement officials did not know them. In 1848, a group of Missouri bounty hunters attempted to kidnap a black acquaintance of Clark's in Muscatine. The threat of abduction constantly alarmed Catharine Clark, who was a native of Virginia. It is not known today if she had successfully escaped from Virginia or if her master had released her from bondage. Either way, Catharine forever bore memories of enslavement and never dismissed the possibility that white bounty hunters might force her back into slavery. Despite the violence and threats suffered by family members in his hometown, Clark refused to give up. He continued to champion democratic governance and pushed white leaders to embrace social equality and diverse representation in government.

Oskaloosa and the Stevens Family

Clark's experience was not unique to eastern Iowa. In the south-central region, few rural neighborhoods welcomed free blacks in 1860. One exception was Oskaloosa. The county seat of Mahaska, eighty miles west of Muscatine, the town was home to a community of Quakers who assisted runaway slaves and endorsed equal rights for African Americans. While most whites in south-central Iowa stood by the Fugitive Slave Act and refused to aid escaping slaves, a brave minority formed a secret network of stationmasters along a so-called Underground Railroad. They aided dozens, perhaps hundreds, of people fleeing slavery.

Prevailing racist sentiment in the area did, however, discourage blacks from settling permanently in Oskaloosa. In 1860, Mahaska County's population approached 15,000, nearly all of them European Americans. The census-taker counted 2,000 residents in Oskaloosa, a fairly substantial figure for a town without a rail link or river access. Oskaloosa's population included a substantial number of unskilled laborers, skilled craftsmen, merchants, and clerks. Carpenter Simeon Stevens and his son Ben counted themselves among the town's skilled tradesmen.[17]

Simeon Stevens's family typified the background of Mahaska County residents. Born in Ohio, Simeon and his wife Elizabeth relocated to Illinois with Ben a few years after their marriage. In the early 1850s, the

Stevens family, which now included three children, crossed the Mississippi River and selected Oskaloosa as their new home. The thriving mercantile center was in need of experienced carpenters, and before the Panic of 1857 Simeon and dozens of other skilled craftsmen built hundreds of homes in and around Oskaloosa using hardwood lumber cut at local mills.

When the credit crisis stalled new construction, Simeon found himself without work and with few assets to keep his wife and children fed. As the depression wore on, family members discussed the pros and cons of relocating to Pikes Peak, Colorado, where the gold rush had created a demand for carpenters and other skilled craftsmen. Rather than relocate to Colorado, however, Simeon and Elizabeth decided to remain in their adopted town and eke out a day-to-day existence on a small acreage outside the city limits, where they raised vegetables to survive. The census-taker listed Simeon as a "farmer" in 1860 even though the out-of-work carpenter did not own any hogs, cattle, or horses and did not grow corn or wheat.[18]

Eldest son Benjamin turned twenty-one in 1860. Having trained as a plasterer in the mid-1850s, he possessed a skill in high demand before the economic collapse. But like his father, Ben found job offers few and far between after 1857. When army recruiters went door to door in the summer of 1861, he was an ideal prospect. In addition to his work skills, the Ohio native had received a good education in the public school system in Oskaloosa. His parents' decision not to join the gold rush to Pikes Peak greatly disappointed him, so he was ready to embark on a new adventure. The disciplined craftsman acted very deliberately in his day-to-day decision making, a practice that made him an excellent follower and leader in the army. Fascinated with mathematics, Benjamin also projected an entrepreneurial spirit. Family members worshiped at a Methodist church in town, and Benjamin's letters home expressed the strong sense of duty he felt toward his family, his god, and his country.[19]

The Dunham Farm in Delaware County

Forty miles west of the port of Dubuque, Ferdinand and Anjelina Dunham operated a farm of moderate size. The Dunhams had relocated to Delaware County in 1855 with their three boys, aged thirteen, seven, and two. Rather than farm in sparsely populated central Iowa, Ferdinand purchased 80 acres of prairie near the projected railroad line running west from Dubuque. Five miles west of the farm lay Manchester, the Delaware County seat of government. In 1855, Ferdinand purchased 240 additional acres several miles away from the homestead. The additional land included 40 acres of wooded ground near the Maquoketa River.[20]

Delaware County had 11,000 inhabitants in 1856, mostly farmers struggling to transform the hilly prairie landscape into ground suitable for agriculture. During the Dunham family's first year in Iowa, Ferdinand planted 16 acres in wheat, oats, and corn, and fed hay to a small number of horses and milk cows. Over the next four years, the number of acres he planted in crops increased significantly, as did the herd size. The 1860 census-taker listed the farm's total value at $1,800, which included $200 worth of farm equipment and $800 worth of livestock. As of June 1, 1860, the Dunham farm consisted of five horses, eleven milk cows, two oxen, twelve swine, and twenty other cattle, a larger-than-average collection of animals for an Iowa farmer at that time.[21]

The Dunham family's hard work did not produce greater financial dividends. Although the railroad was completed from Dubuque to Cedar Falls as they had expected, low regional commodity prices induced the Dunhams and other farmers to try to sell their grain, animals, and butter locally. Bad weather and insect plagues also frustrated the family business plan. To raise money during the leanest years, Ferdinand sold some of the land he owned away from the home farm. Fortunately, Ferdinand and Anjelina did not owe mortgage payments, and they managed to keep their family well fed. They were able to pay their annual county taxes even after 1857. Looking ahead to better years, Ferdinand attended county Agriculture Society meetings and read extensively about progressive farming techniques.

Eldest son Abner Dunham turned nineteen in 1860. When army recruiters came calling, he was among the volunteers in his neighborhood. His background and work experience made him an excellent soldier. He enjoyed farmwork for the most part, during bad times as well as good. Educated in northern Indiana rural public schools, Abner enhanced his learning through day-to-day conversation with his parents. Ferdinand had taught school as a young man in New York, and Abner inherited his parents' interest in books and newspapers. He was a frequent letter writer while in the army, and his correspondence indicates he was an extrovert. Like his parents, he did not drink alcohol. His grandfather had served as an officer in the U.S. Army, and although Abner enlisted as a private, his letters home suggested he followed the campaign in the way a trained officer would. While on the march, he constantly gathered information to understand the broader military strategy in progress. On the eve of a major battle, the concentration of soldiers combined with the anticipation of combat energized the Indiana native to a high degree.[22]

The experience of assisting his parents on their farm developed in Abner the physical and mental skills that served him well in the army. Cutting the tall prairie grass and breaking the thick crust of earth demanded hard, intense labor. Day in and day out during all seasons of the year, he had walked long distances performing farm chores and developed the physical skills necessary to manage livestock. Because his parents' 80-acre farmstead had no native trees, the young man drove a team of horses eight miles to the family's 40-acre woods, where he felled hardwood trees with an axe and saw, loaded the tree trunks on his wagon, and returned the wagon to the farmhouse over a series of dirt paths.

The Musser Farm in Pottawattamie County

Charles Musser joined the army one year after Abner Dunham and Benjamin Stevens enlisted. Although about the same age as Abner and Benjamin, the farmhand from western Iowa was shy and reserved. After joining up in late 1862, he frequently experienced severe homesickness. During his first few months away from home, he yearned to be working on his parents' farm. While on the march, he tended to focus on the task immediately in front of him rather than assess the larger game of military strategy. Educated in country schools in Ohio and Iowa, Charles demonstrated relatively good grammatical skills in his letters home, despite his family's impoverished background.[23]

Family circumstances also distinguished Charles from Abner and Benjamin, and contributed to his late decision to enlist. In 1860, Charles's parents owned a small, 20-acre farm in the Loess Hills, five miles from the Missouri River. Before the war, he and his parents struggled to feed themselves and his six younger sisters, aged two to sixteen. Compared to families in eastern Iowa, the Mussers' community was much more isolated from the regional economic centers of Chicago and St. Louis. The Missouri River represented their only link to the outside world, and the nearest railhead was a hundred miles downstream in the port of St. Joseph. While Missouri River steamboats brought clothing, cooking supplies, furniture, and other goods to Council Bluffs, the Musser family could not afford to purchase much. What extra food the Mussers were able to produce they sold to residents of the port of Council Bluffs, five miles southwest of the farm.[24]

Things had not always been so difficult for the Mussers. John Musser, Charles's father, had come to Council Bluffs in 1854 with the intent of building homes. Like Simeon Stevens, he found that farming was neither his chief nor his preferred occupation. John reluctantly resorted to farming after the Panic of 1857 as a means to ensure his family's survival. Trained as a cabinetmaker in Ohio, John had selected Council Bluffs as his destination in anticipation of tens of thousands of white migrants arriving in this major Missouri River port on their way to settle Nebraska Territory. The Mussers evidently found their way to Council Bluffs through Missouri, where their oldest son took up residence. After arriving in Council Bluffs, John and Caroline purchased three lots in town and attended Sunday services at a local Presbyterian church.[25]

By 1856, 3,000 people resided in Council Bluffs. Although the port's population had grown relatively quickly, as John had expected, the credit crisis suddenly brought the growth spurt to a halt. With no money available to borrow and only a few migrants coming through the area, aspiring cabinetmakers found little work. Unable to make ends meet, John purchased the 20-acre parcel north of the port—land that had been developed for farming by Mormon migrants on their way to Utah in the 1840s. The presence of a spring-fed creek running through the acreage may have convinced John to buy the property for $322. One mile to the north of his farmhouse stood a formidable hill covered in timber.[26] But at least initially, the farm barely kept the family going.

The proximity of Council Bluffs to Nebraska influenced local politics. While virtually every Iowa community endorsed the proposed Homestead Act, enthusiasm for the bill soared to an extremely high level in the Council Bluffs area. The projected transcontinental railroad also sparked enthusiasm for the future. The prospect that thousands of families would disembark here on their way to the Great Plains apparently convinced the Mussers to stay put on their 20-acre plot and wait out the depression. Because the rail line from Iowa City to San Francisco through Council Bluffs and Omaha existed only on paper, families in the Council Bluffs area endured the Civil War isolated from eastern and central Iowa. Until the railroad was built, the fastest route from Council Bluffs to Iowa City involved steamboat travel through St. Louis.

The Mussers' small farm supported only twelve head of livestock (two horses, two milk cows, four cattle, and four hogs). With their oldest son away in Missouri, the family relied more and more on twenty-year-old Charles to attend to the day-to-day operation of the farm. From their small piece of ground, Musser family members harvested 100 bushels of wheat and 350 bushels of corn in 1859. With nine mouths to feed, plus the horses and cattle, the family relied upon the family garden to supplement their spartan diet of milled corn and milled wheat. They did not slaughter any of their animals for meat in 1859, but family members did harvest 140 pounds of potatoes that year. The Mussers also cut 25 tons of hay in 1859 from nearby wilderness land they did not own. By feeding hay to their livestock, they conserved what little corn they could harvest for their own use. The census-taker estimated the value of the farm at $200 plus $60 worth of farm implements and $214 worth of livestock—considerably less than the Dunhams were worth. The four closest neighbors of the Musser family included two impoverished farm families, a Danish immigrant who made shoes for a living, and an aspiring investor who owned $6,000 worth of real estate.[27]

Various circumstances contributed to pull Charles in different directions when army recruiters came around. Council Bluff's proximity to Kansas Territory enticed many southwest Iowa residents to enlist. Reports of bloody violence against free-state settlers in Kansas reached the Council Bluffs area as early as 1855 and sparked much debate in the Mussers' neighborhood. Although a majority of local voters stood by the "popular sovereignty" principle of the Kansas-Nebraska Act, the Mussers and their neighbors worried that proslavery residents in Missouri would migrate northward and impose their will on the majority free-state settlers. If Kansas entered the Union with slavery legal there, the bloody conflict would likely shift to Nebraska, the huge territory immediately west of Council Bluffs. Some slaveowners relocated from Missouri to Nebraska Territory during the 1850s, and the prospect of slave states to the west of Iowa as well as south of Iowa sparked major concerns.

Iowans' perspective as migrants contributed to reinforce expectations of continued national unity. Having relocated from another state or nation, their perspective on life and politics was shaped by substantial knowledge of continental geography. The physical challenges they endured while attempting to tame the wilderness impressed upon them a sense of national purpose and destiny. Whether they came most recently from Kentucky (like the Wittenmyers), Missouri (like the Mussers), Illinois (like the Stevens family), Pennsylvania (like Cyrus Carpenter), Indiana (like the Dunhams), or Ohio (like the Clarks), most saw continental integrity as critical. Whether they were popular sovereignty Democrats or anti-extension Republicans, Iowans perceived unionism as the necessary bedrock upon which to construct a new and brighter world.

"The issue now before us," wrote U.S. senator James Grimes to Governor Samuel Kirkwood on January 28, 1861, "is whether we have a country, whether or not this is a nation." "I know the people of Iowa well enough to believe," he continued, "that they will risk all things and endure all things in maintaining the honor of the national flag and preserving the national Union."[28]

CHAPTER TWO

The Military Frenzy

Iowans around the state demanded military retribution following the bombardment of Fort Sumter by South Carolina secessionists on April 12, 1861. Their collective reaction created a frenzied environment. Iowans of every political stripe—conservative Democrats, moderate Republicans, and radical Republicans—all responded to President Abraham Lincoln's call for volunteers. In the state's Mississippi River ports, huge crowds of civilians turned out to cheer as the boats loaded with soldiers steamed southward. So many Iowans volunteered that officials could not locate enough military rifles and uniforms to outfit all of the citizens-turned-soldiers. Although four more slave states seceded as a result of Lincoln's call for military retribution, only a few Hawkeyes publicly condemned the president's actions.

Anger at the Deep South states had been smoldering for some time in Iowa. One year before the Fort Sumter attack, Democrats and Republicans had expressed harsh opinions about the motives of Southern slaveholders. At presidential campaign rallies, thousands of Iowans donned military-style clothing and paraded through city streets. President Buchanan's veto of the Homestead Act in July 1860 further intensified political passions around Iowa. As Federal election day approached, the partisan rancor in Iowa reached a crescendo.

More than 90 percent of eligible voters cast a presidential ballot in November 1860. Four candidates ran for president that year, two from slave states and two from free states, but 98 percent of Iowa voters selected either Illinois Republican Lincoln or Stephen Douglas, a Democrat from Illinois. The two Southern candidates for president, John Bell from Tennessee and John Breckinridge from Kentucky, collected only 2 percent of all votes in Iowa. Lincoln garnered more than half of Iowa's ballots, and his victory in the Electoral College gave Iowans a greater stake in the outcome of the secession crisis that followed.

Initially, unionism muted Iowans' demands for military retribution. When South Carolina seceded in December 1860, few called for Federal intervention. Douglas Democrats and Lincoln Republicans blamed each other for South Carolina's decision. As time passed, however, and more states seceded, Iowans refocused their anger at the Deep South. Residents anxiously watched and waited on political developments in Washington, and the pent-up anxiety mounted to the boiling point. One night of heavy artillery fire in Charleston Harbor unleashed all of the anger at once. The Confederate bombardment, coming six weeks after Lincoln's inauguration, incited Iowans to turn out en masse and demand reintegration by any means necessary.

Iowans and the 1860 Presidential Election

It is no small challenge to explain how a united nation self-destructed following an election in which each of the four presidential candidates self-identified as a unionist. In hindsight, the disintegration began in the mid-1850s when the two national parties split along sectional lines over issues related to westward expansion. Sectionalism remained a strong dynamic in 1860 even though each of the four parties claimed to represent every section of the nation.

The national voting trends broke down into distinct North-South geographic patterns in 1860, with Bell popular in Virginia, Kentucky, and Tennessee, and Lincoln popular in the nonslave states. East of the Mississippi River and south of the Ohio River, relatively few Democrats cast votes for Douglas, the Illinois senator who championed local control over slavery in the territories. Instead of Douglas, slave-state Democrats stood in line for Breckinridge, who sought to enable slavery's spread westward by means of congressional laws protecting slaveholders. Breckinridge attracted some support in the Northeastern states, but for the most part free-state Democrats picked Douglas over Breckinridge.

A four-way race was not inevitable when local political elites sat down to strategize in early 1860. If Old Line Whigs and conciliatory Democrats had had their way, 1860 would have witnessed a two-way contest between one national Democrat and one national opposition candidate from the old Whig Party. The two-way race never materialized because intra-party friction in both national organizations resulted in a four-way split along sectional lines. Iowans, rather than conciliate, contributed to hasten the demise of the two national parties.

When Iowa Democrats gathered in the late winter of 1860 and discussed their favorite candidates for president, a party schism was the furthest result from their minds. Despite their best intentions, the Democratic national party divided along North-South lines. The sectional split occurred because Iowans and other free-state Democrats in the Western states stubbornly refused to relinquish their support for Stephen Douglas.

Douglas won over Hawkeye Democrats not just because he favored the Homestead Act and opposed Southern efforts to protect slavemasters traveling to Western territories with their slaves. Other free-state Democrats demanded the admission of Kansas as a free state, but Douglas was seen as the most battle-hardened of all popular-sovereignty Democrats. His reputation gained a boost in 1858 when the "Little Giant," as he was known, survived an attempt by President James Buchanan to purge him from the U.S. Senate for refusing to side with Southern Democrats who wanted Kansas admitted as a slave state. The drama in Washington won over the hearts of Iowans who supported local sovereignty and opposed Republican legislation barring slavery in the territories as anti-unionist. But it also made Douglas a demon in the eyes of slave-state Democrats.

When slave-state Democrats threatened to bolt the party if Douglas won the party's nomination for president in 1860, Iowa party leaders refused to abandon their candidate. By pushing their hero's nomination, they sought to recapture control of the national party. They also saw in Douglas the opportunity to defeat the upstart Republicans and permanently reverse the sectionalist momentum in the Hawkeye state.

The schism occurred after the Deep South delegates walked out of the national convention in protest over Douglas's majority strength. The Illinois senator needed a two-thirds majority to earn the nomination under party rules, a situation that ordinarily induced the leading candidate's withdrawal. Although their hero did not have quite enough delegates to meet the two-thirds majority, not a single Iowa delegate changed his vote. One month later, at the second Democratic convention in Baltimore, the same group of Iowans refused to concede defeat. When Douglas supporters managed to reach the two-thirds threshold by disregarding the walk-out delegates, Southern dissenters organized a separate convention and selected Breckinridge to head their ticket.

The split in the nation's most powerful political party should have made it possible for the opposition candidate to capture the White House. That is what had happened in 1848, when Whig Party nominee Zachary Taylor earned a majority of Electoral College votes over his two Democratic opponents. In 1860, the ideal fusion nominee appeared to be Missourian Edward Bates, a Millard Fillmore supporter in 1856 and a longtime Old Line Whig. For those who preferred a candidate who could court Old Line Whigs and anti-extensionists alike, Bates became the runaway favorite. Bates arrived at the Chicago Republican convention having won the endorsement of prominent Republican newspaper editors in New York, Massachusetts, Indiana, and Maryland.

A four-way race ensued in 1860, not a three-way race, because opposition voters in the Western free states refused to support an inter-sectional coalition candidate. Not a single Hawkeye newspaper endorsed Bates, and state party leaders attending the convention targeted Bates for elimination. With so little support from Iowa's delegation and other Western free states, Bates eventually withdrew his candidacy after one round of voting, a development that ensured an anti-extensionist would head the party's ticket. Instead of Bates, the nomination went to Lincoln, an ex-Whig and one of the several anti-extensionist candidates.

With Bates out of the running, the old national Whig Party once again split along sectional lines. Ex-Whig Lincoln was not an acceptable choice to proponents of the Missouri Compromise Line. Rather than support an anti-extensionist in a three-way race against two Democrats, Old Line Whigs rallied around a fourth candidate, John Bell. They predicted Bell would be a popular candidate in the free states as well as the slave states because the senator from Tennessee had voted against the Kansas-Nebraska Act in 1854.

With the Whigs and ex-Whigs working at cross-purposes, Douglas Democrats and Breckinridge Democrats each had a chance of carrying the Electoral College in 1860. So did Bell and Lincoln. Some prognosticators predicted that no single candidate would carry a majority of

Electoral College votes. If that occurred, the House of Representatives would choose the next president. In the end, Lincoln carried enough free states to win the Electoral College. The anti-extensionist candidate not only earned Iowa's Electoral College votes but also garnered a majority of Iowa ballots in this four-way race.

For all intents and purposes, the 1860 election in Iowa played out as a two-way battle between Abraham Lincoln and Stephen Douglas. Bell and Breckenridge received a very small proportion of votes. However, a two-way race was not inevitable. In several states, three candidates earned a substantial number of votes. In neighboring Missouri, all four candidates received at least 10 percent of the vote, and no single candidate collected more than 36 percent. A similar four-way race played out in California. In New England, three-way contests ensued in two states, Connecticut and Massachusetts. A three-way race also played out in Pennsylvania, the home state of President Buchanan. Buchanan pushed for Democrat Breckinridge, who had been his vice-presidential running mate in 1856.[1]

In Iowa, rural Democrats strongly opposed the Kentuckian, even though the Breckinridge camp included several powerful figures in Iowa's Democratic Party. In virtually every Iowa rural district, Douglas handily beat Breckinridge. Among opposition voters, meanwhile, Lincoln out-polled Old Line Whig Bell by a 40-to-1 ratio. Although 9 percent of Iowans had cast their votes for the Old Line Whig in 1856, Bell drew only 1 percent four years later.

The two-way contest reveals much about the mood of Iowans. The final election results reflected voters' impressions that Southern slavemasters dominated the Federal government. Western issues—especially the assurance of Federal support for continued westward expansion—became most important to Iowans. Here, on the free-state frontier, local caucus leaders demanded that Congress pass the Homestead Act and admit Kansas as a state with slavery forever prohibited. Bell did not go on record as favoring the Homestead Act, and Breckinridge opposed both the Homestead Act and the admission of Kansas as a free state. Douglas and Lincoln endorsed both measures, and Iowans rallied around these two candidates.

That the two old national parties had practically disintegrated never fazed most Hawkeye voters. Slave-state voters opposed both Douglas and Lincoln, but Iowans at the polls insisted upon either congressional legislation barring slavery in the Western territories (the Republican platform) or congressional admission of every territory with the status of slavery determined by a majority of the territory's residents (the Douglas platform). The chorus of Southerners calling for secession was growing louder, but Iowans did not take the doomsday rhetoric seriously.

The refusal of a majority of Iowans to support Breckinridge's slave-code bill pending in Congress disturbed some longtime residents. They mourned what they saw as a declining spirit of unionism in Iowa. A majority of Iowans had supported the package of compromise bills enacted in 1850, but since then, it seemed, a parochial perspective had taken root in Iowa that opposed any concessions to slave states. The slave-code bill was popular among slave-state unionists because it granted protection to slaveowners looking to establish plantations in the Western territories. If Iowans continued to oppose protection for slaveowners, conservative unionists wondered how the nation could remain unified.

In fact, unionist sentiment did predominate in Iowa in 1860. When questioned about their patriotism, Republican leaders pointed out that the state party still supported the Federal Fugitive Slave Act and opposed abolitionism. Strategic planning by state party leaders reinforced the appearance that Iowa Republicans loathed sectional discord. Rather than accuse slaveowners of immoral behavior, moderate Republicans cited economic reasons for opposing protection for slaveowners in the territories.

In the two congressional races that year, radical nominees were overlooked in favor of two moderates, former Keokuk mayor Samuel Curtis and William Vandever of Dubuque. Both men had won election to Congress in 1858, and in 1860 the incumbents faced off against pro-Douglas Democrats. As each pair of congressional candidates engaged in a series of public debates around the state, calls for unionism rang out. At a time when radical abolitionists welcomed secession, all four Iowa candidates for Congress fervently opposed any suggestion that the Union be divided.

On the campaign trail, candidates from both parties condemned abolitionists as disunionist traitors. Iowa Republicans joined Democrats in refusing to enact the type of personal liberty laws promulgated in other free states to undermine the Federal Fugitive Slave Act. Disintegration along sectional lines, they believed, would invite the forces of tyranny to seize the reins of power throughout the nation. If democratic government became corrupted by disunion, moderate Republicans believed that individual liberty no longer could be assured. Disunion represented, moreover, a failure of the American experiment with democracy.[2]

No matter which of the presidential candidates prevailed in the Electoral College, Iowa voters were prepared to accept the result as a consequence of democracy. They would grudgingly accept a President Bell or a President Breckinridge, just as they would accept a President Lincoln or a President Douglas. In turn, Iowans expected that Southern unionists would accept a President Lincoln or a President Douglas.

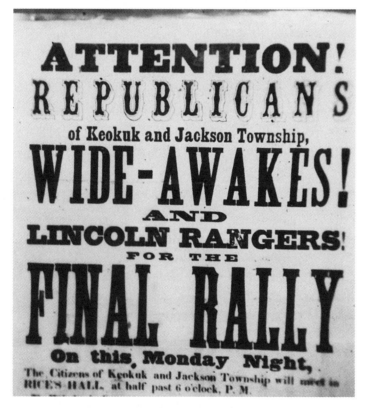

FIGURE 3. Assemblies held before election day included parades by paramilitary units. Across Iowa, Douglas proponents and Lincoln proponents each sponsored rallies. This Republican flyer was posted around the port of Keokuk. *Reprinted by permission of the Keokuk Public Library.*

Iowans' pride in self-governance generated a multitude of local candidate organizations in 1860. Douglas clubs and Lincoln clubs sprouted
across the state, and many of them formed paramilitary units. Groups of
men marched in handsome uniforms in other free states in 1860, but in
Iowa, a frontier jurisdiction so close to Bleeding Kansas, formations of
men in uniform held a special appeal for ordinary voters. Their prolifer-
ation in Iowa symbolized the extent to which Lincoln Republicans and
Douglas Democrats each considered themselves under siege as a result of
the turn of events in the New West during the 1850s.

Decked out in tailored military-style jackets and carrying banners that
proclaimed "Minute Men," "Mounted Rangers," or "Wide-Awakes," the
marchers added a zany flair to the spectacle of the campaign. Lincolnites
and their counterparts, the "Little Giants," marched before and after
campaign speeches. In October, a pro-Lincoln parade in Fairfield drew
Republican paramilitary groups from twenty-two communities, a total of
2,200 men marching in step. When William Seward made an appearance
on Lincoln's behalf in Dubuque, 300 uniformed Wide-Awakes escorted
him from the dock to the Julien House hotel. At one Republican rally
in Keokuk, 2,500 Wide-Awakes from Iowa and Illinois paraded through
town.[3]

Local Voting Results

The two-way contest between Douglas Democrats and Free Soil Republicans proved intense and contentious. On election day, neighborhood
enthusiasm compelled many marginally involved Iowans to turn out and
vote. The total number of ballots cast in 1860 exceeded the 1859 gubernatorial election turnout by nearly 20,000, an 18 percent increase.

Of the six families included in this study, several voted Republican in
1860. Delaware County's Ferdinand Dunham was among the thousands
of rural northeastern Iowa farmers who did so. Dunham, a New York
native, attended the Congregational church in Manchester, an organization whose members nationwide voted Republican by an overwhelming
margin. In Mahaska County, where most residents traced their roots to
the Ohio River valley and not to New York or New England, Simeon
Stevens apparently voted Republican. Native-born skilled laborers in Iowa

embraced Republicanism by a wide margin in the late 1850s, and Stevens's occupation as a carpenter is a strong indication that he stood in line for Lincoln. In Pottawattamie County, John Musser's partisan affiliation is more difficult to discern. A Pennsylvania native who spent much of his early life in Ohio, he had chosen to settle in a traditionally Democratic county after crossing the Mississippi River. Letters sent home from the army by his son Charles indicate that John Musser either voted Democratic or did not affiliate with either party.

One thing is certain. In Muscatine, local authorities denied Alexander Clark the chance to cast a ballot because of his mixed African and European heritage. Had Clark been allowed to vote, he would have stood in line for Lincoln, the most antislavery candidate of the four men running for president. Downstream from Muscatine, black men in the port of Keokuk faced the same racial barrier to voting. Annie Wittenmyer faced a statewide gender barrier. She, like all women, was not permitted to vote, but at least her father could vote because he was white. Three of her four brothers had reached twenty-one years of age, and each of them voted, as far as we know.

We do not know for certain what party the Turner men supported in 1860. Annie Wittenmyer's brothers, whether Republican or Democrat, pledged allegiance to unionism and not abolitionism. The devout unionism of her father rubbed off on Wittenmyer, whose published poetry after the war reflected a devout belief in the virtues of democratic governance. "Above the flags of all nations," she wrote later in her life, "Our beautiful banner floats high . . . The emblem of freedom and right; No star be lost from its azure; No blot on its spotless white."[4]

Unfortunately, there is no historical record of William Wittenmyer's partisan affiliation in 1860, and the town of Keokuk offers little guidance. The kaleidoscope of inhabitants in the town included proponents of Bell, Breckinridge, Douglas, and Lincoln. In many Mississippi River ports, some merchants favored a candidate other than Lincoln or Douglas. Wittenmyer, a Pennsylvania native who had spent most of his life in the Ohio River valley, maintained business relationships in Missouri, Ohio, Kentucky, and Illinois, as well as Iowa. Because he had so many inter-sectional business relationships, he might have feared the consequences if Southern states seceded following a Lincoln or Douglas victory. Cells of

Bell proponents held public rallies in Keokuk and other river ports, as did some Breckinridge proponents. The advocates of Bell and the advocates of Breckinridge included some of Iowa's wealthiest men. Bell strategists selected Muscatine as the location for the state's lone pro-Bell newspaper.

Statewide, religious affiliation tended to drive the voting behavior of white immigrant groups during the prewar period. Controversy over liquor regulation, a measure associated with the Republican Party, worked to the advantage of Democratic candidates. While Catholic Irish and Germans usually endorsed Democrats, British Protestants solidly backed Republican candidates. Anticlerical Germans reluctantly voted Republican in 1860. These libertarian freethinkers opposed liquor regulation, but their antislavery zeal led them to vote for Lincoln. Lutherans in Iowa were divided between Republicans and Democrats. While Scandinavians generally leaned Republican, German-speaking Lutherans split their votes. In Keokuk, immigrant voters endorsed Democratic candidates for the most part, while U.S. natives usually leaned Republican. Immigrant voters in Lee County represented a substantial portion of the electorate, and in the final count the number of Douglas ballots exceeded that of Lincoln ballots by a small percentage.[5]

Keokuk's voting results did not mirror Iowa as a whole. Statewide, Lincoln outdrew Douglas 70,300 to 56,500. New voters preferred Lincoln by a wide margin, and crossover voting patterns also helped Republicans, thanks to developments in Washington. In July, just as the Douglas Democrats appeared to be gaining momentum against Lincoln in Iowa, President Buchanan vetoed the Homestead Act. Republicans lost little time associating Douglas with the Democratic president's veto. Although Douglas himself condemned it in the strongest language, the president's actions on behalf of slave-state Democrats drove many independent voters in Iowa to stand in line for Lincoln at the polling station. In addition to losing independents, Douglas and his Iowa allies witnessed erosion within their own party. The list of defectors included the owner of one prominent Democratic newspaper in Iowa City.[6]

As a result of crossover voting, Pottawattamie County, the home of the Mussers, turned out a Republican majority for the first time in the history of the county. Democrats there had won every election, year after year, until the 1860 presidential contest. In Delaware, the Dunhams' county, Lincoln garnered a majority of votes even though one year earlier most county voters had preferred the Democratic candidate for governor. Meanwhile, in the counties that had voted Republican in 1856, Lincoln prevailed, often by a wide margin. Contests in the river districts tended to be closer than those in the interior counties. In Muscatine County, Lincoln captured 55 percent of all ballots cast.

Riding on Lincoln's coattails, Iowa's two Republican representatives defeated their pro-Douglas rivals. Thanks to support from conservative Republicans in the southern tier of counties, Keokuk's Samuel Curtis beat his challenger by 3,700 votes (roughly 53 percent to 47 percent). In the northern district, Representative Vandever's rival went down to defeat by a wider margin. Compared to the 1858 contest here, the Republican incumbent gained a substantially larger number of votes in 1860. Republicans carried nearly every county in Vandever's congressional district.[7]

Hometown Reactions to Secession

As a result of the telegraph, Iowans learned of Lincoln's electoral victory relatively quickly. Enthusiastic celebrations took place in Republican quarters, but news from South Carolina soon dampened the postelection enthusiasm. When word arrived that South Carolina had scheduled a secession convention, many Iowans expressed dismay. Having voted for Lincoln without regard for the likely consequences in the Deep South, Republicans were stunned by the prospect of disunity. Even after six more Deep South states followed South Carolina's lead, many Iowans could not accept the possibility that the nation would become permanently divided. Douglas supporters, meanwhile, could not agree on who should be blamed for the catastrophe. One easy scapegoat for Democrats was Lincoln, the candidate of the sectional party, who had defeated their beloved candidate. Democrats in Iowa also cast blame on the Southern Democrats who earlier split their national party and now marched in time with the secessionists.

In the nation's capital, the five-month period from November 1860 to March 1861 witnessed a flurry of compromise proposals. Politicians in those slave states that initially hesitated to secede talked of sectional reconciliation and reached out to representatives from the Northern border districts. Much of the behind-the-scenes talk in Congress involved the

Crittenden Compromise, a series of measures sponsored by a bipartisan group of senators (including Stephen Douglas). The group took its name from John J. Crittenden, a Kentucky Whig who, in the tradition of Henry Clay, sought to bring wavering states back into the fold.

Crittenden's list of reforms, introduced in January 1861, rejected the Republican principle of the nonextension of slavery and called for a return to the 1820 Missouri Compromise Line. By reopening the possibility of slavery in territories that were south of the Old Line, the bill's supporters hoped to redirect Southern attention toward national expansion and thereby reverse the momentum of secession. In the Northeastern states, conservative unionists specifically chose Crittenden's reform package as the compromise bill most likely to succeed. Tens of thousands of unionists in New York and New England signed a pro-Crittenden petition circulated in January and presented it to Congress. Their enthusiasm was shared by hundreds, perhaps thousands, of Iowa Democrats. Iowa Republicans, meanwhile, balked. They embraced one proposal or another but refused to accept the premise of Crittenden's plan.

During the months leading up to Fort Sumter, Iowans at home could do little but wait out the impasse. Many still did not think the South would make good on its threats. "You need not be afraid of the secession movement," wrote a Tama County farmer to relatives in Scotland in March 1861. "The western people treat the matter pretty coolly. This thing will blow over in a little while." The task of surviving the winter of 1861 served to distract Iowans and generate skepticism. "The snow has been from two to three feet deep since the first of January and cold most severest weather I ever saw," wrote John Kenyon, a Delaware County farmer, to relatives in New England on March 3, 1861. "All I have did this winter is my chores and I could not half do them some of the time it blowed and snowed so," the farmer complained. "I have lost 17 head [of cattle] and expect 4 more soon." While Iowa's residents went about enduring the season, Governor Kirkwood contemplated summoning the local militia companies and calling a special session of the legislature. As of April 1, he had done neither.[8]

Hundreds of Iowans wrote to the state's two senators and two representatives to offer their advice. Relatively few of the writers, apparently, called for a Federal military response. Even after Lincoln's inauguration in March 1861, Republicans and Democrats in Iowa declined for the most part to promote immediate military intervention. Not until South Caro-lina secessionists bombarded the Federal military installation in Charles-ton Harbor on April 12 did a critical mass of Iowans demand military retribution.

From our modern perspective, the reasons underlying the sudden switch from passivity to military frenzy are not self-evident. Southern militias engaged in several aggressive actions from December to March, yet none of these prompted grassroots demands for retaliation like the April 12 bombardment of Fort Sumter in Charleston Harbor. The short answer to the puzzle is that Iowans' unionist spirit tempered their reac-tion to events in the Deep South states. The same ideological forces that motivated Iowans to conciliate in the early months of the secession crisis fueled their angry response to the blatant military challenge in Charleston Harbor.

If the community debate in Keokuk is any indication, Iowans expressed a high level of dismay and frustration during the four months before Fort Sumter. When South Carolina seceded in December 1860, several Keokuk hawks demanded an immediate military response. Most did not. Instead, they appealed for caution. In January, when the Charlestonians fired sev-eral cannonballs at a U.S. Navy vessel attempting to resupply Fort Sumter, Keokuk citizens hesitated. They hesitated when secessionists comman-deered guns, cannon, and ammunition from Federal armories in the Deep South.

Crittenden's proposal energized local Democrats to demand that the state's representatives and senators support the compromise. In late Jan-uary, with five Deep South states having seceded and two more headed toward secession, Keokuk's Democratic leaders invited all "friends of the Union" to attend a rally for reunion at the courthouse. The port's loca-tion on the border between slave and free states placed its leaders in an ideal position to mediate a peaceful reconciliation, insisted the organizers. Mediation was also in the port's best interest. "It would be a terrible thing," opined Keokuk's Federal judge, "for us to live on the border in case of civil war."[9]

The Union meeting in Keokuk became a significant event because Republicans and conservative Whigs joined the Democrats at the court-house. So many community leaders turned out that organizers quickly scheduled two additional meetings and moved the assembly to a larger venue. Iowans of all parties clearly wanted to find a way to reunify the nation.

After the debate began, Republicans in the audience expressed reluctance at the prospect of making political concessions. Democrats expressed some willingness to negotiate, although they could not agree among themselves on the best terms for compromise. Every Democrat who spoke went on record as favoring compromise, but the lack of obvious solutions divided old friends. When one Democrat proposed the use of military force if all peaceable means had been exhausted, others refused. In the end, dozens of citizens walked out of the meeting in disgust at the lack of consensus. Most disappointed were Democrats who came to realize the scope of disagreement among fellow party members.[10]

No one in attendance spoke up in favor of peaceful separation, a topic hotly debated in the Northeastern states. Only a small fraction of Keokuk residents advocated abolitionism, and there is no indication that abolitionists attended the "friends of the Union" meeting. No one in the assembly expressed support for secession or pointed out the advantages of secession. Instead, speakers referenced the United States in semisacred terms and predicted that disunion would reverse the progress of Western civilization. Attorney William Belknap spoke for many Democrats in the audience when he insisted on taking every possible action to preserve "the glorious and ever to be cherished Union, established by the wisdom and valor of our Fathers." Samuel Miller, a Republican attorney, went so far as to argue that disunion threatened "all the interests of man and society." With Federal unity dissolved, "the ability of government to assert and maintain its own existence and integrity" would be lost. Hugh Sample, Keokuk's mayor, likened the nation to the human body, with the seceded states representing the body's principal limbs. Until all the limbs were reattached, the mayor implied, the body would cease to function. "It is the duty of every patriot," insisted attorney George Dixon, "to act and speak as he shall answer to his God at the judgment day."[11]

Among the mixed assembly of Republicans, Democrats, and Old Line Whigs, a number of speakers expressed a willingness to offer concessions to the slave states. One Republican proposed to elevate New Mexico Territory to statehood with the institution of slavery legal. The most generous proposals came from Democrats, many of whom appealed to Republicans in the audience to support the Crittenden Compromise. The Deep South states would rejoin the Union, Keokuk Democrats insisted, if the free states adopted concessions authored by slave-state senators loyal to the Union.

Despite the best efforts of many in the audience, the Keokuk assembly ultimately failed to find common ground. The fact that secession had already taken place limited the depth of the discussion, and in short order the dialogue devolved into a partisan debate around old campaign slogans. One Republican announced his opposition to extending slavery into any territory. One Democrat accused the Republican Party of plotting to abolish slavery in every state, a goal the accuser claimed had precipitated the Deep South's secession. A newspaper editor raised his voice and accused the Democrats of grossly exaggerating Republican intentions. More than one Democrat insisted the South had been wronged by the North. Southerners could not be compelled back into the Union through force of arms, some insisted. If Republican armies invaded the slave states, Democrats warned, they would not participate in the anti-Southern military crusade. Democrat William Clagett warned Republicans they would "find a hot fire in the rear" if Republicans pursued military intervention. Frustrated by the Democrats' reluctance to use military intervention, a Republican newspaper editor accused them of kneeling "in humble servility to the lordlings of the Plantations." When one prominent community member expressed his willingness to "get down on [his] knees before the South," the editor insisted that doing so betrayed its principles by allowing tyrannical slaveholders to oppress white labor.[12]

On Iowa's far western border, worried citizens in Council Bluffs feared disunion would permanently impede white migration to Nebraska Territory. Lysander Babbitt, a leading Democrat in Council Bluffs, predicted the nation would split into four separate jurisdictions. In the midwestern section of the nation, the Council Bluffs newspaper editor imagined an alliance of slave states and free states, including Iowa, flourishing under the same flag in the Mississippi-Ohio-Missouri river basin. The Deep South Confederacy would eventually attract Virginia, Maryland, and North Carolina, Babbitt predicted, but not Louisiana, Arkansas, Texas, or Missouri. Those states would remain a part of the Mississippi River basin alliance.[13]

Other Iowans offered different forecasts. Rather than split the map into four jurisdictions, antislavery radicals predicted a two-way bifurcation with an east-to-west boundary along the Ohio River, the dividing line between a nation that allowed slavery and one that banned it.[14] Unless Missouri suddenly abolished slavery, abolitionists expected that the Iowa-Missouri border would form the dividing line in the New West.

Most Iowans, however, found any map of separation distasteful. A permanent split would doom American civilization, no matter how many jurisdictions emerged from the chaos. Each of the families included in this study—with the possible exception of Alexander Clark's—refused to consider disunion as a satisfactory result to the sectional political crisis. Although only a small minority around the state demanded immediate military action against South Carolina before Fort Sumter, the bulk of the population refused to rule out violence as a means to restore the nation. Many Iowans willing to consider military action presumed it would not become necessary. From their perspective, Southern secession represented a temporary phase in the long sectional conflict they expected would be resolved by nonviolent means.

Iowans in Congress Reject Crittenden's Compromise

When South Carolina declared its independence, Iowa's four representatives in Congress—James Grimes, James Harlan, Samuel Curtis, and William Vandever—reacted cautiously. They also reacted in a unified voice. Although they came from different backgrounds and represented different towns, they shared a common political path to Washington. Former Whigs all of them, the Iowans had risen to prominence by toeing the moderate Republican line.

Iowa's gang of four began preparing the nation for war in January by enacting naval improvement bills, army equipment bills, and resolutions authorizing the president to take action in response to threats to Federal institutions in the seceded states. Although armed intervention threatened to drive the northern-tier slave states into the Deep South alliance, the Iowans refused to abandon the possibility of forced reintegration. Any approach to reunification had to focus on the Deep South states and not on the slave states still in the Union. With improved Federal military resources, the Iowans expected the seceded states would seriously consider rejoining the Union. If not, the Federal government would be in a better position to engage in military intervention tactics.

The state's congressional delegation kept a close eye on the rival Democrats during the debate over the military bills. The Iowans feared the Deep South secession movement would inspire a new coalition of unionist Democrats to cooperate on a plan to reverse the outcome of the 1860 election. Four long months would elapse between election day in early November and the March 4 inauguration day, and the Republicans in Congress experienced some sleepless nights worrying whether Lincoln would be denied the White House.

For Representative Samuel Curtis, abandoning the White House was not an option. "If the republicans break up and [the Democrats] resume the ascendance," Curtis wrote, "the danger is they will supply anarchy with a powerful military government."[15] Senator James Grimes, from his perspective as a twenty-three-year resident of the first free state west of the Mississippi River, loathed the possibility of Lincoln's resignation. "How rapidly we are following in the footsteps of the governments of Mexico and South America!" he lamented privately in a letter. "[Do] we have any assurance that this is the last demand to be made upon us? Can we be certain that success in this instance will not whet the appetite for new concessions and demands, and that similar threats of secession and revolution will not succeed every future president election?"[16]

Grimes, Harlan, Curtis, and Vandever never seriously considered supporting Crittenden's proposal. In hopes of stopping the spread of secessionist fever, they did, like some other moderate Republicans in Congress, express support for proposals designed to enable slavery to take root in one territory or to guarantee slavery in the states where it currently existed. But to the end, every Iowa senator and representative fought tooth and nail to oppose Crittenden's plan, which, if enacted into law, would have invited further U.S. military expansion south of Texas and Florida.

Why were Iowa's Republican leaders so strongly opposed to the compromise proposal that many free-state residents supported? Because doing so threatened the fragile unity of Lincoln's party. Five years earlier, opposition to the extension of slavery was the common denominator that brought together the several diverse factions that coalesced into the Republican

Party. At the national convention in 1860, every major faction that joined the Republican alliance paid homage to the principle of nonextension—that is, not allowing slavery in any of the new Western territories. Nonextension had become the party's sacred cow. Free Soilers and abolitionists in the party threatened to leave the party in droves if moderate Republicans signed off on any proposal that contradicted the Chicago platform. Even the most modest suggestion—admitting New Mexico as a slave state, for example—threatened to dissolve the national party.

Senator Grimes recognized the long-term implications of Crittenden's Compromise in a January 28, 1861, letter to his friend Kirkwood. The proposal, Grimes noted, would extend slavery "*to all territory that may hereafter be acquired south of that line*"—"that line" meaning the 1820 Missouri Compromise Line. If the measure passed, Grimes expected that "raids would at once begin upon the provinces of Mexico; war would ensue; the annexation of Sonora, Chihuahua, Cohahuila, Nuevo Leon, Tamaulipas, and other provinces, would follow; they would be converted, at the instant of their acquisition, from free into slave Territories, and ultimately be admitted into the Union as slave States." Coming at a time when the nation needed to define the limits of slavery, Crittenden's plan would do the opposite. "Much as I love peace and seek to pursue it," Grimes stated, "I am not prepared to pay this price for it." Kirkwood, a longtime opponent of Cuban annexation, echoed Grimes's concerns. The governor was prepared to accept slavery in New Mexico, but he refused to entertain any thoughts of new slave states south of the Rio Grande or in the Caribbean.[17]

Some historians, notes researcher Robert Cook, criticize Kirkwood, Grimes, and other state Republican leaders for their inflexible stance on Crittenden's proposal.[18] Had Iowa Republicans teamed with conservatives in other states to propel the Crittenden plan forward, goes the argument, the course of American history would have taken a different turn. The Democrats and conservative Whigs who backed Crittenden's proposal were prepared to work with Republican leaders on a bundle of provisions that every party might support. Had Republican leaders done so, bloodshed might have been avoided. While civil war had been averted in 1832 and 1850 through inter-sectional negotiation, in 1861 Republican senators and representatives blocked the possibility of meaningful inter-sectional negotiation. A few Republicans in some states bravely attempted to support Crittenden's proposal, but none of Iowa's party leaders crossed the party line.

In actuality, bloodshed could not have been avoided if the Union was to be preserved. Unlike the situation in 1832 and 1850, in 1860 secession had already crystallized. In all likelihood, successful passage of Crittenden's proposal would not have moved the seven Deep South states to renounce their declaration of independence. And even if they had done so, secession followed by annulment of secession would have prolonged the existing sectional tensions and encouraged other states to threaten secession as a means to improve their leverage in the nation's capital. Annexing Cuba and adding new slave states south of Texas was not a recipe for long-term tranquility, since it invited wars with Mexico and Spain (Cuba's colonial master) and would have exacerbated free-state concerns about the extension of slavery. With or without a grand compromise, military intervention would have been necessary to reintegrate the Deep South states. Representative Curtis and his moderate Republican colleagues understood the futility of Crittenden's proposal, even though the interruption of shipping on the Mississippi River gravely threatened Iowa's economy.

On the floor of the Senate, James Harlan put into words what Grimes and other Iowans expressed privately. On January 11, 1861, three weeks after South Carolina's declaration of independence, Harlan spoke for two and a half hours. He condemned the secessionists for refusing to share power with the duly elected government. Every candidate for the presidency in 1860 had been a sectional candidate, he contended, so any election outcome would have alienated one region or another. Refusing to accept the winning candidate for sectional reasons rendered every candidate for the presidency in 1860 ineligible, the Mount Pleasant Republican argued. The solution was not to offer concessions to the seceded states. The solution was for all slave states to accept the Electoral College results and give the duly chosen executive a fair opportunity to defend the rights of Americans in all sections of the nation.[19]

Harlan went to the podium four weeks later and accused Democrats in the chamber of acting in bad faith: "You have governed this country for the last sixty years. You have controlled its legislation; you have controlled its judiciary; you have controlled its internal policy; you have controlled its foreign relations; you have grown haughty, proud, and—I say it without intending offense—insolent. Being accustomed to command, you have forgotten how to obey. Although you have been fairly beaten at the polls, you refuse to yield the Government into the hands of your constitutional successors."[20]

In Senator Harlan's mind, the threat of secession compromised the political rights of free-state settlers. Conceding the rights of the free states as a "mode of preserving the Union would cost us too much," he warned his fellow senators. "We have the hearts and heads and hands and will to preserve it in a cheaper manner, let the crisis come when it may."[21]

This was not the first time Harlan had made his views known. In a speech before the Senate several months before the 1860 election, the Iowa Republican had replied in a militant tone after one Southern senator threatened to secede if free-state citizens voted Lincoln into office. Rather than "become the political slaves" of the South, Harlan implied that the Western free states would take up arms against the secessionists if necessary to prevent further intimidation.[22]

Concerns over Government Dysfunction

Antislavery sentiment contributed to motivate the Iowans in Congress to stand by Lincoln and oppose Crittenden's proposal, though it was not the primary motivating factor. From their perspective as Westerners, the fear of government dysfunction loomed larger than the amoral institution of slavery. The correspondence of Senator Grimes demonstrates the value he placed on functional government. If threats to secede became common practice during sectional negotiations, he reasoned, the legislative process would become hopelessly gridlocked.

In his January 28, 1861, letter to Kirkwood, Grimes described the slippery slope scenario he feared would unfold, rendering considerable harm to both democratic governance and majority rule. "If Florida and South Carolina can secede because of the slavery question," wrote Grimes, "what shall prevent Pennsylvania from seceding because the Government declines to adequately protect her iron and coal interests, or New England because her manufactures, or New York because her commerce is not sufficiently protected?" For Grimes, neither secession nor the threat of secession could ever be tolerated. Even if politicians threatening secession had no real intent to declare independence, the possibility that such a threat might be used as a negotiating tool to gain political leverage severely disturbed the Iowa moderate. I will "agree to no compromise," he told Kirkwood, "until the right to secede was fully renounced." His language suggests that if the Commonwealth of Massachusetts had seceded or threatened to secede, Grimes would have protested just the same, perhaps with the same degree of fervor.[23]

In the twenty-first century, the word *moderate* often describes nonideologues who employ practical strategies in the pursuit of social progress. That description does not apply to Iowa's moderate Republican leaders in 1860. Although their balance of unionism and antislavery moralism induced them to reach out to both conservative unionists and radical abolitionists, Iowa's Civil War leaders maintained an idealistic approach to the world that was not purely practical. Senator Grimes refused to view compromise as an end in itself. Goodwill gestures such as Crittenden's proposals "tacitly recognize the right of these States to secede," Grimes insisted privately to his friend Kirkwood in January 1861.

Rather than embrace compromise as an end in itself, two powerful ideologies compelled these Republicans to confront secessionism head on: Moral ethics, on the one hand, and unionism, on the other, combined to empower them to reject measures that merely postponed the inevitable decline of slaveholders' political power. Before 1862, the Iowans' unionism militated against their latent antislavery moralism in a manner that maximized the chances of long-term social progress. When the president proclaimed emancipation as a means to end the military conflict in late 1862, the moderates' zeal for moralism merged with their zeal for unionism. The confluence of events transformed them into radical unionists.

Looking back on this critical moment in American history, we can see that the moderate Republicans' dual idealism offered the most practical approach to reuniting the nation. Antislavery radicals reacted enthusiastically to the possibility of secession, while conservative unionists reacted cautiously. Each group initially refused to consider military action to compel reunion, but Iowa's moderate Republicans pursued a plan that condemned the act of secession while anticipating the possibility of military intervention. The moderates understood the larger political dynamics at work. When the seceding states withdrew one by one, like a series of dominoes, the moderates' ability to balance unionism and antislavery sentiment endowed Iowa's leadership clique with the ability to identify the most pragmatic path to reunion.

The Iowans' tactics in Washington directly benefited the long-term interests of the United States as well as of the residents of Iowa. Their actions contributed to sustaining the Republican power base while preventing the nation's sectional divorce from becoming permanent. Had Old Line unionists controlled the state's government and seats in Congress, they might not have resisted the permanence of the Confederate States of America. Although the prospect of permanent disunion saddened Old Line unionists in Iowa, many of them saw negotiation through compromise as the only legitimate means to effectuate reunion.

With the benefit of hindsight, we can conclude that Iowa's moderate Republicans correctly diagnosed the impact of secession threats on functional governance in Washington. The Iowans, however, underestimated the ability of unionists in the Deep South to overcome the secessionists. They also underestimated the ability of slaveowners to operate an orderly government. Iowans assumed that even in times of peace the forces of tyranny would corrupt the infant Confederacy. The four Iowans committed a third major error by assuming that few non–slave-owning whites would risk their lives in the name of sustaining the Confederate States of America. By threatening military intervention but not invading, Representative Curtis believed, unionist sympathy in the Deep South would rebound. In fact, threatening Federal military intervention steeled the determination of Southerners and induced four more states to secede.

To his credit, Curtis did acknowledge the loss of life that would result from a military solution to the secession crisis. A graduate of West Point and a veteran of the Mexican War, he was no stranger to the realities of war. The former mayor of Keokuk mistakenly presumed, however, that any military campaign would conclude fairly quickly. His obsessive hatred of slaveholding politicians blinded Curtis to the political transformation that was taking shape in the Deep South. In fact, non–slave-owning whites volunteered for military service by the thousands with the rise of nationalist sentiment in the South.

Four Months of Maneuvering

No Iowan sponsored a compromise plan during the four-month span between Lincoln's election and his inauguration, but the state's senators and representatives played important roles in the negotiations to resolve the secession crisis. The actions and reactions of James Grimes exemplify the maneuvering that went on within the Iowa delegation following South Carolina's secession. In December 1860, Grimes successfully navigated his way onto the Senate Committee of Thirteen. This ad hoc panel, established to facilitate a sectional compromise plan, included Stephen Douglas, William Seward, John Crittenden, and Jefferson Davis, among others. The Burlington lawyer approved the committee's majority plan to admit Kansas as a free state and split all remaining Western territory into two huge jurisdictions. Under the committee's arrangement, the border between the two territories followed the Old Missouri Compromise Line (the 36-30 parallel) to symbolize parity between free states and slave states. Although the plan did not rule out the possibility of slavery in the southern territory, Grimes accepted the plan because slave-state representation in the U.S. Senate would not increase substantially in the event of U.S. territorial acquisitions south of Texas.

From Grimes's perspective, the dual jurisdiction plan he approved was fair and meaningful. He expected the status of "all the territory belonging to the Government" would be settled sooner rather than later. He fumed when free-state Democrats joined slave-state senators in dismissing the proposal. In a letter to Governor Kirkwood, the former governor expressed his dismay at the missed opportunity for resolving sectional differences under the terms proposed by the Senate Committee of Thirteen. "No reasonable concession will satisfy the Rebels," Grimes exclaimed to his wife in December 1860. Kirkwood, from his perspective in Iowa City, concurred with Grimes's assessment of the secessionists. "It really appears to me," the governor wrote to Grimes on January 12, "as if our Southern friends are determined on the destruction of our Government unless they can change its whole basis and make it a government for the growth and spread of slavery." His phrase "destruction of our Government" entailed much more than a formal divorce. In his January 28 reply letter, Grimes agreed with Kirkwood and expressed his objections in the strongest terms to "this pretended right of a State to destroy our national existence."[24]

In January 1861, the same month Crittenden set forth his compromise plan, Grimes and Kirkwood endorsed slavery in New Mexico. When a bipartisan coalition proposed that Congress guarantee Federal noninterference in states where slavery already existed, two of the four Iowans in Congress approved a constitutional amendment making this provision. The measure ultimately failed to pass both chambers as a result of national Republican opposition, but by approving the measure the two Iowans sought to placate the eight slave states still in the Union. The Hawkeye Republicans' willingness to make minor concessions to the Upper South did not, however, distract them from threatening military action against the Deep South states to compel them to rejoin the Union. Iowans in Congress called for a Force Bill similar to the measure President Jackson had signed when South Carolina had flirted with political independence in 1832.

The composition of Congress changed considerably during the four months between Lincoln's election and inauguration. Election-cycle turnover combined with secession to transform the makeup of both chambers. The biggest impact came in the Senate chamber, where seven slave states withdrew their fourteen members by February. Republicans wasted little time admitting Kansas as a state, thereby gaining two new free-state seats. While the makeup of the Senate changed dramatically, several states sent delegates to Washington to attend a meeting called the Virginia Peace Conference, held in the Willard Hotel in February. Current members of Congress were permitted to attend, but most states assigned former senators and representatives to participate in the conference. The elderly delegates who came back to town from Illinois, Missouri, and other states mingled with members of their current congressional delegations between meetings at the hotel.

Iowa became an exception to the pattern of separate groups of representatives. Instead of former Iowa senators and representatives in attendance at the conference, Iowa's four current members of Congress took turns at the hotel. Governor Kirkwood declined to appoint anyone else to attend, and the Iowa legislature, which could have appointed delegates, was not scheduled to meet until 1862.

The lack of turnover in Iowa's delegation simplified the decision not to appoint others in their place. The composition of Iowa's congressional representation did not change during the secession winter because Curtis and Vandever both won reelection, and Grimes and Harlan happened to be in the middle of their six-year terms. While representatives from other states came and went during the winter, the four Iowans—all moderate Republicans—took advantage of their continuity and their uniform perspective to fill the leadership vacuum. When no one arrived from Iowa to attend the Virginia Peace Conference, Curtis, Vandever, Grimes, and Harlan commuted between the Willard Hotel and Congress, a dual role that enhanced their ability to influence the outcome of the several compromise plans being debated.

In Congress, Iowa's relative influence rose substantially as a result of the confluence of events. Keokuk's Samuel Curtis served on the House Military Affairs panel and represented the state on the Committee of Thirty-three. Like the Senate's Committee of Thirteen, the House committee endeavored to break the negotiation impasse and facilitate a compromise. Because the House committee consisted of one representative from each state, frontier jurisdictions like Iowa enjoyed the same voting power as the most populous states in the Northeast. When the Virginia Peace Conference convened in February, assembly managers adopted the same voting procedure to boost the leverage of less-populated Western states.

The timing of the Virginia Peace Conference—one month before inauguration day—drove Iowa's senators and representatives to take assertive action to minimize the pressure on Lincoln to resign. Senator Grimes put in an appearance at the Willard Hotel as early as February 5, making Iowa the first New West state to participate in the conference. The Iowans' presence proved important because all of the nonseceded slave states were in attendance. Most free-state governors initially reacted negatively to Virginia's invitation, and some of the free-state representatives in attendance favored restoring the Missouri Compromise or enacting a Federal slave code to promote the expansion of slavery. While the House Committee of Thirty-three proposed a modest amendment to the Constitution—restricting congressional power to regulate slavery where it already existed (a measure acceptable to many Republicans)—the majority of representatives at the Virginia Peace Conference favored an amendment similar to the Crittenden Compromise, a measure that would have fractured the Republican Party.

James Harlan represented the Hawkeye state on the all-important Virginia Peace Conference resolutions committee. Caught in the middle of a ferocious debate at the hotel, Harlan faced off against antislavery radicals from the Northeastern states who implored him to reduce the relative power of slave states in Congress. Conciliators from the Upper South states argued, meanwhile, that slave-state interests be expanded so as to balance the collective power of the underpopulated slave states against the collective power of the faster growing free states. One ardent Southern rights proponent attempted to persuade Harlan to embrace a proposal designed to ensure that any antislavery legislation could always be vetoed. In the end, the Iowa senator stood firm with several other moderates on the committee and opposed each of these proposals. Harlan was not able, however, to prevent the majority of delegates from approving a Crittenden-like arrangement that called for extending the Old Missouri Compromise Line to the Pacific Ocean.

In the end, the actions of Harlan and his Iowa colleagues at the Willard Hotel did contribute to prevent an Old Line–based proposal from gaining a majority of support in Congress. The Virginia Peace Conference work product would only become legitimate with the approval of Congress, and the four Iowans joined a united group of congressional Republicans who conspired to table the recommendations. By dragging out the discussions at the hotel, and then ignoring the conference's recommendations in March, they secured the Republicans' electoral victory. Lincoln was sworn in as president without delay on March 4, and without having to negotiate with either the Democrats or the secessionists. Radicals and Free Soilers did not desert Lincoln's organization.

After March 4, Curtis and his nervous colleagues expressed great relief at the turn of events. Once Lincoln entered the White House, Grimes, Harlan, Curtis, and Vandever became less willing to appease the Upper South states. In mid-March, two of the four voted against the proposed constitutional amendment that would guarantee Federal noninterference in states where slavery already existed.

Western Regional Dynamics

Unimpressed by the February peace conference, Representative Curtis continued his military preparations work in the House. One bill submitted by the Iowan would enable the president to call out civilian volunteers and control state militias. Although he understood that further military buildup might trigger a secession movement in the Upper South, Curtis set his sights on persuading the Deep South states to nullify secession. "If the border states are going to prevent us from executing the laws [and prevent us from calling out the militia]," wrote Curtis privately on February 19, "they were better out than in." Considering that Iowa's neighbor Missouri was a border state, the Keokuk attorney's reasoning was quite remarkable.[25]

Looking back, it is striking how unionism drove the Iowans to insist upon reunification. Harlan, Grimes, Curtis, and Vandever continued to demand an end to the secession crisis, even though in purely mathematical terms disunion proved immediately favorable to the nonslave states. With the Deep South no longer represented in Congress, free states could now permanently control the nation's politics. The executive branch would cater to free-state interests, while new judges would be appointed to the Supreme Court. The new members of the court could overrule the 1857 *Dred Scott* decision, the case in which Chief Justice Roger Taney had ruled that the Federal government could not set limits on slavery. With the Deep South senators no longer blocking bills designed to expedite free white settlement of the New West, the advocates of progressive legislation would encounter much less resistance to the Homestead bill, and would benefit from land-grant aid for colleges and a transcontinental railroad through Iowa, among other legislative acts demanded by Northwesterners.

Not even local circumstances could sway Iowa unionists to consider the merits of secession. Given Iowa's relatively small population compared to the New West's slave states, one might have imagined Curtis and other Hawkeye Republicans pursuing more vigorously a nonmilitary approach to reunite the nation after the closing of the Mississippi River to trade. Slave-state residents purchased a substantial portion of Iowa's food exports before 1860, and most Iowans depended upon Mississippi riverboats to haul their produce to market and bring finished goods produced elsewhere back to the state. Despite the regional dynamics, Iowa's geographic circumstances did not compel Curtis to reconsider his militant opposition to secession. In fact, Iowans in Congress saw regional dynamics as a compelling reason to go to war.

Senator Grimes, in his January 28 letter to the governor, summarized Iowa's "peculiar interest" in the unfolding constitutional crisis. "If this right of State revolution be conceded, [Iowa's] geographical position is such as to place her completely in the power of revolutionary States." Grimes expected that Missouri eventually would join the secession movement. Yet for him, with or without Missouri on the side of the Union, there could be only one response. "Will [Iowa] agree," he asked rhetorically in a letter to his friend Kirkwood, "that one State can secede and take from her the mouth of the Mississippi River, that another can take from her the mouth of the Missouri, and that others shall be permitted to deprive her of the right of passage to the Atlantic Ocean?"[26]

Just as Senator Grimes prepared to battle Missouri and Louisiana for control of the Mississippi River, Representative Curtis vigorously pursued Federal armament bills to protect Washington, which was engulfed on all sides by slave states. The nation's capital was in a state of virtual siege as he understood it. Rumors constantly circulated around the capitol that pro-secession forces in Virginia and Maryland were planning to bring down the Federal government. While preparing to defend Washington, Curtis called upon President Buchanan to recapture every fort, every customs house, every Federal courthouse, and every Federal armory taken by secessionists. "When the forts of the Government are taken by lawless mobs," he insisted on the floor of the House on January 19, "I deem it my duty to vote for their recovery."[27] Arguments in favor of invading the seceded states took on a new urgency after the forced surrender of Fort Sumter, one of the few Federal military installations in the Deep South still under the control of U.S. Army troops in April 1861.

The Post-Sumter Military Frenzy

Susan-Mary Grant, in her work *North over South*, argues that an anti-Southern bias drove free-state men to enlist.[28] Certainly, Iowans possessed a deep suspicion if not hatred of slaveowners. But anti-Southern sentiment was not the primary reason Iowans enlisted in the Union Army. They enlisted because the cult of unionism approached something of a religious obsession in their newly adopted state. Had the New England states seceded and dropped shells on a Federal fort in Boston Harbor, Iowans would have enlisted just the same.

As it was, news of the Confederate bombardment of Fort Sumter in April unleashed a contagious militant zeal, a fierce emotional energy that had been brewing for years in the Western states. Iowans could contain their hatred for secessionism no more. Community pressure inspired Hawkeye residents of all types to express their anger—Breckinridge Democrats, Bell Whigs, Douglas Democrats, moderate Republicans, and even radical Republicans. Iowans interpreted the Rebel barrage as a clear signal that secessionists had defeated unionists in the Deep South. If Southern unionists could not drive the secessionists from power by themselves, Iowans would join up with unionists from other states and compel them to rescind secession in order to restore the prewar status quo.

Abolishing slavery would become the noblest moral cause in the nineteenth century. But before 1861, only a small portion of Iowans risked their lives in the cause of abolition. In 1861, thousands of Hawkeye citizens exposed themselves to Rebel gunfire, not in the name of abolishing slavery but in the name of preserving the Union. If disunion became permanent, every section of the nation would suffer immeasurably, Iowans believed. As long as the "whole country" could be maintained, exclaimed one resident near Fort Dodge, "we shall remain a united, happy, and prosperous people."[29] "It may cost me my life," wrote Private W. C. Littlefield, "but if I can't live in a free country [then] I don't want to live at all."[30]

As Private Littlefield saw it, the level of freedom in Iowa had been significantly reduced by the withdrawal of the Deep South states. The young man, who enlisted in the late summer of 1861, feared a culture of corruption would be established in the free states unless the Deep South states rescinded their declaration of independence. "I was born and raised in a free Country," he wrote, "and I still intend to live under the old flag of our union or die in the defense of it.[31]

The reaction of conservative Democrats in Iowa is instructive. Like their Republican rivals, they feared democracy would perish in the wake of permanent disunion. Even for Democrats, who had continuously pushed the principle of local sovereignty in Kansas, it now appeared that every neighborhood in the entire nation was vulnerable to antidemocratic forces.

No Iowans endured the bombardment in Fort Sumter. No Iowans had previously set foot in the fort, and no pictures of the artillery damage to the fort reached the Hawkeye State in 1861. Nevertheless, Iowans' symbolic reasoning allowed frontiersmen unfamiliar with the scene around Fort Sumter to convert the verbal descriptions of the preemptive strike by Charlestonians into vivid mental images. Iowans, upon hearing the news, imagined the national flag flying over the fort being targeted by Confederate artillery shells. They reacted as if they themselves had been guarding Fort Sumter. Feeling defensive and anxious to counterpunch, thousands of Iowans found it nobler to risk their lives in an effort to crush out the revolutionary forces than to stand idly by. Because they perceived their own actions as justified self-defense, retaliation was warranted, they argued, even though the citizens of the Deep South spoke the same language, worshipped the same god, and had contributed to defend the nation in 1776, 1812, and 1846.

Public demands for reunion appealed to every one of the Iowa families included in this study. None of the fathers or young men enlisted immediately following Lincoln's call for ninety-day volunteers, but by all accounts the six families gathered with other members of their respective communities and demanded retribution against the Deep South confederation. With the exception of the Clark family in Muscatine, none saw the plight of African American slaves as a basis for launching cannonballs at Southern troops.

Citizen-soldiers in one Iowa town claimed to be fighting a "holy and just cause for a representative government . . . established and maintained by the will of the majorities." Democratic government could sustain itself, the volunteers argued, only if the nation became reunited under one flag without Southern domination. "[If] not controlled," argued their petition, the will of the Southern minority "affords us the death knell of constitutional freedom throughout the world." In sustaining President Lincoln's call for military volunteers, the Republican editor of one Mount Pleasant newspaper blamed the war on "seventy-five thousand negro drivers" in the South. He condemned them not because they owned slaves but because they were attempting to "compel five million white men" of the free states to abandon the principles of democracy.[32]

In late July 1861, Republican delegates attending the state party convention consolidated Iowans' collective sentiments into a unified plank. The "doctrine of secession is a wicked abomination," began the party's list of resolutions. Secession is "as abhorrent to patriotism, as it is alien to the constitution, demoralizing in its principle, and destructive in its action, a disguise to treason, and an apology for traitors, the ruin of commerce, and the dissolution of political society, the mother of all political crimes and the sum of all villainies, and as such we utterly reject and hold it in absolute detestation."[33]

As the war dragged on week after week, month after month, and year after year, Iowans' deep-seated commitment to reunion bolstered their resolve to continue supporting a military solution to the crisis. Despite the practical opportunities afforded by the Deep South's secession, most Iowans found it extremely difficult to ponder a future without every state united under one flag. Their loyalty to the Union drove most Iowans to ignore the arguments based upon congressional mathematics. As the unionists saw it, the loss of any state, with or without slavery, tarnished forever the immaculate meaning of Union and the image it projected into the future. The Deep South could not be allowed to drift on its own and contemplate the possibility of reunion down the road. Only when Confederate leaders sued for peace unconditionally would the majority of Iowa's military volunteers contemplate a return to civilian life.

CHAPTER THREE

United in Spirit If Not in Readiness

The Iowa governor, more than any other individual, influenced the citizens' response to President Lincoln's first call for troops. Elected in 1859, Samuel Kirkwood was a Maryland native and former Democrat who joined the Republican Party upon his arrival in Iowa in 1855. Taking full advantage of the groundswell of post-Sumter anger, he quickly organized a special session of the legislature and asked both Democrats and Republicans to cooperate with the U.S. War Department.

In his speech before the hastily assembled legislators in Des Moines, Kirkwood cited national reunification as the reason for taking up arms. To avoid any hint that he supported the abolition of slavery as a war aim, the governor declined to comment on the Southern institution. The word *slavery* never appeared in his speech and he did not invite African Americans to engage in supressing the rebellion. Instead, Kirkwood recalled eighty-four years of unity with slavery legal. "For the Union as our Fathers framed it, and for the Government they founded so wisely and so well," he stated, "the people of Iowa are ready to pledge every fighting man in the State, and every dollar of her money and credit."[1]

Legislators in both parties accepted the Republican governor's characterization of the conflict. At the local level, Democrats joined Republicans in embracing national reunification as the sole reason for taking up arms. In Keokuk, citizens associated with the port's military drill team met on April 18, 1861, and passed a series of resolutions to demonstrate their willingness to shoulder the musket in battle. In his diary, one Keokuk volunteer recorded the resolutions approved at the meeting:

Resolved That our Country requires our services and without any Distinction of [political] party we Hereby with our own free will and consent Cheerefully tender our Services to our Country.

Resolved in this contest we Know but two parties: Patriots and Traitors the formor for the Union the Constitution and the Star Spangle Banner; the latter our foes and our enemies.

Resolved That we Hold intestine Traitors in abhorance and would point the Bayonet and Discharge the Musket at them with as much willingness as would a foreign Enemy.

Resolved That while we deplore the Necessity which draws us to this last Resort that we will at all times and at all Hazards Stand by our Country and our Countrey's Flag Right or Wrong.

Resolved That the Name of this command shall be Known as the Union Guards and that we Report ourselves immediately to the Governor of our state as Ready for Duty.[2]

Following their enlistment, Keokuk's Union Guards trained with volunteer companies from other Iowa towns under the flag of the 2nd Iowa Infantry Regiment. Oskaloosa's first wave of recruits constituted a portion of the 3rd Infantry. Iowa's 1st Infantry Regiment included Muscatine volunteers as well as citizen-soldiers from Burlington, Davenport, Dubuque, and other eastern Iowa cities. All total, nearly 3,000 Iowans responded to Lincoln's appeal for ninety-day volunteers. In June and July, thousands more enlisted for three years of service. Remarkably, the recruits assigned to the 2nd and 3rd Infantry did not protest when state officials extended their term of service from ninety days to three years.

Signing up volunteers was not a problem, at least during the first few months of the war. Transforming the mass of three-year recruits into battle-ready condition proved to be an impossible challenge. Without a single military training facility in Iowa, state administrators faced the onerous task of constructing camps to train thousands of novice infantry, cavalry, and artillery units and outfitting them properly. Practically every soldier arrived in camp without a uniform or military rifle. Those who did arrive in uniform wore ceremonial jackets and pants donated by a local paramilitary unit, clothing that quickly disintegrated on the dirt roads in Missouri.

In addition to wearing ceremonial uniforms of many colors, the ninety-day 1st Iowa Infantry Regiment marched through Missouri carrying old Austrian-made smoothbore muskets rather than newly manufactured firearms with rifled barrels designed for long-range accuracy. The heavy smoothbore muskets weighed down the soldiers and had a reputation for being more dangerous to the person firing than to the enemy. Replacement rifles were nowhere to be had.[3]

Frontier Military Resources in Iowa

The scale of the military equipment shortage may surprise some readers today. One might have expected the state to have several caches of military firearms in 1861. Iowa's state militia law required every able-bodied adult male to turn out prepared for battle when local or state authorities issued the call to arms. Most farmers hunted wildlife with guns, and private gun manufacturing firms sold military-grade weapons directly to state officials during the 1840s and 1850s as long as they had the assets to pay for them. Federal authorities periodically offered to sell firearms to state officials at a reduced rate.

In fact, only a few modern military rifles sat in storage in Iowa on the day the Confederates shelled Fort Sumter. The tens of thousands of shotguns and other hunting firearms held on farms used a wide variety of ammunition and could not substitute for military-grade muskets. The few Iowa forts built by Federal authorities in the 1830s had not been resupplied by state officials after Federal authorities relocated U.S. Army units in Iowa farther west to Kansas, California, Utah, Colorado, and Oklahoma after the Mexican War (1846–48). Firearms were still needed in Iowa in the event of a Native American uprising, but frugal state legislators failed to audit existing military supplies.

In the 1850s, when Federal officials offered to subsidize the purchase of new rifled muskets by Western states at a reduced cost, budget-conscious Iowa legislators declined the offer, assuming there were guns already in storage. The error should have been realized in 1858, the year Sioux warriors killed a group of white settlers near the Minnesota border. Iowa's governor contacted Federal authorities after the massacre and asked that they urgently supply rifles to equip the northwestern county militia units, but state officials never followed up to address the gross shortage of military-grade firearms.[4]

The same lack of initiative discouraged militia training during the prewar years. Even though male citizens were expected to perform militia service, the legislature failed to create an infrastructure to facilitate peace-time training. When Iowa's governor proposed a new militia law in 1858 that authorized the chief executive to appoint militia leaders, the legislature declined to pass the overdue amendment. The 1858 General Assembly did vote to establish a company of cavalry for defending the Minnesota bor-der, but it missed the opportunity to ensure that ordinary citizens received proper arms and training. The legislature took no additional action during the 1860 session.[5]

Iowa politicians' inability to comprehend the scale of the sectional military crisis contributed to poor planning. Kirkwood and his colleagues expected a short war in which citizen-soldiers would perform a limited role. Federally trained soldiers already on active duty would assume the primary role, Iowans assumed. If Federal officials set enlistment quotas, state officials intended to rely on the several hundred men already associ-ated with independent military clubs. When Governor Kirkwood learned in April of Lincoln's request for one thousand civilian volunteers, he is reported to have exclaimed, "The President wants a *whole regiment of men!* Do you suppose I can raise that many?"[6]

Two weeks later, the governor no longer worried about meeting the manpower quota. Several thousand Iowans enlisted, and thousands more were leaning in that direction. Instead, it was the equipment shortage that demanded his constant attention. "For God's sake, send us arms," Kirk-wood telegraphed an arms supplier in New York on May 2. "Our First reg-iment has been in drill a week, a thousand strong. It has tents and blankets but no arms. The Second regiment is full, and drilling. *Send us arms.* Ten thousand men can be had, if they can have arms."[7]

The unavailability of military firearms continually frustrated Hawkeye administrators. The lack of trained military officers posed further orga-nizational problems. The War Department expected that administrators in each state would appoint officers to conduct the training and lead the recruits, but no more than half a dozen West Point graduates resided in Iowa in 1860, and Mexican War veterans were few and far between. With no Federal military forts operating between the two great rivers, Iowa administrators scrambled to find trained officers. One potential source was foreign-born residents, but compared to other states Iowa's list of Euro-pean officers was short. A number of migrants to the upper Mississippi

River basin had trained in a European military academy before emigrating; however, most of them resided in Wisconsin or Missouri, states with larger concentrations of central European immigrants.

The lack of trained officers severely delayed the timeline for training Iowa's masses of raw recruits. The state's deplorable tax collection system compounded matters further. Individual states bore the costs of training and equipping their troops at the start of the war, but at this critical time the state of Iowa owed more than $320,000 to creditors for prewar debts. Compared to other free states, Iowa was among the poorest, in terms of both bank assets and the government's ability to raise public revenue through taxes. With no surplus funds available, Iowa's elected leaders turned to wealthy Iowans to shoulder the burden.[8]

The Special Legislative Session of 1861

In this hour of crisis, Kirkwood implored legislators to enact a long list of enabling statutes. State legislators had not gathered as a group since February 1860, and the governor's party held only a narrow 23-to-21 majority in the upper house. Rather than pick a fight with Democratic legislators, Kirkwood and Republican legislative leaders reached across the aisle to the state's most militant Democrats. In the lower chamber of the state legislature, Republicans agreed to appoint Democrats to fill three of the five seats on the all-important Federal Relations Committee. Lee County Democrat Thomas Clagett chaired Federal Relations, and Nathaniel Baker, a Democrat from Clinton and former governor of New Hampshire, chaired the Committee on Military Affairs. Baker proved so adept at drafting war bills that Kirkwood appointed him to fill the key position of state adjutant general after the session adjourned.[9]

Kirkwood's strategy worked remarkably well in achieving bipartisan cooperation. Although cooperation by itself could not overcome the financial crisis, his conciliatory gestures placated Democratic fears that state military units would become an instrument for promoting Republican policies. Legislators in both parties agreed to authorize the executive branch to establish training camps and purchase equipment after the legislative session adjourned. If the war continued into 1862, state administrators now had the means to recruit and train more troops. The legislature also granted Kirkwood's request for criminal statutes authorizing judges to impose sanctions on Iowans who furnished aid to the secessionists, a controversial proposition even within the Republican Party.[10]

Coming at a time when state Democrats still harbored bitter grudges over Lincoln's election, conciliation was no small feat. Yet during the entire 1861 legislative session, the fifty-seven Democrats in attendance avoided making public comments that might be construed as sympathetic to Southern secessionists or critical of the Republican administration. Dennis Mahony, a popular Irish-born newspaper editor in Dubuque, joined the post-Sumter chorus of Democrats who endorsed a military buildup even if it meant that Republican officials in Washington would direct the deployment of Iowa regiments in the field. Kirkwood, in turn, responded by publicly expressing his personal satisfaction with the response of the state's Democratic Party leaders. Writing to the U.S. secretary of war shortly after the attack on Fort Sumter, Kirkwood proclaimed that "ten days ago we had two parties in this state; today we have but one, and that is for the Constitution and Union unconditionally."[11]

Unfortunately, the unified 1861 legislature had no means to generate the large amounts of capital Kirkwood needed to build training camps and purchase military equipment. When legislators approved the sale of $800,000 in state bonds, Eastern investors refused to buy them due to the state's low credit rating. Wealthy Iowans stepped forward to purchase war bonds, but the amount of private capital raised came to a mere $300,000, less than half of the target. By comparison, pro-Confederate bankers in Missouri channeled ten times that amount, $3 million in bank assets, into the purchase of Rebel military supplies in 1861. An increase in state tax revenues would have covered some of the war expenses, but Iowa legislators declined to enact a direct tax in 1861 and continued to rely on county treasurers to forward a share of the county property taxes to Des Moines.[12]

The Profile of Iowa's Citizen-Soldiers

Communities across the Hawkeye State responded with enthusiasm to the governor's call for military retribution. In the Wittenmyers' home county of Lee, on Iowa's border with Missouri, men born south of the Ohio River turned out to enlist. In Delaware County, natives of New York and New England enrolled. In the south-central county of Mahaska, men born in Ohio and Indiana signed up. In Muscatine, German-speaking immigrants enlisted alongside English-speaking residents.

In selecting officers, Kirkwood and Baker appointed volunteers from different political ideologies and ethnic backgrounds with the exception of African Americans. The state's twenty regimental colonels in 1861 represented every Republican faction and a broad spectrum of Democrats. Their nativity profile was also diverse. The list of U.S.–born colonels included men from slave states and free states. The state's 1st Infantry Regiment marched through Missouri led by a Democrat who had endorsed a proslavery constitution for Kansas in 1858. Neither foreign language nor foreign birth disqualified a promising applicant with military experience. Three of the twenty regimental colonels had emigrated from Europe.[13]

In the port of Keokuk, a confluence of forces produced a wide mixture of commanders. Former congressional representative Samuel Curtis, a moderate Republican, commanded the 2nd Infantry Regiment while a John Bell Whig from Keokuk led the 5th Iowa Infantry. The 15th Regiment was led by an abolitionist and former Liberty Party member from Keokuk with a Douglas Democrat serving as its major. Iowa's most talented military leaders—those promoted to brigade commander and division commander later in the war—included several Democrats who had voted for Douglas in 1860. By the end of the war, the list of prominent Iowa generals included many Democrats: William W. Belknap, Cyrus Bussey, James M. Corse, Marcellus Crocker, James M. Tuttle, and James A. Williamson. Many other Democrats served as regimental colonels or company captains. Despite pressure from Republican politicians to promote only Republican officers, Generals Ulysses Grant and William Sherman preferred to nominate officers to the rank of general based solely on merit, and their list of appointments included several Iowa Democrats.[14]

Of the six families included in this study, members of Annie Wittenmyer's family were first to volunteer. Of the four bachelor sons who lived on the Turner family farm five miles west of Keokuk, two enlisted on June 1 for three years of service, including the youngest son, barely sixteen years of age. Both Turner brothers rode with the 1st Iowa Cavalry Regiment, which completed its training in Burlington. In Delaware County, bachelor

Abner Dunham contemplated joining, as did bachelor Ben Stevens in Oskaloosa. Both declined initially.

Census data reveal the challenges faced by military recruiters in a rural frontier jurisdiction like Iowa with a relatively young population. Despite the widespread enthusiasm for military enlistment, family circumstances complicated the recruitment effort. Compared to Connecticut, where one-third of the population in 1860 had not yet reached the age of fifteen, children under fifteen made up 44 percent of the Hawkeye state's total population. Men outnumbered women in Iowa, but males between the ages of twenty and thirty-nine made up less than one-sixth of the state's population. By comparison, a greater portion of Connecticut's male population fell into the twenty-to-thirty-nine age range despite the out-migration of young adult men from the East Coast in the 1850s. If every Hawkeye male age eighteen to forty-five enlisted, Iowa could furnish only about 130,000 troops.[15]

The state's rural economy further limited recruitment. In states with mining, lumber, and industrial operations, military recruiters sought volunteers from among the large concentrations of bachelors already away from their families to work in these enterprises. In Iowa, no large groups of single men lived in rooming houses, with the exception of railroad gangs. Small groups of Mississippi River dockworkers volunteered following Fort Sumter, but that was one rare exception to the pattern of Iowa enlistees. Going house to house, Iowa's military officials had no choice but to solicit multitudes of teenage boys and young men in their twenties who often felt bound to either their parents or their wives or both. Survival in the Iowa countryside required a tremendous output of human labor just to procure basic food and fuel twelve months a year. Many farm families operated at a subsistence level and could not afford to hire replacement laborers. Those families who could afford to hire often struggled to find unmarried men who had not joined the army.

As military recruiters scoured rural neighborhoods in search of male volunteers, mothers and wives endured trials and tribulations. A remarkable number of children had been born in Iowa in the late 1850s, infants and toddlers who needed two attentive parents to survive into adulthood. The propensity of male farmers to marry young placed on their shoulders a multitude of heavy obligations, not to mention the burden placed on the farmwives. Married women typically bore many children. The first child often appeared within a year or two after formal marriage vows were pronounced, and the last when women were well into their forties. Families of eight or ten children were not uncommon. Unmarried women often helped with child care during peacetime, but their chores multiplied when brothers, nephews, and fathers joined the military. Grandparents assisted with child care on the East Coast, but grandparents were relatively rare in Iowa because virtually every family had migrated there.

These kinds of family obligations discouraged enlistment in the Musser and Dunham households. In the Council Bluffs area, John Musser had eight mouths to feed on his small farm. He seems never to have contemplated volunteering. His son Charles was old enough to enlist in 1861, but John needed Charles so Charles stayed put. In Delaware County, oldest son Abner Dunham likewise felt constrained by family circumstances. Although two younger brothers were available to help his parents perform the farmwork, Abner was sorely needed to maintain the 80-acre homestead in its full capacity.

Keokuk's Transformation into a Staging Area

No Mississippi River town witnessed more activity than Keokuk, the state's only port downstream from the rapids. In May, the 1st Iowa Infantry arrived there, a regiment that included several companies of German-speaking volunteers from Burlington, Davenport, and Dubuque, along with English-speaking volunteers from Dubuque, Muscatine, and other towns. As the docks swarmed with activity, business quickened as merchants competed for contracts to supply food, building supplies, clothing, camping gear, and weapons. Previously unemployed laborers cleared flat sections of ground near the port's outskirts and erected crude shacks for barracks. When the first set of barracks quickly filled to capacity, workers cleared more land around Keokuk and erected more shelters.

The task of housing and training the several thousand volunteers overwhelmed municipal leaders. By June 1, three infantry regiments were encamped near Keokuk with two more on their way. Many trainees slept in abandoned warehouses. As Keokuk's logistical limitations became apparent, state administrators established training facilities in Dubuque,

Burlington, Muscatine, Davenport, and Iowa City. In the Council Bluffs area, recruits assigned to the 4th Iowa Infantry drilled on open prairie ground near the Missouri border. With few military firearms available, a majority of recruits performed drills carrying wooden sticks. State officials, desperate to equip the mass of volunteers, accepted any military-style muskets regardless of their age or condition. For those few units able to train with army-grade muskets or rifles, a lack of ammunition limited drill time.

Public health concerns persistently plagued Keokuk community leaders in 1861. During the 1850s, the Gate City endured a series of crises, including a deadly cholera epidemic. In 1861, hundreds of volunteers housed in cramped and unsanitary quarters in the port became infected with one of several varieties of bacteria. The epidemic's first casualties died within a few weeks after their arrival. To isolate the most serious cases, military administrators designated the port's high school, located just a few blocks from the Wittenmyer home, as a soldiers' hospital.

The plight of the hospitalized soldiers instantly transformed the lives of Annie Wittenmyer and other Christian charity workers. As soon as she learned of the shortage of medical personnel, Mrs. Wittenmyer volunteered as a nurse, in which capacity she witnessed the death of the state's first soldier in May. In between her rounds at the hospital, she attended nightly prayer vigils at the Chatham Square Methodist Church, the Turner family's congregation. She and other female charity workers in the port quickly channeled locally donated goods and funds to aid soldiers stationed in the port.

Local Enlistment Efforts

Despite Iowans' hearty response to the call for soldiers to defend the Union, President Lincoln desperately needed the services of more volunteers in the New West states. Although Missouri did not secede after the first call for troops, the secessionists in control of its government received support from the Rebel states of Arkansas, Texas, and Louisiana. More Federal troops were needed to defend St. Louis, but the precarious situation of Washington, D.C., after Virginia's secession prevented a large-scale shifting of forces from the Eastern theater to the Western.

By the winter of 1862, 140,000 trained Rebel soldiers defended the lower Mississippi River valley. Arkansas and Louisiana each raised more than twenty infantry regiments in 1861 plus numerous cavalry regiments. Texas fielded as many cavalry regiments as infantry regiments. Rebel soldiers in the three New West Confederate states, when added to the 15,000 men of the Missouri State Guard under General Sterling Price, posed a considerable threat to Union control of Missouri. Meanwhile, Confederate regiments recruited on the eastern side of the Mississippi River threatened to envelop St. Louis from another direction. Tennessee organized fifty-five regiments of infantry in 1861, twenty-two regiments drilled in Mississippi, and twenty-six regiments in Alabama. Eight regiments of exiled Kentuckians added a dose of enthusiasm as well as fighting prowess to the Rebel army encamped in Tennessee.

When President Lincoln called upon every Union state to supply three-year soldiers in addition to ninety-day soldiers, the War Department calculated its recruitment quotas based on each state's population. Officials in Iowa managed to meet every new Federal quota in the spring and summer of 1861. Military equipment still needed to be found, but state officials had satisfied the manpower quotas, at least for the present. In October, when the president issued another call for three-year soldiers, the total Federal demand for Iowa exceeded 20,000 troops. Although harvest season was in full swing, the state managed to satisfy its 1861 quota, a remarkable achievement for a frontier state with a high proportion of children too young to enlist.

Iowa's experience casts an interesting light on the current debate over enlistment motives. Modern researchers who study this topic contrast sociocultural reasons with political motivations, a dichotomy that allows researchers to compare motivation over time. A thirst for adventure is one example of a social motive. Community pressure, personal economic gain, and religious fulfillment are other examples. The desire to prevent political tyranny or to abolish slavery are examples of political idealism, although the categories are not mutually exclusive. Patriotism has social as well as political implications.[16]

Most researchers today are divided as to the primary motivation of Civil War recruits. Some argue that the legacy of a nonprofessional volunteer military in the United States motivated most recruits, a factor that transcended both sociocultural and ideological factors. Here, on the free-state frontier in the 1860s, a fourth factor—geography—operated to some extent. The Kansas-Missouri conflict in the 1850s fueled a defensive attitude among many Iowans, which recruiters sought to exploit. In addition to Iowans' proximity to slave-state Missouri, the population advantage of New West slave states assisted Hawkeye recruiters in meeting their quotas.

More immediately, fears of a Confederate invasion of the state shaped the rhetoric of Iowa newspaper editors and public speakers in April 1861. These fears continued well into 1862, though no regular Confederate Army units crossed into Iowa. Slavery had almost become legal in Kansas in the 1850s, and many Iowans still feared that it might be established in Nebraska. In 1862, desperate Hawkeye military recruiters suggested the possibility that slavery might become legal in Iowa if Federal enlistment levels were not met,[17] and in 1861 the same fear may have motivated some volunteers to enlist.

That some eligible young men declined to enlist while other civilians signed up raises interesting questions about volunteers' motivations in the summer and fall of 1861. While the scale of Iowa's enlistment bonanza is well documented, the intentions of individuals are more difficult to gauge. Surviving evidence from the period indicates that social and ideological factors both contributed to generate recruits in Iowa, at least in 1861. One available source—weekly newspapers—demonstrates that the state's editors interwove political and nonpolitical motivations into their post-Sumter editorials. Soldiers' diary entries, an even better resource, reveal a range of reasons for enlisting, so much so that one cannot isolate the social factors from the political. As the rationale for pursuing the war evolved in the years ahead, a combination of social and political factors continued to motivate the Hawkeye volunteers who took up arms.[18]

No member of the five white families under examination enlisted in order to hasten the end of slavery. A history of family service in the Federal army motivated Annie Wittenmyer's brothers. Their Virginia grandfather had fought in the Revolutionary War as a young boy and later served as an officer under William Henry Harrison in the War of 1812. In Delaware County, a sense of adventure motivated twenty-year-old Abner Dunham to enlist in September 1861. Like many members of that year's recruiting class, he saw the conflict as a noble cause. He expected the war would be short and feared if he delayed enlisting he might miss the final battle.

The letters of the Stevens family indicate that religion and duty compelled twenty-two-year-old Ben to enlist in October. That his father desired to enlist in 1861 also motivated Ben to sign up and spare his mother the task of becoming a single parent. Discouraging his father from enlisting became a never-ending task for Ben after he left home for training camp. "Father," Ben implored in one letter sent home from Keokuk, "I want you to keep your promise and stay at home. I am perfectly satisfied here [in the army], but if you should leave and go to the Army there would be nobody to take care of the family, and to leave them in that fix I could not be satisfied." Later, Ben's motivations evolved along with the national purpose of the war. In late 1862, young Ben explained in one letter sent home that he had not embraced abolitionism, but he now supported emancipation.[19]

Ben Stevens and Abner Dunham enlisted in the late summer or fall of 1861, the same time thousands of other native-born Iowans volunteered for Federal military duty. State administrators assigned Ben Stevens and his Mahaska County neighbors to the 15th Infantry, a unit made up primarily of rural south-central Iowans plus a contingent of volunteers from Keokuk. Commanded by two lawyers from Keokuk, the 15th Regiment gathered in the Gate City for their initial training. Meanwhile, at the port of Dubuque, Abner Dunham and his Delaware County neighbors trained alongside other northeastern county residents under the banner of the 12th Infantry.

Women Volunteers

Iowa women contributed in their own way to promote military success in 1861. With no established support organizations, women who wanted to help often had to pursue volunteer work on their own initiative. Before the war began, U.S. Army protocol prohibited women from assuming any military tasks, noncombat or combat. Neither the Red Cross organization nor public health care services existed. Initially, women volunteers found a niche obtaining food and clothing outside of the U.S. Army infrastructure. When women collected money and goods within their own communities, male state administrators tolerated the intrusion. When women leaders

FIGURE 4. The earliest known photograph of Annie Wittenmyer. Here she poses (third from right) with fellow charity workers who formed the southeastern Iowa chapter of the Ladies' Christian Association in the late 1860s. *Reprinted by permission of the Putnam Museum and Science Center, Davenport, Iowa.*

proposed to establish local organizations of women volunteers, Iowa's political leaders did not object. However, women were not welcomed in army hospitals, at least at first. This resistance did not daunt the female volunteers. When army officers and state administrators turned a deaf ear to their offers of assistance, Iowa women used their local aid organizations to improve the quality of the army hospitals.

Like women in other states, Iowa's women organized under the banner of the Ladies' Soldiers' Aid Society (LSAS). Keokuk's LSAS organization, one of the first to operate in Iowa, formed in late May 1861. In Council Bluffs, townswomen selected the young Amelia Bloomer to lead the port's LSAS chapter. By 1862, more than 7,000 local LSAS chapters operated from New England to the New West. While many LSAS members contented themselves sewing clothing at home, other members went door to door asking for money, food, clothing, bedding, and medical supplies. The most adventurous women arranged to ship the donated goods to their intended recipients and accompanied the shipments south. The practice of tracking donations to their intended recipients followed the philanthropic practice established in the 1850s, when women charity volunteers undertook to ensure that local donations went to local families in need.

Annie Wittenmyer's star rose as a result of her leadership role in Keokuk's LSAS. By the end of the four-year conflict, Wittenmyer was supervising hospital dietary operations from her headquarters at the Christian Commission building in Louisville, Kentucky. Her path to the diet kitchens began when she became volunteer secretary of the Keokuk LSAS. This organization sent numerous care packages to local volunteers, and Wittenmyer's previous experience had taught her the value of tracking the goods to their intended recipients. Not a single doctor or army officer invited LSAS members to assist with the army camps in Missouri, so she went south on her own initiative to speak personally with soldiers from Keokuk who had deployed to Missouri. Traveling alone to St. Joseph, Missouri, in August 1861, Wittenmyer caught up with the 2nd Iowa Infantry, the regiment commanded by Samuel Curtis of Keokuk.

Wittenmyer's connections and communication talents made her perfectly suited for her role as traveling secretary for the Keokuk LSAS. While in Missouri, she sent back reports to a close friend in town whose husband edited a prominent newspaper there in which he published her letters. While friends back home scrambled to fill her list of needed items, Wittenmyer made her way back to Keokuk, where she oversaw the collection of additional goods. After ensuring the donations had been boxed properly and loaded onto the designated steamboat, she embarked on the vessel and escorted the boxes south to ensure that every item arrived intact and into the hands of the designated unit.

The next time she returned to Keokuk, Wittenmyer expanded the scope of her collection system. In September 1861, a notice "To the Ladies of Iowa" was printed in many newspapers around the state, asking that donated items be routed through the Keokuk LSAS, which "will be in direct communication with the troops . . . through their Secretary." That Keokuk was the hub of the state's mobilization endowed the port's corresponding secretary with considerable influence. To free up as much time as possible, she arranged for family members to care for her son and to provide medical assistance to the indigent women convalescing in her home in Keokuk. By October, Wittenmyer successfully managed the mammoth task of channeling tons of donated bedding, clothing, and food from across the state to the battlefront.[20]

A lack of money discouraged some Iowa women from traveling, but not Annie Wittenmyer. Her divorce from William, which had apparently been made final by April 1861, meant she had to rely on her own ingenuity to pay living expenses. William promised to provide child support for their six-year-old son Charles, but he failed to follow through. Property taxes on her home had not been paid since 1857. Evidently, friends in Keokuk looked out for her economic security by providing cash donations to support her living and travel expenses.[21]

After being rebuffed by male doctors in the army hospitals, Wittenmyer joined the chorus of women leaders who insisted that women be invited to serve in army hospitals, as hospital administrators as well as nurses. Wittenmyer's previous experience had taught her the value of female-led health care, and despite the considerable scrutiny she received from disenchanted males, she continued to collect hospital goods through the LSAS chapter system, convinced that women could manage hospitals more effectively and efficiently than men. Women also devised creative ways to transport perishable food. With no refrigeration available, LSAS members implemented a system for safely shipping eggs, fruit, and vegetables to army camps hundreds of miles away from the point of donation. Because milk could not be shipped safely, they obtained milk cows and transported the cows to the camps.

Immigrant Families

For Iowa to meet its recruitment quotas, much depended upon the ability of native-born community leaders to reach out to immigrant community leaders. Some Iowa residents of European birth had received military training before emigrating, and in a state starved of experienced military officers, Governor Kirkwood and his allies devoted considerable energy to addressing their needs and interests. The successful formation of immigrant regiments in neighboring states led to optimism in Iowa, but it also complicated the task facing military recruiters in the state. While very few immigrants living in other states enlisted in Iowa, some European-born

Iowans enrolled in regiments organized out of state. The all-Irish 7th Missouri Infantry, whose banner displayed the golden lyre emblem on a green background, attracted several Irish Catholic recruits from Keokuk. German-speaking recruits in Keokuk enlisted in the 12th Missouri Infantry, an all-German regiment. Fifty Norwegian-born Iowans from the northeastern corner of Iowa marched in the 15th Wisconsin Infantry, an all-Norwegian regiment that carried an American flag with a Norse inscription.[22]

European natives viewed the conflict from a different perspective than American-born Iowans. The prospect of disunion did not disturb recent immigrants to the same degree that it did native-born Iowans. Among the various ethnic groups, some groups enlisted at a higher rate than others. The reasons for the lower enlistment rates cannot always be discerned, although we do know that religious affiliation was one factor that distinguished one group's reaction from another. When the war began, the relatively small proportion of radical German atheists in Iowa enlisted at a very high rate. Freethinkers welcomed the prospect of slavery quickly being abolished after Fort Sumter, but as the war dragged on and President Lincoln emphasized unionism as the sole war aim, the enthusiasm of the German atheists waned.

The enlistment rate of Protestant immigrant groups tended to be higher than for Catholic communities. In 1861, state officials recruited only Protestant chaplains. The prospect of African Americans migrating to Iowa after a military victory also disturbed some immigrant groups. Rather than enlist, some racist European natives who strongly opposed black migrants refused appeals during the entire war, even appeals backed by threats of conscription.

The challenge for Governor Kirkwood was to customize the state's enlistment spiel in a manner that recognized the particular sensitivities of each immigrant group. Initially, simple patriotism and a thirst for adventure enticed some of Iowa's immigrants to enlist. Marching as part of the 1st Iowa Infantry, Burlington's German Rifles company (which included twenty Keokuk Germans) bore a battle flag that proclaimed: "We Defend the Flag of Our Adopted Land."[23]

Compared to immigrants in Wisconsin, Illinois, and Missouri, relatively few Iowa immigrants volunteered for three years of service in 1861. Most who did enlist spoke English as their first language. The biggest disappointment for Iowa officials involved German-speaking residents. Motivated by the success of German recruitment efforts in Wisconsin and Missouri, Iowa recruiters hoped to fill one or two full regiments with three-year German-speaking volunteers by the end of 1861. About 300 Germans from Davenport, Dubuque, and Burlington volunteered for the ninety-day regiment in April, and several of the state's most talented German-speaking officers reenlisted after the Battle of Wilson's Creek in August. But by the end of the year, only 200 German volunteers had signed up for the 16th Infantry Regiment, the unit designated by state administrators as all-German. Due to the low numbers, English-speaking volunteers filled out the regiment and a non-German was appointed to lead it.

In the final count, Iowa attracted more than one thousand immigrants in 1861 to enlist as three-year volunteers. Protestants born in Britain, Scotland, and Ireland enlisted alongside English-speaking recruits born in North America rather than march in a unit made up entirely of their fellow countrymen. A sprinkling of Hollanders, Scandinavians, and Central Europeans also dispersed among the English-speaking Iowans who signed up for three years of service in 1861. The higher enlistment rate among native-born Iowans meant that interior counties produced more soldiers per capita than the river counties, which were home to larger foreign-born populations.

Southern Iowa rural districts, inhabited largely by native-born Iowans, produced a bountiful harvest of recruits. In addition to Ben Stevens, Mahaska County furnished several hundred recruits in 1861. Pottawattamie County, home to barely 5,000 inhabitants, contributed soldiers to the 2nd Artillery Battery, the 4th Infantry, and the 15th Infantry. Delaware County volunteers marched in three different regiments, including the 12th Infantry, Abner Dunham's unit. In the state's Mississippi River districts, Muscatine and Keokuk both recruited well compared to Dubuque. Muscatine contributed volunteers to three infantry regiments and one cavalry regiment in addition to the state's lone ninety-day regiment. The bulk of the Muscatine County recruits marched in the 11th Iowa, a regiment commanded by Colonel Alexander M. Hare, a local merchant. Horsemen from Muscatine rode with the 2nd Cavalry, a regiment commanded by a Muscatine business leader with prewar military experience.

The Tall Task of Selecting Officers

State organizers encountered considerable difficulty identifying officers capable of training the thousands of raw recruits effectively and leading them into battle. Administrators in every state faced a similar challenge, but the dearth of experienced officers in Iowa was especially severe. When U.S. Army officers stationed in other states declined Governor Kirkwood's appeals and pursued offers elsewhere, state officials turned to Iowans with little or no training or experience to fill out the remaining leadership positions.

The list of twenty Hawkeye regimental colonels included four civilian men with a West Point education. Four U.S. military officers commanded Iowa regiments in 1861, including one Minnesotan and one Kentuckian. Several Iowa politicians won promotion to colonel in 1861, along with several community leaders who had strong political connections. The list of politicians in charge of Iowa regiments included Representative Vandever and state senator Bussey. The list of lieutenant colonels included a greater percentage of political appointees. Several regiments arrived at the war front only one bullet away from being led by a newcomer with no formal military training.

Further down the ranks, the vast majority of majors and adjutants appointed in 1861 had no previous military experience. At the company level, administrators relied upon untested citizen-soldiers to captain a majority of the companies. Lawyers and merchants made up a large proportion of Iowa's officer corps, along with some bankers, teachers, physicians, pastors, millwrights, and farmers.[24]

The dearth of trained officers so frustrated Governor Kirkwood that he advised the legislature to allocate funds to the state university for the specific purpose of establishing a military department there. "The sad experience of the last few months," he wrote in January 1862, "has shown us the necessity of military knowledge among our people. By giving to the young men who may attend the University, military instruction and training, we will not only greatly benefit them, but will also have made provision for what our present experience shows may, at any moment, become a necessity of our people."[25]

The state's heavy reliance upon civilian officers might have resulted in disastrous leadership decisions on the battlefield. Many appointments did prove troublesome. When the real shooting began, some high-ranking Iowa regimental officers panicked and were soon replaced by officers able to cope with the anxiety of battle leadership. On the parade ground, lieutenants and captains often excelled majors and colonels as drillmasters. In some regiments, the most talented leaders happened to be the third or fourth officer below the rank of colonel, civilians such as Major John M. Corse of Burlington and Major W. W. Belknap of Keokuk.

Relatively few in number, Iowa's European-trained officers proved extremely valuable. The list included veterans from wars on other continents who spoke English, German, or Hungarian. A Hungarian-speaking Iowan commanded one of the state's regiments, and among the lieutenant colonels were a Prussian-trained officer and a Scotsman who had served in the Queen's Army in India.

Abner Dunham's regiment benefited from the leadership of a Swiss immigrant put in charge of training. Major Brodtbeck of the 12th Iowa became so popular among the enlisted men that army officials in St. Louis requested he assist in the training of other regiments. Unfortunately, Iowa recruits received very little training in counter-insurgency warfare. Counter-insurgency skills would become particularly critical in Missouri, where many Iowa recruits spent their first months out of training camp marching from one hostile neighborhood to another.

Ready or not, Iowa's recruits shipped off south to face off against guerrillas as well as eager Confederate soldiers. One of the last units out of Keokuk was Ben Stevens's 15th Iowa Infantry. "It would be impossible for me to describe the cheering or our feelings as the Boat left the shore," he wrote home after his arrival in St. Louis. Although Keokuk's inhabitants had turned out many times previously to send off units bound for that city, the embarkation of the 15th Regiment produced another large turnout. "During the embarkation hundreds and hundreds of men, women, and children crowded the [Keokuk] wharf to witness our departure," Stevens wrote. "Many were the 'good byes' and 'God bless yous' that were said to us as we went plunging through the mud to the Boat . . . The Band was on [the hurricane] deck playing Dixey's-Land (quick time), while a thousand and fifty men swung their hats and cheered at the top of their voices, and twice that number responded in the same manner on the shore."[26]

It remained to be seen whether Iowa's citizen-soldiers could withstand forced marches, enemy bullets, and sleeping on the cold ground exposed to the elements. A martial spirit prevailed among Hawkeye recruits, but nearly every unit lacked good organization and equipment. With the benefit of hindsight, it is easy to see that the short period of training combined with the lack of military firearms and ammunition left Iowa's 1861 three-year recruits unprepared for the physical and psychological challenges that awaited them. The state's citizen-soldiers were still more civilians than soldiers. Much of their soldiering would be learned the hard way, through experience. Unfortunately, much of the learning took place while the Iowans were outnumbered and in hostile territory. How they responded when thrust into battle against more numerous foes in the Mississippi River basin would directly affect the Union Army's military status in the New West.

CHAPTER FOUR

Preserving Missouri for the Union

——————•————•——————

Missouri was a constant source of irritation for Federal military commanders. While unconditional unionists in the state sided with President Lincoln, a large number of secessionists sided with President Jefferson Davis. Claiborne Jackson, the slaveholder elected governor in 1860, advocated secession after Fort Sumter. His allies in the Missouri legislature actively supported the Confederate States of America.

The outcome of Missouri's own civil war hinged on the reaction of neutralists—that is, Missourians who chose not to side with either President Lincoln or President Davis. Before the attack on Fort Sumter, neutralists outnumbered unconditional unionists and secessionists combined. President Lincoln's call for troops in April energized some prominent Missouri neutralists to climb on the secessionist bandwagon, including Sterling Price, a popular former governor and Mexican War hero. Price commanded Missouri's militia forces, a large army of volunteers fed and equipped by Missouri bank assets.

Iowa's first wave of citizen-soldiers entered Missouri at a critical time. In early June, when President Lincoln initially summoned men from Iowa, Kansas, and Illinois to deploy to Missouri, Federal forces led by General Nathaniel Lyon consisted of several hundred regular U.S. troops and a few hastily assembled regiments of German-speaking residents of St. Louis. Governor Jackson, having seized the guns and ammunition from U.S. armories in western Missouri, set his sights on capturing the Federal armory in St. Louis, while State Guard militia units under General Price trained in several staging areas. In many rural districts across the state, chaos reigned as groups of local citizens faced off against each other, secessionists who backed the governor and unionists who sought to take control of the militia network away from the governor.

On June 12, 1861, a desperate General Lyon telegraphed Samuel Curtis in Keokuk: "A terrible secession movement, headed by [Governor] Jackson, has commenced. I want you to come at once, with all the force you can command, to Hannibal, Mo. and move over the [rail]road from there to St. Josephs and put down the traitors every where on both sides of the road, and if possible, strike down upon Lexington."[1]

As Lyon captured Jefferson City in mid-June in a bold move, Curtis responded as requested and seized the Hannibal–St. Joseph railroad. By July, however, momentum had shifted in favor of Governor Jackson's forces. That month, Confederate troops from Arkansas, Texas, and Louisiana entered the state and joined Price's Missouri State Guard encamped south of Springfield. In the several battles fought in southwestern Missouri during the summer, Federal forces endured one defeat after another, including Wilson's Creek, where General Lyon died in action. After Federal forces abandoned Springfield and retreated to protect St. Louis, Price marched north to the Missouri River valley, the strongest proslavery region of the state and the site of Jefferson City, the state capital.

Federal authorities relied on Iowans time and time again in 1861 to preserve Missouri as a Union state. In June, the 1st Iowa Infantry—the ninety-day unit—joined Lyon and his hybrid collection of U.S. Army regulars and German-speaking volunteers. Iowa units still training in Keokuk deployed as soon as possible to the rural areas of Missouri in hopes of calming the neighbor-on-neighbor violence there. By the end of the year, more than one dozen Iowa regiments remained stationed somewhere in Missouri. Scattered across the breadth of the countryside, small units of Iowa soldiers performed as military police while the generals kept a sharp eye on Price's Missouri State Guard encamped at Springfield.

Iowa soldiers earned a reputation for hard marching and hard fighting during the first summer of the war. Proud of their status as volunteers, the foot soldiers of the 1st Iowa Infantry competed against the regular army soldiers during Lyon's long marches through Missouri. Very few deserted. The Iowans' ability to out-march the regulars earned them a measure of respect from General Lyon, who called them his "Greyhounds."

The ninety-day soldiers' most enduring legacy was their full participation in the Battle of Wilson's Creek in August. Having enlisted in April, the Iowans' ninety-day clock had already expired by the time Lyon prepared to launch his surprise attack on the large camp of Confederate soldiers near Wilson's Creek. Because the length of their Federal service had not quite reached ninety days, Lyon expected the Iowans to abide by army rules without question and remain in uniform for another week. When some Hawkeyes in the ranks demanded they be discharged, the 800 men of the 1st Iowa Infantry took a vote on August 6 to resolve the dispute.

Rather than allow each company to decide for itself whether to abandon Lyon on the eve of Wilson's Creek, the Iowans determined that the entire regiment would stay or leave depending upon the vote. They had marched over 450 miles without adequate footwear, many days in sweltering weather over 100 degrees, with little food in their knapsacks, but the opportunity to fight appealed to a majority of the Greyhounds. After a majority approved, all ten companies fought at Wilson's Creek, those who had voted to return home and those who voted to fight.[2]

Fighting alongside regular army units and two regiments of Kansans defending the hill overlooking the creek, the 800 Iowans played an important role in the battle. During the retreat to Springfield, the Hawkeye survivors maintained their unit cohesion despite the pounding inflicted by the pursuing Rebel forces. Unit cohesion proved critical to preventing a Union rout during the retreat. Notwithstanding the Rebel superiority in cavalry, the Iowans stuck by their company commanders and maintained an orderly night march back to Springfield and then on to Rolla.[3]

The Paradox of Insubordination and Commitment

In evaluating the performance of Iowa soldiers, we must recognize the scale of the challenge faced by army trainers. Iowa recruits arrived at training camp certain of their knowledge of warfare and military ability. Their overconfidence presented problems. When challenged by the officers in charge of the training, many frontiersmen expressed a general disrespect for military authority and a great contempt for training. Their Western value system instilled in them a great commitment to democratic, collective decision making, a culture of organization at odds with the hierarchical military chain of command. Expected to march in unison to their captain's every command, frontiersmen often found it difficult to follow orders.

Such habits, left uncorrected, would severely compromise a company's fighting effectiveness on the battlefield. In battles fought between two large bodies of inexperienced soldiers, the actions of individual units often decided the outcome. Where unit discipline could be achieved through repetitious exercises, frontiersmen often proved to be excellent soldiers. Industrial technology placed tremendous firepower in the hands of individual soldiers, much more powerful weapons than those used in previous wars. The soldiers, as historian Drew Gilpin Faust notes, had the "responsibility for the decision to kill" at a time when battles still tended to be "intimate, face-to-face" encounters.[4]

Problems posed by overconfident recruits were not limited to Iowa. Compared to their better-trained counterparts in the Northeastern states, Western recruits often appeared in battle for the first time sorely lacking in discipline. To prevent all-out revolts in training camp, army officers in Western states often disregarded the kinds of details West Point faculty considered essential to successful training. In Iowa, many officers—even high-ranking officers—fraternized with enlisted men. Rather than whip soldiers who deliberately violated orders, officers resorted to other means of punishment. At times, officers encouraged enlisted men to pressure their insubordinate comrades into conforming.

Army regiments recruited in Iowa exemplified a Western paradox. Despite their poor training, thanks to lessons learned in civilian life on the harsh frontier, Hawkeye recruits performed at a very high level on the eve of battle. On the march, they reached distant objectives through difficult terrain in harsh weather conditions in remarkably good time. In one battle after another, Iowa's citizen-soldiers maintained unit cohesion after enemy troops initially forced them to retreat to a location to the rear of the original line of defense. Although outnumbered and in hostile surroundings, Iowa units typically regrouped and counter-attacked, regaining the momentum of the battle. After the enemy retreated and they returned to training camp, Iowans maintained their commitment to a military solution despite negligent quartermasters, incompetent doctors, challenging terrain, and the series of Union military defeats in Virginia.

The paradox of insubordination and commitment to performance began as soon as the first Iowans deployed to Missouri. General Lyon, leading his mixed collection of troops in central Missouri, marched the 1st Iowa Infantry alongside his U.S. regular units, a juxtaposition that brought out the worst of the recalcitrant Hawkeyes. Iowa's ninety-day volunteers refused to accept a system that demarcated a wide social gulf between officers and enlisted men, and gave officers unbridled authority to inflict corporal punishment. On Lyon's march to Springfield, recently recruited privates observed army officers punishing regular army soldiers who failed to adhere to strict army rules. When Lyon's staff gave preferential treatment to the ninety-day regiments from St. Louis in doling out food supplies, firewood, and water, and assigning guard duty, the Iowans contemplated rebellion.[5]

The clash of cultures could have spelled disaster for the Federal cause in Missouri. Fortunately, the Hawkeye recruits found the means to cope with brutal army regulations as well as enemy musketballs. Not all enlisted men from Iowa deplored the hierarchical military leadership culture. Of the three individual soldiers followed in this study, Ben Stevens took the most pride in his unit's conformity to rules. In 1862, the duty-bound carpenter's son from Oskaloosa described to his younger brother how his company regularly received compliments from commanders "for our good behavior in camp and on marches and for the neat appearance of our camp." Stevens also took pride in the moral character of the men in his company. "With few exceptions," Stevens wrote, his colleagues did not lie, steal, gamble, or drink alcohol.[6]

Orderliness, honesty, and sobriety did not describe every Hawkeye volunteer. The 1st Iowa Cavalry included some thrill-seeking misfits. It is not known if either one of Annie Wittenmyer's brothers broke military protocol, but many of the young, unmarried horsemen in the regiment did grow tired of the usual camp routine. While on patrol in Missouri, members of the 1st Iowa Cavalry stole valuable items from civilians and forced farm families to serve them food. Some riders deserted. On one occasion in early 1862, members of the regiment's rear guard got drunk on duty after coming upon a wagon loaded with whiskey. For engaging in riotous behavior on one occasion, fifteen Iowa cavalrymen were sent to the guardhouse. One corporal went to jail for expressing his opinion about the colonel's decision to arrest a private for shooting off his pistol in camp.

Later, the colonel himself was taken to jail by his own superiors when questions arose about his ability to manage the regiment. Following the colonel's release, members of one company threatened to murder him.

Tempers flared on another occasion after the colonel pointed his pistol at one soldier who refused to pick up a gun. In an angry letter home, one trooper speculated that twenty shots would have been fired at the colonel if the private had not chosen to pick up the gun by himself.[7]

The record of the 11th Iowa Regiment confirms a common pattern of insubordinate behavior on the part of the three-year recruits. Soldiers in the 11th Infantry, which had a large contingent of men from Muscatine, rioted before they even left the state. The commotion broke out in training camp in Davenport after rumors circulated that camp food supplies were exhausted. Private Daniel Parvin wrote in his diary that he hated army rules and despised the regimental officers, men he considered stupid for enforcing the rules.

Problems did not cease after the regiment deployed. One month after the Battle of Shiloh in 1862, sixteen members of the 11th Iowa Regiment disobeyed orders by not attending drill. When rations were cut as a result of a general food shortage, several infantrymen risked life and limb to steal food from the quartermaster's storage building. As in most regiments, gambling became a regular practice. Alexander Downing, a young recruit from Cedar County, despised the regiment's third colonel, who enforced prewar army disciplinary rules. While on duty in Mississippi, Downing joined a group of fellow soldiers who left camp for one night notwithstanding posted notices warning of severe penalties if caught. Downing and his companions managed to return without being detected, and their success enticed them to violate protocol on other occasions. In 1864, when the Iowans came within sight of one tall mountain near Atlanta, Downing snuck out of his unit and hiked up to the mountain's peak just to see the view.[8]

Like many Iowa soldiers, Delaware County's Abner Dunham despised officers who refused to engage in casual conversation with enlisted men. Officers willing to joke with enlisted men became instantly popular because the informal talk transcended the artificial distinction in rank.[9] Insubordination among the enlisted men encouraged insubordination among the officers, and vice-versa. At times, camp discipline problems stemmed from a lack of patience on the part of regimental officers not accustomed to military red tape. A. M. Hare, the Muscatine businessman appointed commander of the 11th Infantry, received a severe admonition from General

Curtis in December 1861 after the colonel declined to carry out an order. Frustrated by a shortage of ammunition, Colonel Hare refused to march his men. General Curtis saw through Hare's attempt to gain favors for his regiment and would not stand for it. "You must not delay a moment in obeying orders," chided Curtis in a letter to Hare. "Your prompt efforts and obedience to orders you have received will correct what I deem a very improper expression of hesitation in your letter yesterday."[10]

Instilling a culture of obedience in Iowa's citizen-soldiers took considerable time. Curtis, who understood the importance of orderliness, set a high bar. He challenged the pride of his citizen-soldiers in an effort to instill military obedience and raise their standards as they performed routine police duties. Disobedience threatened Iowa's "high reputation for subordination, energy, and gallantry," Curtis explained to the colonel of the 11th Infantry. Impatient citizen-soldiers must do their best with the limited tools available to them. If their "comrades" in the 2nd Iowa Infantry had waited until missing military equipment had arrived before advancing, reasoned the general, "the rebels would have swept the State."[11]

The Battle for the Hearts and Minds of Missourians

Disobedience on the part of the occupying forces threatened to inflame local affairs. Unionists installed a pro-Federal governor in July, an event that pacified some communities but stirred angry emotions in others. Claiborne Jackson still claimed to be the rightful governor, and many Missourians still preferred neutrality. Neighbors who opposed secession did not necessarily welcome Federal troops who arrived to support the unionist war governor. As the bands of guerrillas moved from one neighborhood to another, the military situation remained precarious.

At the time Colonel Hare received his letter of admonition from General Curtis, 8,000 State Guard troops were encamped with Sterling Price near the site of the Wilson's Creek battleground. Rebels from Arkansas, Texas, and Louisiana had left Missouri after the Battle of Wilson's Creek, but the Confederate units remained encamped in northern Arkansas, poised to recross the border. In Neosho, near the Oklahoma border, pro-Jackson state legislators opposed to a Federal takeover of Missouri carried out the day-to-day business of state government in anticipation of returning to the capitol building in Jefferson City.

When green Iowa recruits arrived in Missouri following the Battle of Wilson's Creek, they encountered a very different social and political landscape than they had anticipated. Having completed a few weeks of basic training, many expected to refight Wilson's Creek. Instead, they found themselves thrust into a socially polarized environment where few civilians wore their politics on their sleeves. Instead of clearly delineated secessionist households and unionist households, the Iowans encountered various shades of gray. The breakdown in law and order opened the door for opportunity-seeking criminals called "bushwackers," who formed groups intent on stealing and vandalizing for nonpolitical reasons.[12]

After the war, a captain in the 1st Iowa Cavalry recalled how "our battlefields [in Missouri] were in the byways and waste places, where the human foxes we followed had their holes." Into this setting, Iowa military commanders ordered small squads of citizen-soldiers to patrol suspicious neighborhoods. "Our marches were often in the night time, for from every hill top, and sometimes from the tree tops, looked out a watcher to note our progress and fix the ambush."[13]

The journal and letters of William Gulick, a Clinton County corporal in the 1st Cavalry, testify to the difficult and dangerous nature of counter-insurgency warfare in Missouri in 1861 and 1862. Iowa troopers assigned to the west-central portion of the state initially found the challenges intriguing and provocative. "I like hunting but this is the best game I ever saw," wrote Corporal Gulick. "It is some what exciting." On one occasion, Gulick reflected on the regiment's mission: "I suppose our business is to open the way and establish posts then the State militia will take our place. [They] are not completely organized or drilled yet, and it will be a long time before they can do with out the Iowa boys." A few weeks later he wrote, "Missouri suits me very well now since there is something to do. I shall not want to see other parts until this is cleaned out."[14]

Although this soldier found satisfaction in his work, many of the Iowans who enlisted in 1861 seeking military glory found nothing romantic in the task of policing neighborhoods. As counter-insurgency warfare became a day-in and day-out routine, their enthusiasm waned. "I have seen too many young boys broken down," wrote Corporal Gulick. Homesickness contributed to the situation. "It is hard for so many to leave the home country," he confided in a letter to his sister.[15]

Weeks of dangerous work without immediate gratification challenged the fortitude of the toughest soldiers in the cavalry regiment that included Wittenmyer's two brothers. "I hope we will leave this miserable God forsaken country where we will have something to do," Gulick remarked after several tedious months near Sedalia, Missouri. Some of the men just "lay around camp" and are "never ready for duty, never go a scouting or scarcely anything else, except to [get] their rations, and they are always behind." A few weeks later, the Clinton County corporal confided that he felt "miserably tired." When he was not on the march, he was on guard duty. Twenty-four hours of guard duty was not uncommon, and when the shifts were shortened, soldiers performed guard duty every night.[16]

The lack of immediate success contributed to heighten the stress level. "Many Troops from the South have come up and it seems they are about to over run this portion of the State." Men who took the oath of allegiance to the Union later joined up with the guerrillas. On one occasion, scattered squads of Iowa cavalry encountered a band of guerrillas on horseback led by W. C. Quantrill, estimated at 150 riders strong. Quantrill's seasoned guerrillas easily dispatched the 800 Missouri militiamen who arrived to reinforce the 1st Iowa Cavalry. Frustrated by this turn of events, the Iowa troopers retreated back to camp.[17]

Like it or not, counter-insurgency warfare was necessary to preserve Missouri as a Union state. In the vicinity of Sedalia, where the 1st Iowa Cavalry deployed, the Hawkeye riders entered a landscape strewn with burned-out buildings and abandoned farms. "Everything here looks barren and desolate," noted Corporal Gulick. "The citizens are in a great state of alarm." Members of the 1st Iowa Cavalry rode fifty miles on several occasions, at times through pouring rain while fording streams overflowing their banks with floodwater. Heavy brush and swamp bottoms restricted their access to certain areas.[18]

Guerrillas, many of them dressed in captured blue uniforms, waited behind shrubs to ambush unsuspecting Union troops. When several Iowa horsemen were killed while out foraging for grain, the guerrillas brutally stabbed the victims and left them with their "heads nearly mashed in the ground [and robbed] of every thing they had even boots." On other occasions, captured Iowans would be stripped of their clothes and belongings and released naked as a warning to other Union cavalrymen.[19]

The Iowa cavalrymen persevered notwithstanding the trauma of night rides through unfriendly territory. "Last night had a heavy shower as we were on the ground minus shelter no wonder we were soaked," Gulick wrote in his diary. "But fortunately soldiers are tough so [I] did not mind it." Despite the difficult conditions, the young man refused to become discouraged. "It is in a noble cause, and for noble deeds."[20]

Logistical Delays Prolong Deployments

By October 1861, fresh soldiers were needed to replace Iowa's 1st Cavalry and give them time to rehabilitate before returning to the guerrilla-infested region around Sedalia. Relief never arrived, unfortunately, because of logistical bottlenecks—many of the same difficulties that had plagued Iowa's initial mobilization efforts. Due to equipment shortages, the 2nd Iowa Cavalry remained in training camp. Abner Dunham's infantry regiment, the 12th Iowa, did not leave its camp in Dubuque until early December. When below-zero weather produced ice on the Mississippi River, the regiment's colonel refused riverboat transportation, and the men rode to St. Louis by open railcar. Upon their arrival, they were ordered to do additional training. Ben Stevens's unit waited even longer in camp before departing for Missouri. The 15th Infantry did not leave Keokuk until March 19, 1862.

Despite such delays, as of December 1861, more than a dozen Iowa regiments were deployed across Missouri, either as whole units or spread out in individual companies or in half-regiment battalions. Squadrons of horsemen from the 1st Iowa Cavalry and the 3rd Iowa Cavalry moved from one neighborhood to another. In the central region of the state, the 3rd Iowa Infantry guarded railroad tracks and bridges while the Muscatine recruits in the 11th Infantry patrolled the area near Jefferson City. Near Sedalia, the 6th Iowa Infantry and 8th Iowa Infantry marched alongside units from Missouri, Illinois, and Indiana in anticipation of a Confederate thrust north of Springfield by General Price's Missouri State Guard. Also keeping an eye on Price was General Curtis and his large force at Rolla, which included the 4th Iowa Infantry and 9th Iowa Infantry. In the southeastern region of Missouri, the 5th Iowa Infantry, 7th Iowa Infantry, and 10th Iowa Infantry kept a close eye on the large Rebel forces encamped near New Madrid.

One of the three Iowa regiments deployed near New Madrid participated in the Battle of Belmont, one of the few formal engagements fought in late 1861 in Missouri. In November, the 7th Iowa Infantry accompanied General U. S. Grant and three regiments of Illinois recruits on a water-borne search-and-destroy mission near Belmont, a port across the Mississippi River from the Confederate fortress at Columbus, Kentucky. The regiment fought well at Belmont but suffered severe casualties. Of the ninety Lee County volunteers who fought at Belmont, twenty-five were killed, wounded, or captured. The battle losses affected families back home in Muscatine, Keokuk, and Oskaloosa, as all three communities had contributed volunteers to the 7th Infantry.[21]

In the final count, far more Iowans died of disease than battle wounds in 1861. By the time Abner Dunham's regiment arrived in St. Louis from Dubuque, the Delaware farmboy, like many of his colleagues, had contracted some form of bacterial infection. Despite his "bad cold," he and his colleagues remained enthusiastic. "I often think of home and if god sees fit hope to return to it, but I do not for once regret enlisting in the noble cause in which I am now engaged. I would not miss sharing the glory of victory which we are sure to gain, for hardly any thing." The 12th Infantry trained with new Enfield rifles manufactured in Great Britain, but other regiments had to rely on old smoothbore muskets with a limited firing range, made in Austria, Belgium, or Prussia. The 11th Infantry was one of the units that arrived in Missouri carrying nonrifled muskets.[22]

Lack of equipment also delayed the deployment of the 15th Iowa Infantry. An anxious Ben Stevens spent much of his four months in Keokuk worried that he might miss out on the last battle of the war, because in late 1861 people still expected the war to be short. As of November 27, 1861, Private Stevens had received one standard shirt and one pair of pants but was still waiting for blankets and an overcoat. In his letters home, the professional plasterer described the poor quality of the wood barracks. He itemized camp rations much like a bookkeeper, the profession he would pursue after the war. Despite his having no culinary training or experience, Stevens was ordered to cook for his eighty-two-man company in November.

After spending several weeks in an unheated building designed to house one hundred trainees, Stevens's unit relocated to a heated warehouse in the port of Keokuk.

The coats and blankets finally arrived sometime before March 19, 1862, the date the unit shipped out, but they could do little to keep the men warm on the deck of the steamboat headed for St. Louis. "We were so badly crowded that one half of the boys had to stand up. I tell you now," Ben wrote home, "it was disagreeable. There was a cold wind from the northwest, with a drizzling rain. Many of the boys were wet and cold and had to go without their suppers, but they stood up to it without a murmur."[23] Once in St. Louis, the recruits in the 15th Infantry received tents and clothing in addition to Springfield rifles, with which they drilled six hours a day. Despite the months spent in camp at Keokuk, the men of the 15th Infantry had not been taught how to load and fire a modern military firearm.

The long delay wasn't all bad. By spending so many weeks in Keokuk, the 15th Iowa resided for only a short time in the disease-ridden barracks in St. Louis before reboarding the steamboat for deployment in Tennessee. Nevertheless, many soldiers in the 15th Iowa succumbed to disease. During their brief stay in St. Louis, the green Keokuk recruits encountered the original recruits from their town, who had been tramping around Missouri with the 2nd Iowa Infantry for more than nine months. Military police work had taken a severe physical toll on them. Of all the Iowa units deployed in Missouri, the 2nd Infantry endured the most hardships.

During the regiment's first two months in the state, they traveled the line of the Hannibal–St. Joseph railroad from one village to another, sleeping on the ground without tents much of the time and eating cornbread for the most part. After reaching the Missouri River, the regiment shipped down to St. Louis, where they boarded a steamship bound for a port on the Missouri side of the Mississippi River. After landing west of Cairo, Illinois, the 2nd Iowa patrolled rural southeastern districts in case General Price chose to strike out east from Springfield toward St. Louis. Deployed to Sedalia in west-central Missouri in October, the 2nd Infantry traveled 200 miles in open railcars in cold weather. When the Iowans arrived back in St. Louis in December, 400 soldiers (approximately half the regiment) were on the sick list. According to one Iowa soldier in another unit, the 2nd Infantry "presented a hard sight" upon their arrival in St. Louis.[24]

The regiment's greatest enemy was not guerrillas but unsanitary camp conditions. Soldiers slept not far from open latrines, horse manure, and piles of decomposing food. While on assignment, soldiers of the 2nd Iowa camped without adequate clothing and tents. Of the roughly one hundred Keokuk volunteers who enlisted in Company A after Fort Sumter, nearly one-quarter were gone from the unit by January 1862, never to return. Five Company A soldiers had died of disease and ten more came home permanently because of poor health. At least a dozen more lay in hospital. Despite the grueling conditions, only two of the company's hundred men deserted.[25]

The Origins of Army Hospital Reform

It was not just the camp conditions that undermined soldiers' health. Unsanitary army hospitals killed some of the Iowans who had been placed there to recover from illnesses contracted on the march or in camp. The gruesome hospital conditions in Missouri shocked Annie Wittenmyer and other civilian observers.

Wittenmyer discovered that ignorant managers located hospitals near the same unsanitary camps that had infected the soldiers. Hospital water supplies often contained harmful bacteria, and no system existed to ensure basic standards of cleanliness. In the surgery tents, battle wounds became infected, as the surgeons cleaned wounds with untreated water, dressed wounds with infected cloth, reused bloody surgical instruments, and rarely cleaned their hands with soap. Following surgery, infected patients lay side by side in cramped quarters on dirt floors. Patients suffering from diarrhea received the same fatty meat fed to soldiers in camp.

At a time when a system of scientific practices and centralized regulation was desperately needed, Federal officials declined to assume responsibility for the task. A manual of army hospital standards did not exist, and Congress had not allocated Federal funds to cover the expense of treating citizen-soldiers recruited by state officials. State military administrators, convinced the war would end soon, refused to stock the cupboards with medical supplies or invite female nurse volunteers to support the work of male health care professionals. Without enough bandages, pillows, and mattresses to go around, wounded soldiers slept on straw with their sores exposed to the contaminated air. Wittenmyer and other women working on behalf of the war effort looked on in horror.

From a modern perspective, the state government's slow response to the health care crisis is difficult to explain or defend. Governor Kirkwood did not establish a state oversight board until October 1861. Kirkwood appointed men to manage the organization, called the Iowa Army Sanitary Commission (IASC), despite the contributions made by women.

The IASC desperately needed state revenue, but the Iowa legislature was not scheduled to convene until January 1862. When they did convene, legislators failed to adequately fund the commission, with the result that the IASC remained quasi-private. With few state resources available for medical expenses, directors appealed for private donations.

Iowa's sanitary board operated independently of the organizations that cared for soldiers in St. Louis and Chicago. It also operated independently of the LSAS network, whose female leaders had realized the seriousness of the problem weeks before Kirkwood established the IASC. During the fall and winter months, the loudest protests came not from the IASC board but from LSAS leaders like Annie Wittenmyer.

The magnitude of the crisis was already evident in August 1861, when Annie Wittenmyer arrived at St. Joseph, Missouri. She personally comforted several dozen members of the 2nd Infantry who had been left behind there after the healthy men in the regiment shipped downstream to St. Louis. When she saw homesick young soldiers no longer able to answer the drum roll, she facilitated their return home.

When Wittenmyer toured other Union hospitals in the upper Mississippi River basin, she discovered that the primitive hospital conditions in St. Joseph were standard across the region. As a result of "hordes of dishonest army contractors," according to Wittenmyer, a portion of funds allocated for medical supplies never reached the hospitals. The supplies and equipment that did arrive were often substandard.

Hospital encounters with Keokuk soldiers, including her own brother, galvanized Wittenyer's determination to pursue major reforms. The scale of the war's medical crisis compelled her to embrace sanitary administration with all her might. When she observed morbid conditions in the hospitals, she confronted doctors and insisted that the facilities be drastically improved. Late at night, she wrote letters to top administrators complaining of incompetent hospital doctors and demanding that more army resources be allocated to cover health care services. Lacking a typewriter or an assistant to do her secretarial work for her, Wittenmyer persevered, utilizing her public speaking ability and writing skills to influence army officers.

Her prewar experience managing charity work in Keokuk had taught Wittenmyer to be firm but effective in negotiating with men. Perhaps most important, she possessed a supreme level of self-confidence and fearlessness, as well as a strong work ethic. Wittenmyer knowingly took risks few other women dared to take in an age when male-on-female assault was not uncommon. Despite the dangers that women who traveled alone faced, the LSAS secretary did not hesitate to book a steamboat passage by herself and travel near the front lines. In those moments when she might have hesitated, strong religious convictions compelled her to move forward.[26]

Family connections nurtured Wittenmyer's gift for hospital administration. Brother Will Turner had attended the Iowa Medical School in Keokuk in the mid-1850s, and for years afterward Will and Annie conversed on topics related to disease prevention and patient rehabilitation. She never completed a single training program for nurses, yet Wittenmyer, like many other housewives, had become quite adept at understanding complex human biological phenomena while serving her family and her community's health needs before the war. Letters between the two siblings indicate that they commiserated as they shared observations about medical practices considered barbaric. Both loathed incompetence and corruption, and neither was afraid to speak out and protest intolerable conditions.[27]

Wittenmyer, although she ended the war as a hospital administrator, was perfectly comfortable talking one on one with patients confined to bed. While calling on individual patients, she provided ministerial care to the dying, a task for which she was well suited. While praying with soldiers on their deathbed, she came to realize the war's impact on orphaned children back home. Although doctors and army officers often regarded her presence as a threat to their authority, the reaction of ordinary soldiers ensured she would not be denied entrance. When Wittenmyer traveled to the 2nd Infantry's camp in southeastern Missouri, one Keokuk sergeant noted her arrival in his diary and expressed relief.

The cause of humanity as well as the cause of unionism benefited from Wittenmyer's intelligence and personality. The putrid condition of the army hospitals never deterred her from trying to help, and when she returned to Iowa, her magnetic charm invigorated unionist women across the state and compelled them to contribute their time, money, clothing, and food in an effort to conquer the health crisis. "I have gloried in your courage, independence, and ability," Amelia Bloomer wrote to Wittenmyer from Council Bluffs. "I have rejoiced that it is a woman that is doing so much and has gained the confidence of State and National governments." So many Iowans, male as well as female, came to revere Wittenmyer by the winter of 1861–62 that the critical mass of support created a new political dynamic.[28]

The health care crisis expanded Wittenmyer's sphere of influence. When supplies were needed, she turned to her female colleagues back in Iowa for assistance rather than rely upon male authority figures. In a letter published in several Iowa newspapers in November 1861, she offered a long and detailed list of needed hospital items, including clothing, bedding, bandages, food, and medicine. Local LSAS chapters were still forming across the state at this time, and as groups formed, dozens of women leaders, from Council Bluffs to Dubuque, wrote to the Keokuk chapter's secretary asking for her assistance with local regiments.

Wittenmyer took full advantage of her Keokuk connections to ensure that donated goods reached their intended destinations. Her initial circle of friends, which included Samuel Curtis, grew wider as the war progressed. By 1862, many prominent military leaders and male politicians supported the LSAS network. When obstacles stood in her way, she shrewdly utilized her acquaintances to obtain special favors.

In the hospitals, Wittenmyer's leadership style encouraged male doctors to disclose their own concerns regarding the deplorable hospital conditions. As early as October 1861, one brigade surgeon wrote to her asking for her assistance in improving the quality of the meals served to hospital patients. When other doctors rejected her assistance and did not share her concerns about hospital meals, she persisted in her efforts to improve conditions. When the chief surgeon in Sedalia appeared before Wittenmyer under the influence of alcohol and ordered the future temperance crusader to leave the premises immediately, she reported the incident to the top military brass, who saw that the intoxicated doctor was removed from his post.[29]

Wittenmyer's commitment to the idea that women had a particular and important contribution to make contributed to her success. Despite the tall barrier of sex discrimination, she insisted that she be allowed to serve as a volunteer nurse and tour the hospitals. She also insisted that women be recruited to volunteer as nurses and hospital cooks. At least two women nurses should be assigned to every Iowa regiment, she recommended in 1861. Underutilizing women compromised the Union war effort, she argued, at a time when thousands of soldiers were suffering unnecessarily. "Womanly hearts and womanly tact can lay hold of influences men cannot reach," wrote Wittenmyer in 1861. "They are received with a degree of confidence and cordiality that no man, however great his military or medical reputation, can command."[30]

Collective action by LSAS chapters was so successful that it spawned a chauvinistic backlash. When Governor Kirkwood created the IASC, men who believed they could best manage the system began directing the operations of the local LSAS chapters. Some women's groups did cooperate with the board secretary, who maintained his office in Davenport, but many chapter presidents ignored his instructions and instead sent donated goods to Wittenmyer in Keokuk. As a result, two separate systems for routing goods to soldiers operated concurrently. Governor Kirkwood tiptoed around the controversy, hoping a coalition of men and women would come to agree on a compromise plan. Unfortunately, a system of well-supplied hospitals had not yet been realized by April 6, 1862, the day thousands of wounded Union soldiers cried out for help on the Shiloh battlefield in Tennessee.[31]

The Balance of Power Shifts in Missouri

By the winter of 1861–62, Iowa's military volunteers had improved substantially the status of Federal military operations in Missouri. Their counter-insurgency work stabilized the state long enough to allow Missouri unionists to outfit more than twenty regiments for three years of service in the Federal army during the late fall of 1861. Especially in the northern counties and around the St. Louis area, Federal military recruiters reaped a windfall of volunteers.

Although the battle for the hearts and minds of Missourians was far from over, Union commanders in St. Louis could now contemplate offensive operations in the Mississippi and Ohio river valleys. Henry Halleck, the top U.S. commander in the Western theater, set his sights on several Rebel forts guarding the Mississippi, Tennessee, and Cumberland rivers. At Columbus (Kentucky), 100 Confederate cannon looked down on the Mississippi River from the Iron Hills facing north. Seventy miles east of Columbus as the crow flies, forts Henry and Donelson blocked passage up the Tennessee and Cumberland rivers, respectively. General U. S. Grant, fresh off his daring raid on the Rebel camp at Belmont, commanded the closest Union staging area at Paducah, Kentucky. For Grant to successfully carry out a deep thrust up the Cumberland or Tennessee rivers, he needed more troops to be transferred to him out of the St. Louis area.

Because General Halleck's first task was to keep St. Louis in Union hands, the timeline for invading western Tennessee ultimately depended upon events in Missouri. At Springfield, Sterling Price and his 8,000-strong Missouri State Guard went into camp expecting to strike east or north as soon as an opportunity presented itself. As long as Price posed a direct threat to St. Louis, Halleck hesitated to shift any units from his base in St. Louis to the Ohio River valley.

Neutralizing Price required the movement of Union troops close to Springfield, and as of December 15, 1861, the largest Union force in the vicinity was in Rolla, one hundred miles to the east. General Curtis commanded the approximately 12,000 Union troops here, who sat in winter quarters guarding a railroad terminus. If Price's force at Springfield could be neutralized, General Halleck was prepared to honor Grant's request and transfer more bluecoat reinforcements to Paducah in anticipation of a deep thrust up the Tennessee and Cumberland rivers.

The series of events that would culminate in the capture of Fort Donelson in Tennessee began at Rolla in late December. Rather than wait for warmer weather, Curtis pressed forward toward Springfield, ending his advance at Lebanon, fifty miles northeast of that city. From this point, Union forces could effectively counter Price, should he move north to threaten the Missouri River valley or east toward the railhead at Rolla. To Halleck's satisfaction, Price stayed put in Springfield and prepared to defend the town rather than pursue offensive action against Curtis at Lebanon.

With Price neutralized, Halleck transferred Union reinforcements from St. Louis to Paducah to support Grant's initiative. He then proceeded south against Fort Henry and Fort Donelson near the Tennessee-Kentucky border. Grant's army included a mixed collection of Ohio River valley regiments and New West regiments, including several from Iowa that had previously deployed in Missouri.[32]

Historians William Shea and Earl Hess give Curtis high marks for his leadership during the winter march from Rolla to Lebanon. Undertaken during one of the coldest months of the year, the march forced the men to trudge over mud roads hauling supplies by wagon in lieu of railroad cars. While en route, Curtis managed to resolve a serious internal staff dispute. Nearly half of the 12,000 Union troops spoke German. German officers, convinced that one of their own, General Franz Sigel, should be in charge of the expedition, refused to heed Curtis's orders. Sigel had lived in St. Louis before the war, and many of the German-speaking recruits came from the St. Louis area. The rebellion within the ranks required considerable diplomacy on the part of the former mayor and member of Congress. Through delicate handling of the dispute, Curtis kept his brigades functioning long enough to pose a threat to the Missouri State Guard commander. Iowans made up two of the nine English-speaking infantry regiments with Curtis, two of the six cavalry battalions, and two of the eight artillery batteries.[33]

Halleck's decision to reassign Union regiments from Missouri to Tennessee did not mean that the battle for the hearts and minds of Missourians was over. With the state still bitterly divided between neutralists, secessionists, and unionists, cells of dissenters resided in every county when 1861 came to an end. Confederate officials in Richmond entertained grand designs of restoring Governor Jackson to power. The pro-Jackson rump legislature continued to meet in Neosho, from where they appealed to neutralist Missourians as well as secessionists.

Confederate military recruiters, meanwhile, found hundreds of Missourians willing to fight with Price against Federal forces in Missouri and Arkansas. With Missouri's best Union troops assigned to fight in the Ohio River valley, the task of managing the risk posed by Missouri dissenters continued to fall largely on the shoulders of unionists from other jurisdictions—Kansas, Minnesota, and the Old Northwest states—but particularly Iowa.

CHAPTER FIVE

Blood Sacrifice

⸻

Three major Union military victories in early 1862 turned the course of the war in favor of Union forces. Fort Donelson, the first of the three, propelled Ulysses S. Grant to fame and placed Union forces in control of much of Tennessee. The second resounding Union victory took place in northwestern Arkansas at a village called Elkhorn Tavern near a ridge of hills. Known as the Battle of Pea Ridge, the intense two-day engagement produced a Union victory despite the Confederates holding a two-to-one advantage in numbers at the tavern on day one. Pea Ridge occurred one month after the capture of Fort Donelson and one month prior to the Battle of Shiloh in Tennessee, the third major Union victory. During the fighting on the first day at Shiloh, Iowa soldiers blunted the Rebel attack long enough to prevent a Union rout. Called by some postwar observers the "Gettysburg of the West," the two-day Battle of Shiloh produced more casualties than all previous Civil War battles. At least temporarily, military momentum shifted away from the Confederate States of America.

Iowa soldiers found themselves in the thick of the heaviest fighting at all three battles. On the second day at Fort Donelson, Iowans led the charge on the line of earthworks closest to the fort. In northwestern Arkansas, General Samuel Curtis's regiments successfully protected the vulnerable Union supply wagons near Elkhorn Tavern. Isolated, outnumbered, and outflanked, the Iowans held the Union line near the tavern until Union reinforcements arrived. At Shiloh, officers from Iowa commanded five Union brigades during the critical first day of battle. The eleven Hawkeye infantry regiments present at Shiloh included Abner Dunham's 12th Iowa and Ben Stevens's 15th Iowa. Keokuk, Muscatine, Oskaloosa, and Manchester were all represented at Shiloh, and each community paid a dear price in human terms.

The Capture of Fort Donelson

Few Union victories stirred the enthusiasm of unionists like the surrender of 15,000 Rebel soldiers guarding the walled fortress of Fort Donelson, situated on a bluff overlooking the Cumberland River. It was the first major Union triumph of the war, and Nashville came into Union hands shortly thereafter. From Maine to Iowa, church bells rang out following the news of the victory.

In the Hawkeye state, residents took pride in the performance of the 2nd Iowa Infantry, the regiment most closely associated with the victory. The Iowans' charge on day two of the battle so impressed General Grant that he assigned them the honor of raising their regiment's national flag over the fortress. Governor Kirkwood made a special trip to the fort and returned home with the bullet-riddled flag. The 2nd Infantry's Stars and Stripes was paraded through a series of Iowa towns from Keokuk to Des Moines, after which it adorned the state capitol building.

The contest for Fort Donelson might have taken a very different turn. Confederate general Simon Buckner's troop strength roughly equaled the size of the Union army, and until the successful charge by the Iowans on the second day of the battle, nothing had gone right for Union forces. On day one, Confederate artillery fire repelled the Union Navy ironclads as they attempted to advance slowly upstream toward the fortress on the bluff. When General Grant ordered his infantrymen forward, they encountered a series of earthworks, a three-mile arc of trenches surrounding the stone installation that overlooked the river. An impassable creek that split the battlefield into two sectors prevented Union commanders from rapidly shifting forces from one sector to another. In both sectors, deep gullies limited the avenues of assault on the outer line of Rebel trenches, and tall trees blocked Union cannon fire.[1]

At not a single point on day one did Union forces breach the outer defense perimeter. The situation appeared grim, as Grant did not have the logistical resources to maintain a siege. Having prepared an interior line of trenches in case the perimeter trench became breached, Rebel forces might have successfully resisted a Union Army three times its actual size.

The onset of a blizzard in the middle of the battle compelled Grant to

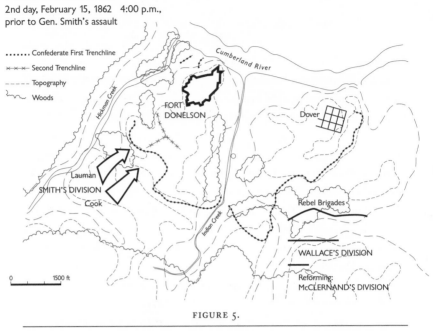

FORT DONELSON

2nd day, February 15, 1862   4:00 p.m.,
prior to Gen. Smith's assault

······· Confederate First Trenchline

×—×—× Second Trenchline

– – – – – Topography

ꙭꙭ Woods

Cumberland River

Hickman Creek

FORT DONELSON

Dover

Lauman

SMITH'S DIVISION

Cook

Rebel Brigades

Indian Creek

0 ———— 1500 ft

WALLACE'S DIVISION

Reforming:
McCLERNAND'S DIVISION

FIGURE 5.

contemplate a retreat to Paducah. Despite the miserable weather, he maintained a line of troops around the Confederate earthworks on day two.
His patience paid off handsomely when Buckner chose this moment to
concentrate his forces on the southern side of the creek and counter-attack
in hopes of forcing Grant back to Paducah.

The Confederate leader nearly achieved his goal. By mid-afternoon on
the second day, both Union divisions on the southern sector had reached
a breaking point. To relieve the pressure on his southern sector, Grant
ordered the lone Union division north of the creek to assault the Rebel
entrenchments closest to the fort. Seizing the initiative, the Union officers in charge of the assault sought to punch a hole through the northern
perimeter trench line and seize the fortress two miles away (fig. 5). To lead
the assault, the division commander chose the 2nd Iowa Infantry.

Military fame came to the 2nd Iowa unexpectedly. If all had gone
according to General Halleck's original plan, the 2nd Iowa would have
been tramping over muddy Missouri roads with General Curtis into
northwestern Arkansas. Sent to support Grant's assault on Fort Donelson instead, Curtis's old regiment missed the first day's battle and avoided

the Rebel counter-attack on day two because Grant assigned them to the northern sector, the same ground where three other Iowa regiments were deployed, including the 12th Iowa, Abner Dunham's unit.

Burlington's Jacob Lauman, the top-ranking Iowan on the northern sector, recommended that the 2nd Iowa spearhead the assault instead of his old regiment, the 7th Iowa. The 2nd Iowa had the reputation of being the best-drilled unit among the Hawkeye regiments under Grant. Newly arrived by steamboat from St. Louis, the 2nd Iowa brought with them warm clothing to protect them from the elements, while the men in the other units, including Dunham's regiment, spent a sleepless night without a campfire to keep them warm. "We only had our blankets, our overcoats being left in Fort Henry," Abner Dunham wrote home, "and I tell you we had a tough night of it. It rained until we were all wet and then it commenced snowing and freezing."[2]

The cluttered terrain protecting the outer Rebel trench line allowed just enough room for a line of 300 men to charge the earthworks. Six hundred fifty men of the 2nd Iowa took part in the assault at Fort Donelson, roughly 65 percent of the regiment's original strength. The four other regiments in Lauman's brigade prepared to follow them up the gully. On their right, a second brigade aimed for a series of earthworks south of the 2nd Iowa's point of attack. When the lead columns of the 2nd Iowa stepped forward, four hours of daylight remained.

Given the physical obstacles before them, the slaughter might have reached epic proportions. Confederate gunners had inflicted numerous casualties during the failed assault on day one, and Union commanders assumed the second day's assault would be just as bloody. Fortunately, General Buckner had transferred nearly all of his northern sector units across the creek to the southern sector to increase the chances of breaking the Union line there. Only two companies of riflemen (approximately 130 Rebel infantry) defended the earthworks facing the Iowans, and not a single Confederate artillery battery had a line of sight to fire on the 2nd Iowa Infantry.

As soon as Union artillery on the northern sector announced the attack, Buckner redirected several infantry units to return at once to their previous place of deployment. The Iowans leading the charge did not realize it, but the fate of the battle depended upon how quickly they could seize the opportunity and how quickly the Confederate troops could move to block them. As the Iowans struggled to make it through the dense rows of obstacles, several Confederate regiments in the southern sector hustled north to cut them off while Rebel reserve artillery sped to the point of attack.

Fortunately for the Union cause, the 2nd Iowa captured the outer Rebel trench in short order. The thin detachment of Tennesseans broke and fled in the face of the Iowans' disciplined charge. At this critical juncture, the 2nd Iowa's top officer, James M. Tuttle, saw an opportunity to capture an interior line of earthworks that commanded a higher elevation. A lateral trench connected the exterior and the interior lines of earthworks, and Tuttle wasted little time rushing his men forward to the inner line of trenches.

Tuttle's Iowans stopped in their tracks when the hustling Rebels arrived on the scene to block their advance toward the inner trench line. Despite the sudden appearance of Rebel reinforcements, the Iowans pushed forward toward the fort. Heavy fighting ensued in the lateral trench between the two lines of earthworks. "These Confederate troops," writes historian James Hamilton, "while equal in number to the Iowans . . . did not possess the moral impetus which imbued the victorious Union striking force."[3] The Rebels broke ranks after receiving a burst of rifle fire from the unwavering Iowans, who then entered the second line of earthworks. More Rebel troops arrived, enough to prevent the Iowans from advancing out of the trench toward the fortress. Outnumbered, the Iowans now prepared to defend their portion of the interior trench line against a series of desperate counter-attacks.

As Grant had hoped, Buckner pulled back all of his forward units in the southern sector in response to this direct threat to the fortress. Their withdrawal to the outer line of Rebel trenches allowed the Union troops in the southern sector to reorganize their forces. Fresh Union units, including the 8th Missouri and the 1st Nebraska, joined the battle-worn brigades in the southern sector and counter-attacked. Buckner's army remained in control of most of the fortified positions, but Union forces now could block any Rebel infantry units that attempted to escape Grant's trap.

The soldiers of the 2nd Iowa, the Union regiment closest to the fort, fought tooth and nail in hopes of securing the interior line of earthworks. Exposed to Rebel artillery fire and facing four Rebel infantry regiments, Colonel Tuttle reluctantly retreated back to the first line of Rebel rifle pits.

There, the 12th Iowa joined the firefight, supported by the 7th Iowa and the 14th Iowa. Their position was supported by Union artillery, which had relocated to forward positions during the fight for the inner trench. As nighttime approached, Lauman's brigade clung desperately to the outermost Rebel trench line, beating back every attempt to dislodge them.

Throughout the bitterly cold night, the Iowans stood by with guns ready. When morning dawned, Union cannoneers took aim at the fort. With the Confederate inner defense network exposed to artillery fire, Buckner realized his strategic position was vulnerable. Prepared to resume the battle on the third day, Grant demanded Buckner's unconditional surrender. The Confederate leader presented his reply under a flag of truce delivered to the Iowans clinging to the only Rebel earthworks in Union hands. He accepted Grant's demand, handing him the first major Union victory of the war, east or west.

Fame at Fort Donelson came at a high price to the 2nd Iowa Regiment. During the two most intensive hours of fighting, 30 percent of the regiment was wounded. Of the seventy-some Keokuk volunteers present for duty in Company A, fourteen were hit by fire. Two died from their wounds. "I took a mule yesterday and rode around over the battle ground [of Fort Donelson]," Abner Dunham wrote home after the surrender, "until I got tired and then did not see half but it makes me feel bad to see some of the sights." He survived the battle without a scratch but was horrified by the carnage, particularly in the southern sector. "To see the dead heaped up by the dozens not yet buried and they cannot get them buried before tomorrow night," he explained to his parents, "to see how they are mangled and then just tumbled into holes by dozens gives a person a good idea of the horrors of war. And the wounded are not all got into good hospitals yet and the ambulances are running night and day doing their best for them."[4]

Future Union victories would carry names more familiar to twenty-first-century schoolchildren, but no other Civil War battle had more immediate consequences than the capture of Fort Donelson and nearby Fort Henry, the two Rebel bastions blocking access to the Tennessee and Cumberland rivers. Six thousand Confederate cavalry and infantry escaped Fort Donelson to fight another day, but the surrender of 15,000 first-rate infantrymen created a huge void in Rebel general Albert Sydney Johnston's western defensive network. A week later, Confederates abandoned the capital of Tennessee. On the Mississippi River, Rebel forces evacuated the Iron Hills at Columbus, Kentucky, without a fight, allowing Union gunboats to venture as far downstream as Island Number 10 near the Tennessee-Kentucky border.

Grant's victory "resounded in bitterly hushed tones across the South," notes historian B. F. Cooling. "Larger and more famous battles would eclipse the infamy of Forts Henry and Donelson, perhaps, but the gall of ultimate Confederate defeat by 1865 could be traced directly to those early, shocking setbacks in Middle Tennessee."[5]

The victory at Fort Donelson also relieved pressure on Union forces in Missouri. Tens of thousands of Rebels stood ready in Arkansas prepared to invade Missouri, but after Buckner's surrender, Confederate general Johnston shifted New West Rebel regiments from Arkansas to the east side of the Mississippi River. With twenty-three Confederate regiments already transferred from the Western theater to Virginia, Johnston's decision to relocate more Texans, Louisianans, and Arkansans to Corinth, Mississippi, reduced substantially the number of Rebel units deployed in Arkansas. Confederate commanders in Arkansas still managed to assemble nearly 14,000 troops to stage a reinvasion of Missouri, but the figure would have been much higher without the surrender of 15,000 Rebels at Fort Donelson.

In the end, Richmond's decision to strip the New West states of so many regiments had immense strategic consequences. In the summer of 1862, several Louisiana regiments marched with Stonewall Jackson through the Shenandoah Valley, but only one Louisiana regiment fought in Arkansas alongside Price's Missouri State Guard at the Battle of Pea Ridge. With some of their best troops no longer available, Rebel commanders in Arkansas turned to Native Americans recruited in Oklahoma to make up the numerical difference. The hybrid group of Arkansas Confederates, Missouri Guardsmen, and Oklahoma Indians faced off against Curtis's hybrid Union army of German-speaking units and English-speaking units recruited in Iowa, Illinois, and other Great Lakes states.

The Battle of Pea Ridge

Of the three major Union victories in the Western theater in early 1862, the Pea Ridge campaign stands out as the most impressive. Not only did

Confederate forces outnumber General Curtis's troops in northwestern Arkansas, but the terrain and the low population density there increased the likelihood of a Union defeat. Compared to the rolling terrain of western Tennessee, crisscrossed by railroads and close to navigable rivers, the rocky heights between Fayetteville, Arkansas, and Springfield, Missouri, challenged soldiers, horses, and mules alike. The nearest railroad junction lay hundreds of miles away, and Rebels controlled the Arkansas River, the only navigable watercourse. Logistical barriers forced invading Union soldiers to live off the land, but few towns dotted this remote portion of Arkansas, and only a fraction of the wilderness had been converted to farming. Weather further complicated matters for Curtis, who elected to follow Sterling Price's Missourians across the Arkansas border despite the threat of snowstorms and other winter conditions.[6]

The tenuous political circumstances in Missouri raised the stakes for Curtis. Earl Van Dorn, the Rebel commander in Arkansas, had every intention of capturing St. Louis when he arrived at Little Rock on January 29, 1862. If Curtis's bold decision to pursue Price into northwestern Arkansas resulted in a resounding Rebel victory, guerrillas would be emboldened and thousands of Union soldiers would have to be transferred back to Missouri to protect St. Louis. Compared to Grant's campaign in Tennessee, the Union Army had more to lose in northwestern Arkansas. While the Ohio River afforded Union forces some protection from Rebel invasion, a defeat in Arkansas in the late winter of 1862 would have directly undermined the security of Missouri and compelled Halleck to recall Grant's force from Tennessee.

Curtis crossed the Missouri-Arkansas border with fewer than 10,000 soldiers, all of them former civilians. His support staff included only two West Point graduates plus a few European-trained officers. When he realized he had no means to supply his troops with food in Arkansas, Curtis scattered his forces over a distance of twenty miles in the northwestern quadrant of the state to forage. He was unaware that Rebel units stationed near the Mississippi River in New Madrid had advanced to join Van Dorn north of Little Rock.

After the war, the veterans of Pea Ridge recalled the campaign in northwestern Arkansas as the most physically demanding of the entire conflict. Despite the many disadvantages they faced, Union forces prevailed in the end. Historians assign most of the credit to several Iowans: Cyrus Bussey,

Grenville Dodge, Frank Herron, William Vandever, James Williamson, and of course Samuel Curtis.

Pea Ridge proved a baptism of fire for Council Bluffs soldiers in the 4th Iowa Infantry and for Delaware County recruits in the 9th Infantry. These two regiments suffered more casualties than any other bluecoat infantry regiments at Pea Ridge. Just as impressive was the Iowans' prebattle marching. When Dodge and Vandever pushed their infantrymen hard, the citizen-soldiers responded magnificently.

Two days before the firing began, the 9th Iowa marched forty-two miles in sixteen hours through snow and mud and icy watercourses with little food. Marching was dirty work, but it was not unfamiliar work to the Iowans. When food became scarce, they foraged the wilderness for wild nuts and berries, and slaughtered wild animals for meat, the same tasks that had ensured their survival at home before the Civil War. Despite the physical challenges posed by the terrain, every soldier made it to the battlefield. When Rebel cannon shells began landing on the Elkhorn Tavern, the inexperienced volunteers held their formations like veterans.[7]

Thanks to the soldiers' hard marching, Curtis pulled together his scattered units in time to avoid piecemeal destruction at the hands of General Van Dorn. Once they achieved concentration, Union troops headed north toward Springfield, Missouri. Expecting that the Confederates would attack him by moving south to north, Curtis dug in and established a defensive position along an east-to-west line of hills called Pea Ridge just south of the Missouri state boundary. The Union defensive line lay several miles south of Elkhorn Tavern, one of the few villages in the area.[8]

Van Dorn, rather than risk a head-on attack, ordered an all-night flanking march around the hills north of Elkhorn Tavern. At sunrise, the Missouri guardsmen at the head of the Rebel flanking movement found themselves within striking distance of the vulnerable Union supply wagons parked near the Elkhorn Tavern. The outcome of the campaign ultimately hinged on the contest near the tavern on day one.

Fortunately for the Union cause, Van Dorn's plan to assault the tavern from two directions fell through. At Leetown, two miles west of the tavern, a group of Confederate troops failed to dislodge the Federal soldiers guarding the crossroads. This successful defense at Leetown provided a fighting chance to the one thin Union division protecting the supply wagons near the tavern. When Rebel general Price struck at the tavern from the north, his 6,800 Missouri guardsmen held a two-to-one advantage in numbers. Union forces guarding the supply train included two full-strength Iowa regiments and three half-strength regiments from Missouri and Illinois. One Illinois cavalry regiment and two Iowa artillery batteries provided support.

At Elkhorn Tavern the best troops in both armies battled for possession of the Union supply wagons. The surviving elements of the Missouri State Guard included Price's most talented officers and fighting men, many of them veterans of Wilson's Creek. The Union division at the tavern, the "most battleworthy unit" in Curtis's army, made up in training and fortitude for what they lacked in battle experience.[9]

Dodge deserved most of the credit for their battle-readiness. A graduate of Norwich Military Academy in Vermont, he personally recruited the officers in the 4th Iowa and trained them in the art of military drill and maneuver. By the end of the war, the 4th Iowa had earned a reputation as one of the best infantry regiments in Sherman's army. Much of Dodge's training rubbed off on the soldiers in the 9th Iowa, who marched alongside the 4th Iowa for the remainder of the war.

In the days leading up to the battle, Dodge made several timely command decisions. The railroad surveyor from Council Bluffs was the first Union officer to recognize Van Dorn's envelopment strategy. Without his keen insight, the supply wagons would have been left undefended. As it happened, Dodge's brigade was the only Union force prepared to defend the supply wagons the night before the battle. By the time Van Dorn ordered Price to launch an all-out attack, Dodge had put together a defensive line. The 9th Iowa Regiment guarded the west side of the tavern, while to the east soldiers in the 4th Iowa stacked tree limbs to shore up a fencerow on their portion of the front. When Price attempted to outflank the Union line, Dodge re-formed the line at a 90-degree angle.

Prewar farmwork, in combination with Dodge's training, prepared the Iowans for the difficult task of holding back Price's experienced shock troops. The Iowans were conditioned to cope with the inevitable setbacks they would encounter on the battlefield. They prepared for battle "as the farmer does his preparation for harvest," noted one Iowan. Working men considered soldiering as "a job to be done, not thought about, and demonstrations of concern were taboo," historian Earl Hess points out.[10]

The rural working culture also enabled inexperienced officers to be aware of the shifting dynamics of the battle. While they were stationed in the thick of the fighting, the officers' prewar experience working the countryside taught them to be mindful of what was happening elsewhere on the battlefield. Time and time again, the Iowans repositioned their men in good order so as to prevent an all-out rout. However, the officers' bravery itself contributed to high casualties. Confederate fire wounded four of Iowa's eight top-ranking men at Elkhorn Tavern. Into their place stepped lower ranking officers who stood firm in the face of the concentrated fire from Price's intrepid Missourians. Despite heavy casualties, the bluecoats retreated slowly and methodically to prepared positions when the Missouri guardsmen breached the initial line of defense.

The contest for the Union supply wagons reached a critical moment when simultaneous Confederate flank attacks prevented Union officers from shifting units from one spot to another to fill gaps in the defense line. Price's Confederates gained control of the tavern and bore down on both flanks, but a half-strength Indiana regiment arrived just in time to close one gap in the Union line. Another breach was about to develop when General Curtis hustled 500 infantry reinforcements and 8 cannon from Leetown to the tavern.

The 4th Iowa and the 9th Iowa retired in relatively good order—despite having fought for more than four hours—to a new line 600 yards southwest of the tavern, anchored by the 500 reinforcements from Leetown. With the Union supply wagons nearby, this would be the final Union defense line. General Price continued to press for the vulnerable supply wagons, but the 9th Iowa repulsed the final assault on the new line. With the sun about to set, Curtis ordered Dodge and the 4th Iowa to charge and retake the tavern. Out of ammunition, the Iowans fixed their bayonets and prepared to advance. Giving a wild cheer, Dodge's men threw their hats into the air before advancing pell-mell toward the tavern. The surprise counter-attack drove Price's Missourians back to the tavern, far enough to discourage any further action until the next day.

When day two dawned, the prospects for a Union victory did not appear promising. During the night, Arkansans, Texans, and Louisianans had marched from Leetown to join Price's Missourians. Curtis refused to be discouraged by the turn of events, and as it happened, Van Dorn's supply train failed to arrive with the rest of the Rebel army. Curtis had plenty of artillery ammunition while the Rebels had little, and that gave the Federals a fighting chance to preserve their supply train.

After Union artillerymen fired continuously for two hours without letting up, Van Dorn abandoned the field, setting out east down the Huntsville Road rather than renewing his infantry assault. The tired and hungry Union troops, elated by this turn of events, celebrated their unexpected victory with wild shouts of joy. Some compared the mood of victory to a religious revival meeting.

The Pea Ridge victory exacted its highest toll on Iowa's infantry regiments. Altogether, 440 Iowans died or sustained wounds. That only ten Iowans turned up missing after this, their first battle, attests to their fortitude. Unfortunately, few medical personnel were on hand to treat the hundreds of wounded. Many of them lay on the cold ground for several hours before receiving care. Rebel wounded left on the battlefield lay interspersed with Union wounded as Van Dorn marched his survivors into eastern Arkansas.

Stung by his defeat at the hands of Curtis, Van Dorn could not resist appeals from Confederate commanders on the east side of the Mississippi River to cross over and join forces in an attempt to threaten St. Louis from that direction. His departure from northwestern Arkansas ultimately affected the deployment of troops in the entire theater of military operations west of the Appalachians.

Union commander Halleck, in response to the Confederates' shifting of forces, relocated his headquarters to Tennessee and maneuvered more Union troops from the New West into that state. The Union veterans of Pea Ridge joined other bluecoat units redeployed there. Upon their arrival on the east bank, some marched to Nashville and joined the Army of the Cumberland, while others (including the 4th Iowa and 9th Iowa) fought in Grant's Army of the Tennessee.[11]

The Battle of Shiloh

The 40,000 Confederate soldiers concentrated near Corinth, Mississippi, in late March 1862 posed a formidable challenge to the overconfident Union Army encamped thirty miles north, near Pittsburg Landing on the Tennessee River. The Rebel army included twenty-five infantry regiments from Louisiana, Arkansas, Missouri, and Texas. Those New West units, combined with forty-nine infantry regiments from Tennessee, Mississippi, Alabama, and Kentucky, provided General Johnston with enough manpower to overwhelm Grant, provided that they carried out their attack in a well-organized fashion and before Union reinforcements arrived.

The regiments under Grant came primarily from Indiana, Ohio, Illinois, and Kentucky. Fortunately for the Union cause, nineteen bluecoat regiments from Iowa, Missouri, and Nebraska Territory arrived around April 1 to raise Grant's total force to a size roughly equivalent to that of the Confederates. Iowa's Pea Ridge veterans did not arrive in Tennessee soon enough to participate in the Battle of Shiloh, but the majority of the state's 1861 volunteers did participate. On the day the Rebels launched their attack, eleven of Iowa's fifteen three-year infantry regiments—a mixture of Fort Donelson veterans and green troops—were encamped within a mile or two of the river docks known as Pittsburg Landing. On the battle's second day, thirty-four Ohio River valley regiments arrived to lead the Union counter-attack.[12]

Shiloh's significance as a battle is undisputed. Its importance is magnified by what might have been, for a Rebel victory would have reversed Union momentum in the Ohio River theater of operations. While historians still debate the relative merits of the Confederate battle plan, most researchers agree the Rebel commanders missed a grand opportunity to drive Grant's isolated force into the river on day one. The outcome of the battle hinged on the fighting on the first day, the time period when Iowa regiments defended the Union right flank while other Hawkeye units defended the Union left flank near the Sunken Road.

The defenders of the Sunken Road deserve much of the credit for frustrating Confederate plans to reach the Tennessee River by the early afternoon. While some historians challenge the significance of the Union defense of the Sunken Road,[13] Hawkeye units actually served at several battlefield locations on day one. The Sunken Road had the highest concentration of Iowa units, but several others fought on the Union right flank. Former regimental colonels from Iowa commanded five brigades at Shiloh, and all five were heavily engaged by noon.

Few researchers question the active involvement of Iowa troops on day one. Nearly every Hawkeye regiment had encamped well away from the point of the initial Rebel attack, and as a result the Iowans played a prominent role after the initial panic on the Union perimeter. After the most exposed bluecoat regiments from other states disintegrated in the face of a surprise Rebel attack, the Union units, encamped closer to the river landing, stepped forward to form a defense line and secure the landing.

The number of Iowans engaged in action around noon on the first day is striking. Five Hawkeye regiments participated in the noon counter-attack on the right flank, while six Hawkeye regiments guarded the Sunken Road on the center-left portion of the Union line, approximately one mile away from the river landing. The units defending the Sunken Road included Abner Dunham and his colleagues in the 12th Iowa. Lee County soldiers in the 2nd Iowa and 7th Iowa stood nearby.

The first Rebel infantry attack hit the Sunken Road about ten a.m. The 2nd Iowa's Colonel Tuttle, riding his horse back and forth along the dirt path, eased the nerves of his soldiers by reminding them to "keep cool and remember that we are from Iowa."[14] After the initial wave of Confederates retired with heavy casualties, a fresh Rebel brigade launched an attack at noon. Four times the Rebel brigade attacked, and four times the defenders sent them reeling back in disorder. On the Union right flank, meanwhile, the brigade commanders prepared to launch a counter-attack. Three Hawkeye units on the right flank, including the 11th Iowa, sustained their attack before withdrawing in relatively good order. The same could not be said for the 15th Iowa.

While Colonel Hare of Muscatine directed the 11th Iowa on the right flank, a half mile away two Keokuk lawyers led the charge of the green 15th Iowa, which included Ben Stevens. Still in training camp when Fort Donelson capitulated, the 15th Iowa arrived by steamboat on the morning of the Battle of Shiloh. The 15th disembarked as a growing crowd of shell-shocked bluecoats took refuge near the wharf. In the middle of the chaos, General Grant personally directed the 15th Iowa to march to the front line. As nervous as anyone would be in such a situation, Ben Stevens and his fellow soldiers from Oskaloosa headed toward the sound of distant cannon fire.

Grant, who had no more than 25,000 effective soldiers on the front line at any point on day one, relied on the eleven Iowa regiments to stem the Rebel attack. With many Union regiments already out of action, at least 25 percent of Grant's noon defensive line consisted of Iowans (fig. 6). Even if the contest over the Sunken Road did not define the battle, Iowa's soldiers as a whole contributed a disproportionate share to the ultimate outcome. Because every Hawkeye regiment engaged in several hours of combat on day one, the state suffered an extraordinary number of casualties.[15]

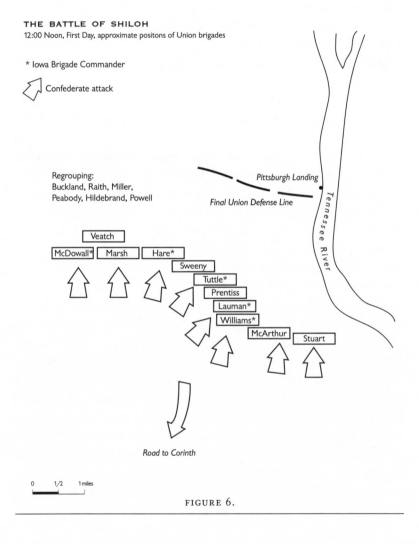

THE BATTLE OF SHILOH
12:00 Noon, First Day, approximate positons of Union brigades

* Iowa Brigade Commander

Confederate attack

Regrouping:
Buckland, Raith, Miller,
Peabody, Hildebrand, Powell

Pittsburgh Landing

Final Union Defense Line

Tennessee River

Veatch

McDowall*   Marsh   Hare*

Sweeny

Tuttle*

Prentiss

Lauman*

Williams*

McArthur   Stuart

Road to Corinth

0   1/2   1 miles

FIGURE 6.

The 15th Iowa fared perhaps the worst. After taking a position on the Union right flank, the overconfident soldiers in the 15th Iowa engaged the enemy on open ground without artillery support. Confederate fire struck the regimental colonel, the major, and many junior officers. Two hours of fighting seemed like an eternity to the inexperienced Iowans. When a Rebel counter-charge drove back the units protecting the flanks of the 15th Iowa, individual members began to panic and withdraw without orders. Dozens of men in the 15th Iowa left the sector in small groups and fled back to the security of the river landing, leaving behind more than 200 wounded and dead Iowans from the 15th Regiment.

Ben Stevens was among those who fled. He survived unscathed, and in the days that followed, the Oskaloosa carpenter came to realize the lack of fortitude shown by his regiment. The battle "was terrible, words cannot express the scene," the twenty-two-year-old wrote in a letter home. "I was in the midst of a continual shower of shot and shell, and when we was ordered to fall back I must confess that I felt weak in the knees. I thought we would all be taken [prisoner]."[16] Major William Belknap rallied several hundred survivors and re-formed the 15th Iowa, but in psychological terms the regiment's enthusiasm was spent. They could no longer be relied upon to lead an attack. If called upon to defend a sector, the 15th Iowa might not be able to hold down the position.

While units on the right flank reached a point of near-collapse, the Iowans guarding the Sunken Road continued their stubborn defense on the left-center of the Union line. The Rebels' inability to penetrate Colonel Tuttle's position convinced General Johnston to shift four Confederate brigades toward the far left of the Union line near the Peach Orchard.

The attack on the Peach Orchard began about one p.m. The persistent graybacks eventually forced the bluecoat regiments there to fall back one by one toward the landing. As the attackers worked their way around the end of the Union left, the flanks of Tuttle's soldiers guarding the Sunken Road became exposed. Tuttle refused to retreat at three p.m., when the Confederates resumed their attack on his portion of the line. Battery after battery of Rebel artillery launched salvos at the defenders of the Sunken Road, but despite the barrage the bluecoats managed to repulse an attack by one Rebel brigade and then another. Remarkably, the defenders incurred relatively few casualties despite the length of time they were deployed along the road. As long as they had ammunition and as long as their flanks were protected, Union troops would hold the position.

Troops protecting their flanks did not hold out. The center of the Union line—to Tuttle's right—collapsed about the same time that General Lauman on the far Union left retreated with his brigade from the Peach Orchard. By the time Tuttle realized the danger to his flanks, approximately half the Confederate Army surrounded his position on the Sunken Road. The Iowa colonel managed to escape the encirclement with about half of his brigade. The other half—including Abner Dunham's 12th Iowa—surrendered. Dunham was among the 1,200 Iowa soldiers taken captive at the Sunken Road.

In his 1974 book on Shiloh, Wiley Sword singled out the leadership of Colonel Tuttle in preparing the final Union line of defense.[17] By the time the hero of Fort Donelson escaped the Confederate trap at the Sunken Road and arrived back at the landing, Grant's battered army was disorganized and vulnerable to attack. At 4:30 p.m., one hour before Tuttle completed his mile-long retreat from the Sunken Road, Grant had tried in vain to inspire thousands of stragglers huddled near the riverbank. When they refused to rally, Grant's fate fell into the hands of the battle-weary soldiers falling back to the landing.

Tuttle's soldiers arrived near the landing around 5:30 p.m. Several dozen Union cannon guarded the top of the bluff over the landing, but a cohesive and mutually supporting defensive line had yet to be formed. Unless the disorganized groups of Union infantry could be inspired and redirected to support the line of artillery, Rebel units could seize the unsupported canon or maneuver around the cannon and attack the landing from several directions simultaneously.

Tuttle immediately rallied the survivors of his brigade near their original campground, one-half mile from the Tennessee River. From here, the 2nd Iowa and 7th Iowa regiments joined with Iowans who had fought their way back from the Peach Orchard through a gauntlet of Confederates. To fill gaps in the line, bluecoats who survived the fighting on the Union right flank stepped in. Several regiments from Illinois and Ohio joined the Iowans near the center of the new Union line. General Sherman's bloodied regiments formed to the right of the Iowans away from the river, thus extending the makeshift line into the woods. On the bluff above the landing, regiments including the 11th Iowa and 15th Iowa stood at the ready behind a row of cannon. General Lauman deployed near the landing with the remnants of his battle-worn brigade of Indiana and Kentucky volunteers.

By the time Confederate troops stormed forward toward the landing, a Union defensive line was intact. The final Rebel assault of the day failed to penetrate the line at any point. The successful defense of the landing enabled thirty-four fresh Union regiments to reach the landing during the night. While Grant relied primarily on the new arrivals to lead the counter-attack on day two, some Iowa units, including Tuttle's survivors, contributed to push General Beauregard's depleted Rebel units away from the landing and back toward Corinth. The 7th Iowa captured one Rebel artillery battery, while the 2nd Iowa charged headlong into a line of enemy infantry. Union commanders held the 15th Iowa in reserve on day two.

Despite the Rebel retreat at the end of day two, Ben Stevens felt a sense of failure. Yet he should have been ecstatic. The Confederate Army suffered a staggering 10,000 casualties during the two-day conflict. Hundreds more Rebel volunteers deserted in the days that followed. General Beauregard eventually abandoned Corinth and with it any hope of shifting his forces back to the west side of the Mississippi River for a drive into Missouri. Memphis fell into Union hands soon after Shiloh, and Grant set his sights on Vicksburg. With Nashville and Memphis lost, the Confederate Congress passed the Conscription Act, a desperate measure President Davis hoped would reverse the course of the war in the West.

The High Cost of Victory

The total casualty list at Shiloh appalled Iowans back home. Hawkeye units incurred only light casualties on day two, but the state of Iowa paid an unusually heavy price as a result of the sustained fighting on day one. In all, 2,400 Iowans were killed, injured, or captured at Shiloh, nearly one-fifth of all Union casualties. Roughly half the state's casualties came at the Sunken Road in the form of prisoners. Most of the wounded and dead fought on the right flank (away from the Sunken Road). The Iowa regiments on the right flank, including the 11th and 15th, lost nearly one-third

FIGURE 7. *Steamboats at Pittsburg Landing*, ink drawing from a photograph taken a few days after the Battle of Shiloh. The steamboats arrived from Cincinnati, Ohio, and other ports, loaded with supplies for wounded soldiers. Originally published in *Century Magazine* in 1886.

of their men (166 dead, 780 wounded, and 92 missing or captured). Fewer Iowans defending the Sunken Road received wounds. Tuttle's units, which narrowly avoided capture (such as the 2nd and 7th regiments), survived the battle with only a modest number of casualties.[18]

Because recruits fought in the same units with their neighbors, the impact of the battle varied from community to community. Nearly every Delaware County soldier in the 12th Iowa spent the remainder of 1862 in a Confederate prisoner of war camp. Those from Lee County experienced a different form of terror. While few were taken prisoner, more than 100 were wounded or killed. The list of Muscatine soldiers struck down by shot and shell included Colonel Hare, who received a severe wound. Mahaska County families grieved for several dozen casualties in the 7th and 15th regiments.

Sadly, the sorely understaffed Union medical corps was ill equipped to handle the scale of Shiloh's carnage. Annie Wittenmyer, who happened to be on a hospital boat moored at the landing when the battle began, worked night and day with other women, tending to the thousands of wounded soldiers. To feed the multitude of injured soldiers, Wittenmyer made soup using what few resources she could find. In the hospital, she prayed alongside individual men as they died from their wounds.

By one account, Wittenmyer worked twenty-four hours straight without stopping for a meal or a change of clothing. Her floor-length dress absorbed mud and moisture up to her knees. In her few spare moments, she furiously penned a series of letters imploring LSAS chapter presidents to seek immediate assistance. Her spirits revived when her brother, Dr. William Turner, arrived in Tennessee after joining the medical staff of the 2nd Iowa Regiment.[19]

Shiloh forever altered the career path of Annie Wittenmyer. The scale of the medical crisis generated considerable debate among civilian volunteers, and in the end Wittenmyer emerged as the state's most influential advocate, male or female, for hospitalized soldiers. In late 1862, the all-male state legislature passed a bill specifically naming her as one of two designated agents for the Iowa sanitary commission. Her talents as a sanitary administrator catapulted her upon the national stage. Within a few weeks after the battle, high-ranking Federal officials facilitated her access to hospitals and ensured her safe passage between army bases. Greater access empowered her to more actively manage the transportation of donated supplies. Historian Lisa Guinn notes that Wittenmyer now entered the public world where she could "experience independence and usefulness as part of a new self-identity."[20]

Back home in Keokuk, women from the LSAS worked day and night to facilitate an emergency plan to treat Shiloh survivors. LSAS members quickly took possession of the Estes House, a large but unfinished hotel, and outfitted 179 empty rooms for medical purposes. Within a few days, 112 beds had been installed in anticipation of boatloads of wounded Iowans arriving from Shiloh. Eventually, 652 beds filled the Estes House. When the first boat arrived April 19 carrying 200 wounded and sick soldiers, Keokuk's fire bells tolled its arrival. Two hundred more wounded arrived April 23, most of them destined for the Estes House. By January 1863, 5 hospitals housed 1,440 patients.[21]

As Wittenmyer's leadership role expanded, objections from rivals escalated. Women as well as men conspired to undermine her authority, influence, and credibility. The long Shiloh casualty list prompted complaints as well as proposals for changing the LSAS system of collecting and transporting donated goods. As the war continued in a stalemate, a faction of Wittenmyer opponents crystallized within the LSAS network and the state Republican Party. Ann Harlan, the wife of Iowa's senior senator, led the anti-Wittenmyer faction.

Herself a hospital volunteer and veteran of Shiloh's aftermath, Mrs. Harlan advocated that the LSAS join the U.S. Sanitary Commission (USSC), a national organization supported by her husband. The USSC routed donated goods through central distribution hubs in urban centers such as Chicago. However, there was no USSC hub in St. Louis, the point through which most Iowa donations passed. Wittenmyer opposed a USSC merger and led a large faction of Iowa LSAS officers in opposition. In 1863, a friend of hers warned that "Mrs. Harlan is your sworn foe."[22]

The reasons behind Wittenmyer's opposition to the USSC are not entirely clear. Historian Judith Giesberg notes that in other states, LSAS leaders feared the loss of autonomy that would occur if donated goods were routed through a central distribution center.[23] There was also the question of efficiency. Wittenmyer and her allies insisted that a town-to-regiment system generated more donations at home and improved the soldiers' spirits.

Disagreement over the USSC first arose in mid-1862. Wittenmyer, anxious to resolve the dispute within the state LSAS network, organized a convention for Iowa LSAS leaders. The meeting ended on a positive note, as far as she was concerned. Rather than merge with the USSC, the IASC board specifically instructed donors to direct their goods to "Mrs. Annie Wittenmyer care of Partridge and Company in St. Louis." As the war dragged on, however, the Harlan family and others renewed their efforts to route Iowa donations to the USSC.

As the debate continued, municipal rivalries dating back to the 1840s stirred the pot of acrimony. Men and women from Davenport, the lone river port with a rail connection to Lake Michigan, pursued a Chicago-based model of transporting donated goods, while the steamboat-based port of Keokuk preferred to work through relief agencies in St. Louis. When the USSC office in Chicago appealed to Iowans for money and goods, many

Davenporters responded enthusiastically, while society leaders in Keokuk preferred the status quo arrangements through St. Louis.

In the midst of the dispute, Wittenmyer's home life became disrupted by two family deaths in 1862. Her father died in Keokuk, and she apparently missed his funeral as a result of her relief work. Meanwhile, in St. Louis, one of William's two daughters by his first marriage died while she was still in her twenties. Financial obligations, meanwhile, continued to trouble her, since she never considered women's work as employment and never received a monthly salary. The property taxes due on her home in Keokuk remained unpaid.

Fortunately, as word of Wittenmyer's good reputation spread, money came into her hands through unexpected sources. To help her defray expenses and minimize barriers to women, General Curtis, General Grant, and President Lincoln issued her unlimited transportation passes. Since she did not have a husband to provide companionship, members of Wittenmyer's family stepped in to provide much-needed consolation in the form of regular letters. Sister Alice looked after her home in Keokuk and nurtured son Charles. Her brother Will also kept in contact. Stationed in western Tennessee, he visited Annie from time to time during 1862. Will noted in one of his letters that the war would likely last "for another year and it may be longer."[24]

Coping with the Prospect of a Lengthy War

Southern reactions to the Union military success in early 1862 raised the prospect of a long military conflict. Despite three major Union victories in the West, Confederate leaders refused to surrender. In northern Mississippi, General Beauregard's Rebel army prepared to fight another Shiloh while in Richmond Jefferson Davis appointed Robert E. Lee to command Rebel forces in Virginia. When the Union Army on July 1 retreated from the gates of Richmond back to Washington, many Iowans realized the sectional conflict would not resolve itself in short order as they first thought. Volunteers who had responded to Lincoln's call for three years of service realized that the war might last even longer than their enlistments.

Like Dr. Will Turner, Cyrus Carpenter arrived at this gloomy conclusion after the Battle of Shiloh. Having returned to Fort Dodge in

November 1861, Carpenter utilized his partisan connections to obtain a spot as captain in the U.S. Quartermaster service. The former Republican state legislator initially expected a short war, but a few months of work in western Tennessee changed his mind. In one letter home, Carpenter remarked that "few of us have yet risen to the conception of the giant strength of this Rebellion." He confided to his brother, "I tell you Judd, I have seen enough of war to satisfy my curiosity. It makes me shudder barely to think of the waste of life, loss, of health, and the destruction of property which this war must result."[25]

The prospect of extended service fueled homesickness in many Iowa soldiers. The gnawing stress worsened as relatives appealed for them to return home and assist them in their struggle for survival on the frontier. The longer they remained away from home, the greater the toll their absence took on their parents, siblings, wives, and children. The boredom of camp life challenged homesick soldiers, as did repetitive military drills. Although recruits had been drilling for months, the critical period for training was now commencing in earnest.

Just as the military exercises became more intense, the persistent logistical deficiencies undermined the psychological well-being of soldiers. Before Shiloh, Hawkeye soldiers had to endure poor leadership, inadequate equipment, and bad food. After Shiloh, thousands of wounded soldiers died from inadequate medical care. Any reasonable person might have given up and gone home to protest the scandalous condition of the field hospitals.

The threat of capture and confinement added to the psychological stress. Stories of captives being mistreated in the Deep South found their way back to the Union lines. Abner Dunham was one of hundreds of Iowans languishing in Southern prisoner of war camps with no guarantee of release.

Along with 400 other members of the 12th Iowa captured at Shiloh, Dunham stepped aboard a railcar destined for Tuscaloosa, Alabama. During the long journey, angry citizens jeered the Union prisoners while a few sympathetic people offered them food and tobacco. The old Alabama state capitol, with no indoor plumbing facilities, housed more than 1,000 prisoners packed into cramped rooms without any bedding or eating utensils. The Shiloh veterans shared space with soldiers captured at Belmont and Fort Donelson, along with some political prisoners from eastern Tennessee. Food was sparse, and disease killed some of the prisoners. The soldiers of the 12th Iowa coped with the drudgery by helping each other clean the lice off their clothing and bodies every morning.[26]

As 1862 dragged on with no end in sight to the war, a final dilemma—a political and moral challenge—suddenly presented itself. Lincoln threatened to emancipate enslaved African Americans in late September, just a few weeks before the Battle of Corinth and the fall congressional elections. For those Iowa troops who had enlisted in 1861 for the specific purpose of preserving the status quo, the war suddenly took a new direction—a battle to end slavery. This more radical war aim posed an immediate challenge to Western conservative values. Being called a "Yankee" by the Rebels was one thing; embracing the abolitionist cause of the northeastern states—a cause most Iowans deemed anti-unionist—was quite another. How Iowans responded to the new debate over slavery directly influenced the outcome of the War of the Rebellion.

CHAPTER SIX

Radical Impulse in the New West

C yrus Carpenter spoke for thousands of Iowa soldiers when he questioned the humanity of African Americans in 1862. His first encounter with blacks occurred after he joined the U.S. Quartermaster service at an army warehouse in Tennessee. By 1862, former slaves performed much of the work hauling huge quantities of supplies to and from the warehouse. From the perspective of the former Iowa legislator, their dedication to family members corrupted their work ethic. He criticized the former slaves for their habit of circulating back and forth between the Union Army camp and their former plantations. "Negroes" have no courage to fight, the Pennsylvania native concluded in his diary. "They don't want to be set at liberty . . . A Negro slave with his wife and children is attached to the plantation upon which he was born [and] he would rather be a slave a thousand times than surrender one local attachment."[1]

Alexander Clark disagreed entirely with Carpenter's assessment of the potential contribution of African Americans to the war effort. For some months, Clark had been agitating in hopes of persuading Iowa's legislators—all white men—to enroll free blacks in the state's regiments. Thirty-seven years of age, the longtime Muscatine resident stood ready to enlist, as did other African American residents of Muscatine and Keokuk.

Their calls to enlist fell upon deaf ears in the summer of 1862. White Iowans in charge of the state's war administration were not ready to recruit black residents. Had they done so, hundreds of white Iowans would have refused to serve in nonsegregated units, they feared. Creating black-only units and assigning them to patrol backwater regions of the South away from the primary staging areas might have reduced white opposition to black recruitment. But recruiting blacks symbolized to some people a final act of desperation in the quest to reunite the nation.

Iowa's war leaders also expressed concern about the public's perception of the purpose of the military conflict. Because arming blacks in the spring of 1862 would have invited more charges that Lincoln aspired to abolish slavery rather than reunite the nation, Republicans led by Governor Kirkwood firmly opposed arming nonwhite volunteers. They refused to seek out African American volunteers despite the shortage of Union troops in the New West.

Clark's efforts to amend state civil rights laws encountered the same obstacle of fear. A referendum on equal rights had gone down to defeat at the polls in 1857, and in 1862 state Republican Party leaders still presumed that advocating on behalf of free blacks would undermine the party's popularity among Iowa voters.

Not all Republicans feared a public backlash. Abolitionists, labeled traitors before the war for demanding immediate emancipation, had for decades lobbied the Iowa legislature on behalf of equal rights. Iowa's radical leaders, encouraged by the prospect of a war to end slavery, renewed their demands for equal rights legislation in 1862. Moderate Republicans expressed no interest, however, in reopening the debate over black civil rights.

Continued enforcement of the Fugitive Slave Act after Fort Sumter symbolized Iowans' commitment to unionism as well as the lack of respect for human rights. In the state's southern border counties, white unionists turned over to authorities several Missouri slaves caught trying to escape to freedom. The rate of successful escape apparently increased following the chaos of 1861, but those African Americans able to cross the border found little comfort in the Hawkeye state. Those able to reach a safe sanctuary struggled to survive in a state where social oppression infected the quality of life.

White sentiment changed dramatically in late 1862 with regard to slaves held in the Deep South. Angry at continued Confederate military resistance, Republican moderates did what had been unthinkable in 1860 by urging the Federal government to make the emancipation of slaves the penalty for Southern resistance to forced reunification. The progressive trend accelerated as the war continued into 1863. More good news for black Americans would follow in 1864. By the end of the war, many conservative unionists embraced a radical position on black civil rights and opposed the so-called colonization bills designed to forcibly deport freed blacks. In Washington, representatives and senators from Iowa, Missouri, and other New West states enthusiastically endorsed an amendment to the U.S. Constitution eradicating slavery.

Pre-Proclamation Politics in Iowa

Lincoln issued his Emancipation Proclamation on September 22, 1862. That carefully tailored statement declared: "On the first day of January, in the year of our Lord one thousand eight hundred and sixty three, all persons held as slaves within any State, or designated part of a State, the people whereof shall then be in rebellion against the United States, shall be then, thenceforth, and forever free."[2] Despite its high moral tone, the proclamation did not free a single slave. Most slaves in North America were held captive in the seceded states. Slaves within the nonrebellious states of Missouri, Kentucky, Maryland, and Delaware did not fall within the scope of the proclamation. No slaves would be freed, moreover, if the rebellious states rejoined the Union. Although Lincoln implied he would follow through and declare the slaves free in 1863, he was not bound by his promise to issue an executive order abolishing slavery if the Confederate states refused.

Notwithstanding these severe realities, the proclamation instilled in Alexander Clark and other Iowa African Americans a belief that slavery would be abolished ultimately. For white unionists, however, the proclamation at this point was merely a political gesture designed to expedite the resolution of the military conflict. If slaveowners continued to maintain their independence as of January 1, 1863, the president would have a difficult decision to make. In the event that Lincoln followed up on his threat and abolished slavery on paper, such a bold action might permanently alienate slave-state unionists, thereby complicating the Federal government's military mission.

Abolishing slavery on paper might also alienate militant free-state Democrats. In Iowa, militant Democrats had played a critical role in sustaining the Hawkeye state's commitment to the war effort as of September 15, 1862. Samuel Kirkwood won reelection in August 1861 thanks to the support of multitudes of Democrats. Kirkwood did not lose a single county he had carried in 1859, while the Democratic candidate lost several major counties that had polled for his party in 1859.

To court militant Democrats, Kirkwood deliberately avoided any suggestion during the 1861 campaign that he supported calls for the abolition of slavery. At the state party convention that summer, the governor and his moderate colleagues succeeded in adopting a unionist platform for the party, which never once mentioned the word *slavery*. "We heartily invite cooperation with us of men of all parties," stated the final platform draft, "whatever their former political ties." In several Iowa communities, Republican candidates ran on a "Union Party" ticket to distinguish themselves from their neighbors who endorsed radical nominees for office.[3]

Kirkwood's appeal to militant unionists in 1861 caught his Democratic rivals at a vulnerable moment. Although most grassroots Democrats in Iowa supported the war effort, a majority of party leaders preferred a pro-negotiation candidate for governor, who advocated on behalf of a peace conference. The peace conference proposal reflected the deep unionist sentiment in the Hawkeye Democratic Party, but it bitterly divided long-time Democrats into two distinct factions. The most militant Democrats opposed holding a peace conference at this early stage of the conflict, while the less militant faction feared that any blood shed in the name of unionism would permanently alienate Southerners. Party leaders eventually settled on a militant Democrat to head their ticket—the lieutenant colonel of the famed 1st Iowa Infantry—but his party's flirtation with the peace conference proposal poisoned the well in the eyes of the public.

Jacob Ritner was one Iowa Republican enamored with his party's decision to emphasize unionism and deemphasize black civil rights in 1861. A moderate from Henry County, he had marched in the 1st Iowa Infantry Regiment that summer. Although he personally opposed slavery on moral grounds, he accepted orders not to disturb any slave quarters they encountered as they marched through the central Missouri River counties. Writing home to his friends on June 22, 1861, Ritner highlighted his unit's efforts to placate unionist slavemasters and pacify the Missouri countryside. "Several runaway Negroes came into camp, but the Colonel sent them back; and by this means we created quite a revolution in public sentiment, and encouraged the Union men greatly."[4]

The 1862 Legislative Session

In the final count in 1861, Kirkwood defeated his Democratic rival by a decisive margin of 11,000 ballots, having collected 55 percent of all votes cast. The results of the legislative contests brought more good news for Republicans. Riding the governor's coattails, most Republican candidates defeated their Democratic opponents. After holding a slim two-seat majority in the Senate following the 1859 election, Kirkwood's party gained a commanding 31-to-14 margin in the fall of 1861. In the House, the Republican margin improved from a 50-to-36 majority to a 65-to-30 majority. Only 44 Democrats served in the 1862 legislature, down from 57 in 1860–61.[5]

When the legislators convened in the winter of 1862, Democrats joined Republicans in renewing the bipartisan spirit that had prevailed one year earlier. Both parties endorsed a long string of military measures put forth by Governor Kirkwood and Adjutant General Nathaniel Baker. New laws facilitated tax collection, improved the local militia, and authorized the payment of funds for war matériel. Hoping to increase the enlistment rate, legislators exempted soldiers from having to pay property taxes.

Democrats marched arm in arm with Republican legislators for the most part. Wary of being labeled as disloyal, Democratic legislators declined to submit a resolution calling for a negotiated peace. The legislators' actions reflected the sentiment of grassroots Democrats. Across the state, Democratic newspaper editors and local party leaders expressed their support for Iowa's troops in the field.[6]

The bipartisan cooperation continued through the spring months of 1862. Democratic newspaper editors encouraged party members to enlist. In Dubuque, former state party chairman Dennis Mahony continued to harangue the Lincoln administration. But he also insisted in his newspaper columns that Democrats act as true war heroes and lead the fight against secession.[7]

As Democrats and Republicans competed for the title of most loyal party during the first half of 1862, the cause of black civil rights suffered considerably. Nearly every reform measure sponsored by radical Republicans went down to defeat in the state legislature. Blacks did not gain the opportunity to enlist, and a resolution demanding Federal action against slavery died on the floor without a vote.

Equally concerning, some Iowa Republican legislators voiced their approval of the Federal colonization bill pending in Congress, sponsored by Frank Blair, Jr., a conservative St. Louis Republican. Similar to colonization bills submitted before the war, the Blair bill proposed to facilitate the deportation of former slaves to Africa or Central America. No formal vote was ever taken in Des Moines on Blair's bill, but a portion of Republican legislators would have voted for the plan in the months before the Emancipation Proclamation. Colonization found strong grassroots support across the state. Some Iowa newspaper editors suggested that a successful conclusion to the war might include forcing all blacks out of North America.[8]

Emancipation and the 1862 Congressional Elections

In Iowa, the congressional campaign was in full swing when news of Lincoln's proclamation echoed from one community to another. With four new U.S. House seats on the line, Iowans had been captivated by the election drama since the early summer months. Twelve nominees, selected by their respective party caucuses, were stumping around their districts when word arrived that Lincoln intended to eliminate the institution of slavery in the Deep South states unless the slavemasters rejoined the Union. Congressional polling took place three weeks later, on schedule. With radical Iowans voting at a higher rate than in previous off-year elections, and with the army's balloting system organized, the number of ballots cast in 1862 exceeded the number for the 1861 gubernatorial election.

Before the proclamation, Republican candidates had stopped short of endorsing emancipation. In all six districts, moderates outnumbered radicals at the district party conventions. The moderate candidates chosen at these events embraced the 1861 strategy of encouraging conservative independents and Democrats to join the Union Party bandwagon. At the state Republican convention during the summer of 1862, moderates in charge of the platform committee included a quotation from Stephen Douglas, Lincoln's longtime rival, who had died the previous year. "Every man must be for the United States or against it—There can be no neutrality in this war—only patriots and traitors."[9]

The Emancipation Proclamation, coming when it did, immediately compromised the Republicans' cautious strategy. Kirkwood and other moderate Republicans supported Lincoln's proclamation, but they worried that conservatives in their party would either abstain from voting or cross over and vote for Democratic candidates. Just as they predicted, many Hawkeye Democrats did express outrage at Lincoln's proclamation.

The Emancipation Proclamation raised the level of hate rhetoric in Iowa to its highest mark to date. On the campaign trail, Lincoln's opponents redoubled their efforts to characterize the political contest as a clash between abolitionists and patriots, between whites and blacks. Under their polarized definition of patriotism, Democrats were the true patriots. Candidate D. O. Finch spoke for many Democrats when he predicted that tens of thousands of free blacks would migrate to the state if Lincoln carried out his threat of emancipation.[10]

The debate over emancipation smoldered in every Iowa locale. The Democratic message intermixed predictions of Eastern economic oppression with fears of a large-scale African American migration. Democrats stumping in Mahaska County during the late summer of 1862 charged that emancipation would lead to economic enslavement of the white man. Competition with free black labor will "reduce your already scanty earnings," predicted one Democrat at a public rally in the county. "You would not be able to pay your taxes at all," warned one opponent of emancipation.[11]

Mahony, Grinnell, and the Media Circus

When the bombshell of emancipation exploded in late September, one of the six Democratic candidates sat in jail in the nation's capital. Dennis Mahony, running for his party's nomination in the Dubuque district, had been arrested in mid-August by the U.S. marshal for publishing newspaper editorials attacking the Federal Conscription Act. Six days before the start of the Democratic district convention, marshals seized Mahony in the early morning hours, hustled him out of state by train, and locked him up in an East Coast prison.

By the time Democrats in Mahony's district gathered to select a nominee for Congress, the circumstances of the Dubuque editor's arrest had become the talk of the state. In point of fact, the prominent Irish American had never explicitly urged Iowans to resist the draft. Because Mahony crafted his editorial opinions carefully to avoid charges of incitement, Republican prosecutors found it difficult to formulate a charge of treason. In the end, no charges were filed. Rather than pursue criminal charges, War Department officials held Mahony in Federal prison through the conclusion of the election, at which time they released him without official explanation.[12]

The Democrats' decision to nominate Mahony for Congress even as he was held in jail had far-reaching implications for Iowa politics, in Des Moines as well as northeastern Iowa. So did the Republicans' decision to nominate Josiah B. Grinnell in the south-central district, which included Mahaska County. The Democratic editor of the *Oskaloosa Weekly Times* took particular delight in badmouthing Grinnell, the "bosom friend of John Brown" who dared run for Congress.[13]

Grinnell had, in fact, sheltered John Brown before the war. He also sheltered several escaped slaves Brown was shepherding from Kansas to Illinois. Grinnell wished to keep secret his involvement in the Underground Railroad, but when his name appeared on the Republican ticket for Congress, the truth could be concealed no longer. The prewar stigma associated with violating the Fugitive Slave Act worked against the Congregational church minister. Abolitionist Brown was considered a traitor for having attempted to incite a slave rebellion in 1859, and in many Iowa neighborhoods in 1862, Grinnell's prewar association with Brown undermined his credibility as a unionist.

Neither Mahony nor Grinnell deserved the label of extremist in the fall of 1862. Grinnell opposed black civil rights laws in Iowa, while Mahony aspired to see the nation reunited. The storm of public criticism that followed their nominations illustrated the extent to which the two parties had split over the purpose of the war and the definition of loyalty. Each party looked to label their opponents as extremists, and Mahony and Grinnell became the scapegoats during this most ugly campaign.

Of Iowa's twelve candidates running for Congress, public debate focused primarily on Mahony and Grinnell. Mahony's name appeared on the ballot in only one district, but the Dubuque editor became the primary symbol of dissent across the state. Republican newspaper editors targeted him in an attempt to smear all six Democratic candidates as traitors. Meanwhile, Democratic editors in every corner of Iowa ridiculed

Grinnell, whose prewar association with antislavery radicals in Kansas was public knowledge by 1862. The Congregational minister's association with the Underground Railroad prompted Democratic publishers to characterize every Republican candidate as an abolitionist.

At the polls, most Iowa voters recognized that the candidates nominated by their own party were true unionists. Mahony's bitter anti-Lincoln rhetoric compromised his reputation in the minds of some war Democrats, but in the end hundreds held their noses and reluctantly voted for the jailed newspaper editor.[14] In Grinnell's district, meanwhile, most conservative Republicans reluctantly voted for Grinnell over his Democratic rival.

The location of the district boundary lines added an interesting dimension to the election drama. Given regional voting patterns, Lincolnites might have conceded one or two congressional districts to the Democrats to ensure their capture of at least four seats. Republicans rejected the cautious approach, however, in favor of an all-or-nothing strategy shrewdly calculated to contend in every district. During the spring, Republican leaders in Des Moines split the southern tier of counties into three districts and combined the Republican-strong counties of Henry, Washington, and Louisa into the same district with Lee and Des Moines counties, offsetting Democratic strength there (fig. 8).

The competitive boundary plan, although designed to ensure a Republican sweep, might well have backfired had independent voters cast their lot with the Democrats. While they had not garnered a majority of votes in either congressional district since 1854, the Democrats had come close, particularly in the southern district. Republican legislators, anticipating a strong Democratic turnout in Dubuque, split off neighboring Jackson County into a separate district, while placing a multitude of interior rural counties into the district with Dubuque.[15]

Conservative Support for Emancipation

Despite the best efforts of Democrats to utilize unionism against their competitors by condemning the president's pledge to emancipate slaves, Iowa Republicans survived the 1862 fall elections. Moderates such as Jacob Ritner came around and endorsed Lincoln's proclamation. The Henry

1862 ELECTION MAP OF IOWA

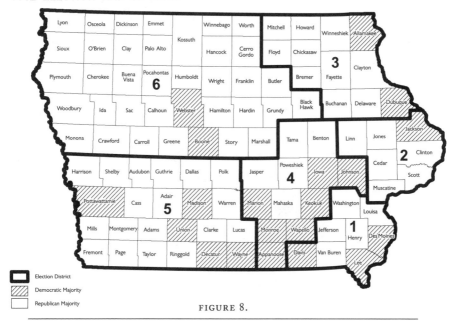

FIGURE 8.

County farmer and former private in the 1st Iowa Infantry preferred to integrate slaves into the Union war machine instead of returning them to their masters. Having recently reenlisted in the army, he saw emancipation as a means to expedite the war's conclusion and increase the likelihood that he himself would return home alive.[16]

Ritner's change of opinion was common among Iowa soldiers. After September 22, a substantial number wrote home endorsing the Emancipation Proclamation. Instead of returning slaves to their Missouri masters, many Iowans in uniform encouraged slaves to report to Union Army work stations. Some of the most conservative Iowans went on record in favor of emancipation. "The most proslavery men of former times are now among the <u>most radical</u>," wrote an officer in the 1st Iowa Cavalry Regiment in Missouri.[17] In nearby Illinois, two entire regiments of Democrats resigned from the army en masse in response to the Emancipation Proclamation, packing up their personal belongings and marching back home. Among Iowa units, no such mass defections took place.

The state's Republican newspaper editors responded much as its soldiers did. To the surprise of many, they spoke in a positive, unified voice in favor of emancipation. In contrast, Democratic newspaper editors failed to agree on a unified response to Lincoln's announcement. While several prowar editors condemned the Emancipation Proclamation as anti-unionist, others endorsed it as a necessary means to reunify the nation, with or without slavery.

Prominent party leaders who had publicly split from the Democratic organization earlier in the year stuck by their decision to defect. The list of notable defectors included Nathaniel Baker (the adjutant general), George Tichenor, and C. C. Cole. Tichenor, a political opportunist, had previously served as secretary of the Democratic state central committee. Cole, a widely respected lawyer, had run for Congress against Samuel Curtis in 1860. Among Democrats in the army, the list of those who voted Republican in 1862 included such prominent Iowa colonels as Marcellus Crocker, James A. Williamson, and H. H. Heath.[18]

To a man, every one of the six Republican candidates for Congress accepted the challenges posed by Lincoln's announcement and endorsed the president's support for emancipation. John Kasson, the most conservative pro-Lincoln candidate, proposed that Congress only grant the president authority to free slaves owned by Rebel slavemasters. Emancipation was not the primary goal of the war, Kasson held, but continued resistance by Confederate military forces justified emancipation as a war measure.[19]

Republicans responded in such a positive way partly because the seeds of support for emancipation had been planted long before September. Eight months earlier, during the winter of 1862, Iowa's Republican leaders commented publicly on emancipation and speculated on its impact on the Deep South states. Rather than alienate Southern unionists, some Republicans believed the threat of emancipation would inspire slave revolts throughout the South and precipitate the region's military collapse.

Senator James Grimes was among the first moderates in the state party leadership to promote emancipation as a war measure. His anxiety over the slow pace of the war spread to other moderates within Iowa's party leadership circle. Governor Kirkwood talked publicly of pursuing a more radical course in response to news of Rebel victories in Virginia. As early as January 1862, the governor mentioned slavery in his call for new strategies to end the rebellion. "My deliberate convictions are that to prosecute this war successfully, we must strike directly at Slavery," noted Governor Kirkwood. "The time must soon come when every man must determine for himself which he loves most, the Union or Slavery, and must act accordingly."[20]

Language echoing that in Kirkwood's January address appeared in the state Republican platform in July. Two months before Lincoln issued his proclamation, party convention delegates approved a resolution declaring its willingness to embrace emancipation in the Deep South. "If, as a last measure for the preservation of the republic, it shall become necessary to blot out the institution of slavery from the soil of every State, we will say Amen, letting the consequences fall upon the wicked authors of the war and leaving the final issue with God."[21]

Religious leaders joined the chorus of unionists who supported emancipation as a war measure. Several weeks before Lincoln's proclamation, ministers and lay leaders of the popular Iowa Methodist church issued a statement declaring that slaves owned by secessionists should be freed and employed to further the war effort. With no end to the war in sight, a majority of Methodists in Iowa's southern counties—moderates and conservatives for the most part—no longer defended the rights of slavemasters.[22]

For conservative Republicans wary of bearing the radical banner, Lincoln's announcement provided a convenient alternative to endorsing abolitionism. The proclamation did not grant political rights to African Americans. It did not call for arming blacks as soldiers, and if the slaves did become free, nothing in the proclamation precluded colonization, the means by which some Western Republicans sought to ensure a white America. In short, it was neither a proclamation of abolition nor a proclamation of black equality.

The prospect of emancipation as a means to end the war did not inspire a great deal of moral idealism in Iowa. Republican candidates for Congress defined themselves as "emancipationists" in lieu of "abolitionists" and refused to advocate the repeal of laws barring blacks from settling in Iowa. John Kasson spoke for many Republican candidates in 1862 when he strongly denied Democratic assertions that freed blacks would inundate the state once slavery had been vanquished. Iowa would remain a white state, Kasson insisted.[23]

Despite the moderates' refusal to embrace equal rights, Iowa's long-frustrated radicals were thrilled at the turn of events. They celebrated Lincoln's announcement, but for a different reason than did the unionists. For radicals, the proclamation represented the fulfillment of a lifelong dream. In October, radicals turned out in droves to hear Republican moderate candidates on the stump. Some Iowa radicals who had previously shunned elections now contemplated voting for Republican candidates at the polls. Senator Grimes, a personal friend of many Iowa radicals, corresponded regularly with Salmon P. Chase, the most radical Republican in Lincoln's cabinet. In October 1862, Grimes confided to Chase how Lincoln's announcement induced "the radical element" in Iowa to stand in line at the polls. In fact, moderates' positive reaction to the proclamation enticed Grimes to step up his antislavery rhetoric. "We took the bull by the horns and made the proclamation an issue," Grimes wrote to Chase. "I traveled the state for four weeks, and the more radical I was the more acceptable I was."[24]

Regional Voting Patterns

With all six congressional races staunchly contested by the Democrats, there was a real possibility of a Republican defeat. To avoid a Democratic majority in Congress, Lincoln desperately needed Iowa Republicans to sweep all six congressional races. Voting results in other free states in the fall 1862 elections severely eroded the Republican majority established in 1860. In New York, Pennsylvania, and Ohio, Democrats gained a substantial number of U.S. House seats previously held by Republicans. Republicans lost eight of eleven House contests in Indiana in the fall of 1862, nine of fourteen seats in Illinois, and three of six contests in Wisconsin. Democrats in Indiana and Illinois now controlled a majority of seats in their respective state legislatures, forcing Republican governors, elected the previous year, to negotiate with uncooperative state legislators.[25]

The new wave of Democrats elected in other free states came to Washington with numerous complaints against the Lincoln administration. Prowar Democrats charged the War Department with incompetence and extravagant spending. One subgroup demanded peaceful reconciliation, and within this cohort emerged some Democrats convinced the nation could not be reunited. While Democrats debated among themselves on the best course of action, most Democrats in Congress—both the prowar faction and the negotiators—condemned the president's emancipation pledge in the harshest terms. Lincoln was accused of being a traitor, blasphemer, disunionist, and promoter of interracial sex.

Election results in Iowa might have produced six Republican members of Congress, six Democrats, or a mixed delegation of Republicans and Democrats. Consistent with previous elections, the counties of Lee, Jackson, and Dubuque voted in the Democratic column. So did a majority of voters in the interior counties on Iowa's border with Missouri. With so many men away in the army, Democrats collected a majority of votes in some counties that had supported Kirkwood in 1861, including Pottawattamie County.

In the end, the final vote count confirmed the value of the Republicans' risky undertaking. Iowa Democrats failed to carry a single congressional seat. By drawing the congressional district boundary lines as they did, the Republicans produced a shutout.

Hawkeye soldiers cast approximately one-fifth of all ballots in the 1862 congressional election. Despite Republican fears of a backlash within the ranks, nearly 80 percent of the state's soldiers at the polling line voted Republican. Ben Stevens was among the Mahaska soldiers who stood in line for Grinnell. Despite his unrelenting unionism, Ben endorsed Republican candidates, notwithstanding Lincoln's radical proclamation. "I have changed my mind but very little in Reference to the Abolition question," Ben wrote home. "I would rather see our country as it once was than as it now is." At the same time, "I feel proud that we have so great a Republic to sustain and that we are able to help do it."[26]

The magnitude of the South's defiance led Stevens and other Iowa soldiers to support emancipation as a means to expedite the resolution of the military conflict. Despite Union victories on several Western battlefields, the rebellious spirit of the Confederates had not diminished. At Shiloh, Iowa soldiers had watched with disgust as triumphant Rebel soldiers gleefully dragged captured Federal flags through the mud for the specific purpose of desecrating the Stars and Stripes. Horrified, some soldiers proposed arming former slaves. "If a [colored] man will dig trenches and chop down timber and even fight the enemy he is just the fellow we want," wrote one sergeant in the 15th Iowa Infantry in August 1862. "And the sooner we recognize this the quicker the war will end."[27]

In the army camps down south, thousands of Democrats in uniform contemplated how to cast their ballots. Back at home, Democrats tended to stand by their party's candidate. Dubuque County voters turned out in huge numbers for the jailed Mahony. In the army camps, however, only a very small percentage stood in line for Mahony. In the northeastern district, where most soldiers' families lived in rural neighborhoods away from the port of Dubuque, 95 percent of all voting soldiers chose the Republican candidate, W. B. Allison. The voters in Delaware County, the home of the Dunham family, lined up against Mahony.

In the five remaining districts, Democrats and Republicans tended to cast straight party ballots, a voting pattern that ultimately helped the Republicans. In the contests for state auditor, treasurer, and secretary of state, Republican candidates garnered a comfortable 56 percent of all nonmilitary ballots statewide. Republicans drew particularly well in the northwestern district, the largest of the six districts geographically. Here, in the region that included Cyrus Carpenter's hometown of Fort Dodge, A. N. Hubbard, a Sioux City Republican running for Congress, carried all but two counties. In the east-central district, which included Muscatine County, Republican Hiram Price mustered consistent majorities in his bid for Congress. In the port of Muscatine, a majority of voters backed Price, the Davenport banker who had made a name for himself by financing the war effort in 1861.[28]

In the southwestern district that included Des Moines and Council Bluffs, John Kasson earned a seat in Congress. Although a majority in Pottawattamie County rejected Kasson, in the final districtwide count the Des Moines lawyer came out on top among both military and nonmilitary voters. Similar election dynamics operated in the southeastern district, which included the port of Keokuk. Lee County remained in the Democratic column in 1862, but in the districtwide vote Republican James F. Wilson, who had replaced Curtis in 1861, retained his seat in Congress by a comfortable margin.

A victory for Grinnell in the south-central district would complete the Republican sweep. Here, the race was tighter. The Democrats experienced a resurgence of support following the Emancipation Proclamation, and Grinnell's secret radical past worked against him in many neighborhoods. In Mahaska County, nine rural townships voted against the

Vermont-born Congregational minister. Although the Democratic candidate lost Mahaska thanks to a strong Republican turnout in Oskaloosa, Grinnell's rival won seven of the ten remaining counties in the congressional district, including Johnson (Iowa City), Marion (Knoxville), Appanoose (Centerville), and Wapello (Ottumwa). Had the district's soldiers not been permitted to vote, Grinnell's Democratic challenger would have captured the congressional seat.[29]

Soldiers from Grinnell's south-central district voted 3-to-1 in favor of the Congregational minister. Although the voting rate fell below the statewide average of 80 percent, Grinnell polled well enough among the soldiers in his district to propel him to Washington. The combination of military and nonmilitary votes produced a Grinnell victory by a margin of 53 percent to 47 percent.[30]

The end result of the 1862 election cycle produced a strikingly pro-Lincoln delegation of New West members of Congress. Sixteen of the twenty U.S. House seats assigned to Kansas, Missouri, Iowa, and Minnesota sang in the Republican choir in Washington, as did all eight senators. The New West's representatives did not always harmonize with one another, but President Lincoln certainly appreciated their presence. Their numbers helped offset the Democratic gains in the Old Northwest states and preserved Republican majorities in both chambers of Congress.

The Emancipation Proclamation was much on the minds of the members as they gathered in Washington. In several respects, new political terms replaced traditional designations. Within Democratic ranks, members who questioned the utility of continued military action became known as peace Democrats as opposed to war Democrats. Peace Democrats adopted the name "Copperheads," a badge of honor for dissenters who expressed sympathy for the Confederates. Like the peace Democrats, war Democrats feared the country could never reunite as long as the Republicans remained in charge of the Federal government. But the war Democrats increasingly came to view antiwar Democrats as traitors. Republican party strategists, always looking for opportunities to improve their public image, defined every Democrat as a Copperhead.

Republicans faced a classification dilemma of their own. Because so many radicals endorsed the Emancipation Proclamation, Democrats began referring to all Republicans as radicals. Some moderate Republicans willingly embraced radical principles by advocating the recruitment of black soldiers and granting them equal rights at home. Others, however, still found the radical label repulsive. Having opposed the radical faction for so long, Republicans who loathed the term *radical* could not bring themselves to support equal rights laws. To distance themselves from the radical faction, cautious Republicans self-identified as "emancipationists" as opposed to "abolitionists." In Iowa, the distinction between the two factions lasted for an extended period of time.

Lingering Racism

Alexander Clark became restless during the early months of 1863. Despite the six-nil Republican victory in 1862, the Emancipation Proclamation was not producing the social revolution he had imagined it would. The moderate Republicans' willingness to embrace emancipation did not bring an immediate improvement to the rights afforded black Iowans. While the proclamation brought new hope for enslaved persons in the Deep South, state officials in Iowa still refused to accept Clark's offer to enlist in the U.S. Army. When he wrote a personal appeal to Kirkwood, the governor's secretary advised him not to press his luck. "You know better than I the prejudices of our people for you have felt them more severely," wrote the secretary to Clark, "and you know your color would not be tolerated in one of our regiments."[31]

Racism lingered to such an extent that Clark and other radicals wondered if Iowans' support for emancipation in the Deep South would soon evaporate. Based on the correspondence of Cyrus Carpenter, Clark had every reason to worry. Carpenter, in a private letter to his brother, called the threat of emancipation "a good joke on the rebels."[32]

Carpenter's pessimism was a common response among Iowa soldiers in the army camps close to the front lines. Many white soldiers loathed African Americans as much as they had at the start of the war. In February 1863, members of the 15th Iowa Infantry expressed contempt for the ex-slaves who appeared at their camp in droves seeking assistance. "The men in our camp treat them worse than <u>brutes</u>," noted one sergeant in a letter home. "When they come into camp cries of 'Kill him,' 'drown him,' etc. are heard on every hand," he recorded in his diary. "The prejudice against the race seems stronger than ever. The Proclamation of the President has strengthened this feeling."[33]

By the spring of 1863, political developments at home gave Alexander Clark more reason to worry. At dozens of rallies around the state, peace Democrats openly demanded a nonmilitary solution to the war. At the Republican Party state convention, radicals once again lost their bid to select the party's nominee for governor to succeed Kirkwood. Radicals had united behind Fitz Henry Warren, the original colonel of the 1st Iowa Cavalry, but instead of Warren's name on the ballot, it was that of William M. Stone, the moderates' candidate.

Once again, in designing the party's platform, state Republican delegates approved a platform of resolutions that ignored black civil rights and the enlistment of blacks. The words *slavery* and *emancipation* did not appear in the 1863 platform, and nothing in the platform suggested any interest in abolishing the Fugitive Slave Act. Instead, the platform read: "We declare that the preservation of the constitution and the Union is above and beyond all other interests, and that all questions of party, of life, and of property, must be subordinate thereto." On the campaign trial, Republican candidates denied any suggestions that emancipation would unleash a flood of African Americans into the state.[34]

That a substantial proportion of Hawkeye Democrats continued to reject emancipation as a war aim also frustrated the state's black citizens. Both war Democrats and peace Democrats defended the institution of slavery. When peace Democrats organized rallies in the early months of 1863, thousands of Iowans turned out to hear critics of President Lincoln renounce military force as a means to resolve the secession crisis. One rally held north of Oskaloosa in Mahaska County attracted some 6,000 participants. Despite having to stand outside on a cold January day, attendees listened for several hours to dissenter Henry Clay Dean as he made his argument for a negotiated resolution to the conflict.[35]

The increasing level of white-on-white violence must have alarmed Alexander Clark. In this frontier state, threats of violence by white citizens against other white citizens escalated at times into shooting matches. In some communities, war Democrats, peace Democrats, and Republicans began carrying weapons to local political rallies. When a group of anti-war Democrats paraded through a largely Republican village in Keokuk

County in the summer of 1863, random shots fired by onlookers killed the Democrats' chief spokesperson. Word of his death spread quickly, and when hundreds of Democrats across the district assembled to protest in Sigourney, the Keokuk County seat of government, Governor Kirkwood called in militiamen from other counties to ensure that the town did not burn to the ground.

A few Iowa dissenters took the negotiated peace argument one step further and justified disunion. Some outspoken Iowans actively interfered with the Union war effort by openly discouraging young men in their neighborhoods from enlisting in the army. "We *will not* render any support to the present administration in carrying on its wicked abolition crusade against the South," proclaimed one group of Davis County dissenters. "We will *resist to the death* all attempts to draft any of our citizens into the army."[36]

Alexander Clark, undoubtedly disillusioned, looked beyond Muscatine for greener fields to form his all-black regiment in another state. One promising location was St. Louis, the home of Missouri's new senator, B. Gratz Brown. Brown, a Republican, pursued a more radical path in Washington than Grimes and Harlan, a plan that included arming blacks. Kansas presented another possibility for Clark. There, military organizers recruited slaves escaped from Missouri and Arkansas as early as 1862 and trained them for battle. White Kansans were also moving forward to grant blacks the right to vote.[37]

After much consideration, Clark decided to stay put in Muscatine and demand formation of an all-black Iowa regiment. While Clark pursued his black regiment, Kirkwood worried about the reaction of white soldiers recruited before the Emancipation Proclamation. He also worried about their lack of military experience. It was far from certain how the novice soldiers would react in the face of Rebel bullets. The latest group of enlistees included Charles Musser of Pottawattamie County, Dr. Will Turner of Keokuk, and Simeon Stevens of Oskaloosa, the father of Ben Stevens. None of them affiliated with the radical wing of the Republican Party.

Iowa's 21,000 military recruits of 1862 did not disappoint the state's radicals and moderates. In many respects, Iowa's new soldiers pursued the goal of emancipation far more vigorously than many had imagined they would. The six Iowa Republicans in the U.S. House of Representatives did not join ranks with the radical faction in Washington. But Iowa's last-minute wave of volunteers did come around to embrace the abolition of slavery as a war aim. The soldiers also contributed directly to the successful prosecution of the war. The ultimate demise of the Confederate States of America might not have come about without the Iowans' dedication to unionism and the abolition of slavery.

CHAPTER SEVEN

The Militant Class of 1862

U nion military success in 1863 could not have occurred without the large-scale enlistment of civilians in the summer of 1862. Of all the Western states, none enlisted a higher proportion of citizen-volunteers after July 1 than Iowa. Many husbands and fathers left their families for an extended period to enable the state to meet its Federal recruitment quota. Muscatine County alone furnished 800 soldiers, nearly one full regiment of men, and Mahaska County enrolled 650 men.

Given the challenges facing the state's executive officers in the summer of 1862, it is astounding that Iowa outfitted such a large number of three-year regiments in 1862. Military equipment remained in short supply, the harvest season was fast approaching, and a Sioux uprising in Minnesota diverted resources and threatened the security of the state's northern counties. Lincoln's call for 21,000 additional citizen-soldiers in July and August arrived just as administrators were scrambling to find 8,000 replacements to revitalize the nineteen three-year regiments that had been formed in 1861. Two dozen new regiments would have to be organized in Iowa to meet the new quota, more regiments than in 1861. Two thousand Iowans had enlisted in early 1862, but these volunteers did not reduce the state's enlistment obligations.[1] How would the state's leaders meet the challenge?

The Rhetoric of Conscription and Enlistment

With barely 100,000 men of military age remaining in the state by the summer of 1862, the Kirkwood administration needed to attract thousands of married men as well as bachelors, Democrats as well as Republicans, and immigrants as well as native-born. Without a substantial enrollment by men in their thirties and forties, the August 1862 quota would not be met.

The governor and adjutant general contemplated the advantages and disadvantages of randomly enlisting Iowa men of military age. Although the new Federal law empowered state officers to conscript men, Kirkwood realized the shortcomings of this approach. Not only did volunteers make better soldiers, but any attempt to draft frontier settlers inevitably gave rise to local protests. Pockets of resistance might force militiamen to guard local recruiting stations and track down draft dodgers, distractions likely to drain resources from the front lines. Although they did not intend to conscript soldiers in 1862, Iowa's war administrators used the threat of conscription as the primary means to fill the state's quota.

The draft threat succeeded in frontier Iowa because the label "draftee" marked a man with an unpatriotic stigma. Aware of this, Kirkwood traveled across the state warning of the consequences of nonenlistment. On the stump, the governor noted that Rebel forces now held an advantage on the battlefield as a result of the Confederate draft act passed by Richmond in April 1862. "The enemy, by a sweeping conscription, have forced into their ranks all men capable of bearing arms," declared the governor on July 9. "Our government has yet relied upon the volunteer action of our citizens. But if need be, the same energies must be exerted to preserve our government that traitors are using to destroy it."[2]

Kirkwood recognized the manpower challenge facing the state and implored every resident to participate in some way to further the war effort:

> Our harvest is upon us and we have feared a lack of force to secure it. But we must imitate our brave Iowa boys on the field, meet new emergencies with new exertions. Our old men and our boys, unfit for war, if need be, our women must help to gather harvests while those able to bear arms go forth to aid their brave brethren in the field. The necessity is urgent. Our national existence is at stake. The more promptly the President is furnished the needed troops the more speedily will this unholy rebellion be crushed, and the blessings of peace again visit our land. Until then we must expect the hardships and privations of war.[3]

State and local officials understood the importance of assuring prospective volunteers that their families would be kept secure. Kirkwood personally pledged to protect and feed the wives and children of volunteers. Neighbors, township officials, and county leaders pledged to look after the financial interests of the soldiers' families. Once the harvest of 1862 had been gathered, the governor appealed to farmers to bring meat, fruit, vegetables, baked goods, and clothing to the training camps. LSAS chapter leaders enlisted the support of farm women and town women to facilitate the collection of money and donated items. To house the new recruits, new training camps popped up in Oskaloosa and other medium-sized interior towns, while additional land surrounding the state's river ports was converted to camps. Five regiments trained simultaneously in the several camps around Davenport.[4]

Iowa's mobilization required that government agents at every level assume new duties on a scale never before seen. The brunt of the new responsibilities fell upon the shoulders of the county administrators—elected officials who traditionally enjoyed considerable autonomy. To ensure the Federal quota could be met, the Kirkwood administration imposed new regulations governing the means by which local authorities administered enlistments. Every county now had a recruiting office staffed to answer questions and enroll volunteers. Unofficial recruiters continued to scour the countryside looking for volunteers, but by the summer of 1862 all enlistments had to be approved by state officials.

The number of volunteer enlistments each county had to provide was based on a per capita calculation. The imposition of a quota on each county gave local officials an incentive to find creative means to meet the state-imposed expectations or risk the dishonor of conscripting reluctant citizens. To assist local recruiters, state administrators invited war veterans back to Iowa for short leaves of absence and arranged for them to speak at village assemblies in their home districts.

Because some districts—particularly counties with large immigrant populations—struggled to find enough local volunteers to meet their district quotas, state officials encouraged officials in high-enrollment counties to exceed their quotas. To assist counties with large immigrant populations, state rules permitted recruits to enlist in counties other than the one they lived in. Because state rules credited the county of enrollment for each enlistment, regardless of the volunteer's place of residence, districts with a smaller proportion of U.S. natives met their quotas by enticing residents of other counties—usually by offering them money.

Federal policy forced state officials to choose between filling new regiments and revitalizing old regiments. On this question, state officials opted to prioritize filling new regiments, to enable the most successful recruiters to be commissioned as officers. Enlistees who signed up for old regiments entered the service as privates, but every new regiment required a colonel, lieutenant colonel, major, and adjutant, as well as ten captains, twenty lieutenants, and several dozen sergeants and corporals.

The governor appealed to family ties in hopes of replenishing the old 1861 regiments while filling the multitude of new infantry units. So that they might fight alongside family members, Kirkwood offered brothers and cousins of 1861 recruits the opportunity to choose the regiment they would serve in. Despite the kinship opportunity, the appeal to family netted only a modest number of new enlistments for the old 1861 regiments.

When the first wave of new recruits declined to enroll in old regiments, state officials concentrated their energy on organizing new ones. After starting in July with the modest goal of filling five new regiments, state officials changed course and designated twenty-five new infantry regiments, numbered 19 to 43. Because artillery batteries and cavalry regiments were more expensive to outfit, only a few of them were organized in 1862.

Kirkwood's willingness to assign recruits to new regiments made the difference between success and failure in 1862. It also helped that administrators embraced the practice of concentrating recruits by residency rather than scattering them to different units. Civilians seeking to fight alongside their neighbors did not come away disappointed. Eight companies of volunteers from Muscatine County marched in the 35th Iowa Infantry along with two companies from nearby Cedar County.

As in 1861, recruiters solicited immigrants with promises that they could march alongside their fellow countrymen regardless of county residence. Adjutant General Nathaniel Baker designated two regiments exclusively for Irish Catholic volunteers with the promise that Roman Catholic priests would be assigned to the regiments rather than Protestant clergymen.

One recruiter sought to form an all-sharpshooter unit. Horsemen were offered the chance to carry a lance. One regiment restricted its membership to men who vowed not to drink alcohol. For those Democrats who preferred fighting alongside fellow party members, Republican administrators reluctantly agreed to combine several groups of volunteers recruited by Democrats into one regiment.

Another example of Iowa resourcefulness was the "Graybeard" regiment. When some Mexican War veterans expressed a willingness to fight in a unit that would not march long distances, state officials received special permission from the secretary of war to recruit a regiment made up entirely of volunteers forty-five years of age or older.

As in 1861, the lack of experienced officers confounded military administrators, who searched high and low to find enough former soldiers willing to train and lead the masses of inexperienced volunteers. Men with only three months' experience marching with General Lyon in Missouri in 1861 were elevated to officer status as long as they agreed to serve a three-year term. To fill out the higher ranks, state officials solicited lower-ranking officers in the state's existing three-year regiments. Captains were elevated to lieutenant colonels, and sergeants donned a captain's uniform. Several newly appointed colonels had been majors or lieutenant colonels in one of the state's 1861 regiments.

To their credit, Kirkwood and Baker emphasized quality over quantity to the extent possible. Military administrators personally inspected the training camps looking to disenroll disabled men and boys who were not likely to be able to endure long marches through rain and snow. Dozens of teenagers were turned away despite their high level of enthusiasm.

The governor and adjutant general also refused to cut corners when it came to explaining the conditions of enlistment. Army rules prohibited new enlistees from walking away from their three-year service pledge, but some local recruiters preferred not to explain army rules to prospective recruits. To avoid misunderstandings and prevent mass defections, state officials instructed local officials to read the terms of enlistment in their entirety to every interested recruit.

The governor's decision not to accept nine-month recruits further contributed to quality control. While some Union states met their quotas by signing up thousands of these short-term soldiers, the Hawkeye state produced not a single nine-month regiment. With the exception of several hundred two-year volunteers, every Iowa enlistee in 1862 became a three-year soldier. Kirkwood and Baker had the foresight to recognize the long-term value of three-year recruits in the event of a long war. They also realized that signing up three-year recruits reduced the likelihood of a draft. Under Federal rules, one three-year volunteer counted the same as four nine-month soldiers, a formula that rewarded Iowa's long-term recruitment strategy.

The Response of Women to Super-enlistment

Much of the credit for Iowa's recruitment success must be attributed to the thousands of farmwives who enabled their male family members to enlist. Historian J. L. Anderson's research documents the prominent role Iowa women assumed when their husbands, brothers, and fathers went south to fight. Diaries and letters reveal that farm women successfully negotiated disputes with neighbors and relatives, and managed their family's farms while still performing the traditional household tasks of preparing meals, raising children, and caring for older family members.

In the absence of their husbands, Iowa women "confronted tenants, creditors, and debtors, and sometimes marketed livestock and crops," notes Anderson. Livestock management posed a particularly daunting challenge, yet many wives and older daughters handled it competently. "I am willing to work to raise corn, to pay taxes, to help sustain the government, and to carry on the war," Mary Alice Vermilion wrote to her husband stationed in Arkansas. "A sacred cause makes even the humblest labor dignified and holy." Some wives, including Elizabeth Stevens of Oskaloosa, commended their husband's decision to enlist despite the disruption it would cause to their home economy. After Simeon's unit deployed to Missouri, Elizabeth wrote, "Do not let the hard scenes of war demoralize you in any way but keep your eye on the path of duty . . . O, my dear Simeon, if you know the anxiety I feel both for your spiritual and temporal welfare, it would stimulate you to duty."[5]

In reality, outdoor farmwork combined with indoor housework proved insurmountable for many wives. Concern for their wives' health weighed heavily on the minds of the thousands of Iowa men contemplating enlisting in the late summer of 1862. Herding cattle, harvesting corn, and chopping wood were tasks traditionally performed by men, and it is not surprising that wives of volunteers relied upon nonenlisted males in their neighborhood to perform much of the heavy work.

Letters written by Helen Maria Sharp, a farmwife in central Iowa, testify to the severe psychological and physical strain of farm management.

When her forty-one-year-old husband John enlisted, Helen had to care for four children ranging from six months to twelve years old. Her younger sister moved in to help supervise the children, but even so Helen had to rely on a few men in her neighborhood to provide wood, plow her garden, and harvest corn. She also had to rely on women neighbors for extra food.

With this assistance, Helen found she could manage the farming operation—as long as the family cow provided milk and husband John sent her money. "I have got everything I need up here so far by going in debt some," she wrote to John. "Mary Waldo has let me have butter all along and her and Aunt Nancy both says that I shall have as long as they have anything to eat." Some letters testified to the time Helen spent caring for the cow and chickens. Weekly prayer meetings at the local church alleviated her fears for her husband and her children. "If you do fall you will fall Zionward," she assured John, "and we will try to meet you in heaven."[6]

Many of Helen's letters reflect a despondent rather than a patriotic mood. Weather extremes exacted a particularly hard toll. One day in January, when the temperature fell to 15 degrees below zero, Helen wrote to John, "I have but little wood . . . I don't think that I ever lived in as cold a house in my life. It is all I can do to keep from freezing." Rather than downplay the hardship of the cold spell, Helen bluntly told her husband the honest truth. "I have frosted one of my feet" chopping wood, she wrote. "No one comes in the house [with food] unless I beg for it and sometimes not then . . . Every week you are gone I am more lonely and I feel the war won't end soon."

In July, six months later, a despondent Helen announced to John that she was seriously thinking of returning to her family in Indiana. "Today is one of the hottest I have ever saw," she remarked. "My baby is a good deal of trouble this hot weather and I have to get the children to school and you know how hard hot weather sets on me . . . I have not got anything but dress and hoops on and the sweat just pours off me like rain." She concluded her letter, "Come home soon . . . Three years seems a long time if you ever come back."[7]

Helen Sharp's anxiety and loneliness were not unusual. Mathilde Hoffbauer, a German-speaking housewife who lived near Muscatine, became despondent in October 1862 at the thought of her husband being drafted. Three of her sons already served in the army, and Mathilde feared her

FIGURE 9. Ladies' Soldiers' Aid Society members in Fairfield process apples for distribution to Jefferson County soldiers in the South in 1863. These women worked with other LSAS women leaders around the state to collect and transport donated food, clothes, and medical supplies. On one trip alone, 37 tons of supplies were transported from Fairfield to army camps down South. *Reprinted by permission of the Carnegie Historical Museum in Fairfield, an Iowa Century Museum.*

husband Hugo would be taken from her involuntarily. "You can probably imagine the kind of fear and anxiety I am suffering constantly," Mrs. Hoffbauer wrote to her daughter. "We expect an order for Hugo to have to leave at any moment. I worry that he might suffer a premature death as well." The three sons, who had enlisted one year previously, were still alive, but the separation anxiety continued to sap their mother's morale. "My dear boys—I wish I had all three of them home again," Mrs. Hoffbauer wrote, expressing particular concern about son Fritz, who "seems to be tired of the soldier's life." She told her daughter, "Father should attempt everything possible to try and get Fritz back—if he is still alive."[8]

In Mahaska County, Simeon Stevens enlisted, notwithstanding the strain imposed on his wife Elizabeth and their young daughter. An early July recruit, he trained with the 18th Infantry, a regiment formed in the late spring along with the 17th Infantry. Three months later, he wrote home from Springfield, Missouri, hoping to console Elizabeth, who had supported his decision to enlist. "I am sorry to hear of your being sick and disconsolate," Simeon began. "Well, you must keep your spirits up and receive all news for the best . . . Now don't worry and grieve for my absence," Simeon added. "I am doing very well, in good health, spirits and God grant the same to you. You must pray that not only for me to come home in full health and strength but that I may discharge all the duties incumbent on me with fidelity and honor to my country and friends, as the greatest calamity would be, I consider, to bequeath the name of a coward to my family and children, which by the blessing of God I never will, but borrow no trouble for me."[9]

In Pottawattamie County, John Musser never seriously considered enlisting. Struggling to feed his large family, he had not welcomed the news that Charles, the only Musser son still at home, enlisted in September 1862. The young man joined the army despite the hardships his absence imposed on his family. His letters home indicate that other young men in his neighborhood pressured him to enlist. When the twenty-two-year-old entered training camp in Council Bluffs, he expected the military conflict would end within a year. "Soldiering is a hard life, but it agrees with me and I with it," he wrote to his parents on December 14, 1862. "I think we will all be at home next fall at farthest, at any rate, I hope so."[10]

County Recruitment Rates

As the draft deadline of August 15 approached, Governor Kirkwood announced the details of his conscription plan should a flurry of last-minute volunteers fail to materialize. County assessors prepared to post lists of male citizens between the ages of eighteen and forty-five eligible for service who had not enlisted. Posters warned that conscripted men who did not report by the deadline would be classified as deserters. However, under proposed exemption rules, eligible men could hire substitutes. Male citizens on the conscripted list could avoid service by paying a substitute $300, a relatively high price for most Iowans. By comparison, those who enlisted voluntarily before the draft selection date received a guaranteed $100 Federal bounty.[11]

By late August, twenty-four of the twenty-seven designated regiments were operational. The 8,000 vacancies in the 1861 regiments remained unfilled, but at least the state met its August quota without having to conscript a single soldier. Hoping he could avoid having to randomly draft citizens to fill out the older regiments, Kirkwood appealed to the War Department for leniency. Remarkably, the department granted his request. That other states failed to organize new regiments on the scale that Iowa did worked to the governor's advantage. Iowa enlisted more new soldiers in the summer and fall than did Missouri, Kentucky, Wisconsin, or Michigan, each of which had a larger population than Iowa.[12]

Within the state, the picture was mixed. Some counties met their quotas, while others did not. Muscatine County achieved the highest rate of recruitment in the state. Mahaska, another high-enrollment district, enlisted 650 new recruits, bringing that county's two-year total to 1,100. At the low end of the spectrum, Dubuque County fell short by some 1,300. Most of the shortage came from the port of Dubuque.

Lee County, after producing 1,000 recruits in 1861 and another 150 volunteers in the late spring of 1862, signed only 330 three-year volunteers in the late summer. A similar pattern emerged in Scott County (Davenport), where almost 1,000 had signed up in 1861. Had it not been for the heavy enrollment of men in the state's south-central rural counties, the August quota would not have been met. The Mississippi River counties had two to three times as many residents, yet the rural interior counties contributed a significantly greater number of recruits per capita.

Cultural factors largely accounted for the disparity. Immigrants, who lived predominantly in the river cities, did not consider draft status a stigma. But for U.S. natives, the threat of conscription created a formidable inducement to enlist, an incentive more compelling than monetary bounties. In the nonimmigrant districts of south-central Iowa, U.S. natives by the thousands came forward to enlist in mid-August rather than endure the disgrace of conscription. "Recruiting is going on in this State magnificently," remarked Adjutant General Baker. "I like a draft."[13]

In the final count, some neighborhoods heavily populated by immigrants produced few recruits. Muscatine County officials had some success in attracting immigrants, but army recruiters encountered resistance in many neighborhoods. While a substantial number of Protestant immigrants from the United Kingdom did volunteer, few German and Irish Catholics did. In the county of Dubuque, home to more than 2,000 natives of Ireland, historian Russ Johnson counted only 41 Irish volunteers in 1861 or 1862. With such a low turnout in the state's most Catholic county, the two promised Catholic regiments never became operational.[14]

The 300 new recruits from Delaware County included some natives of the British Isles. Some of them marched in the 21st Infantry, one-quarter of which was composed of foreign-born volunteers, mainly natives of England and Scotland. Lee County's 330 recruits, mainly U.S. natives, marched in the "Graybeard" regiment or in one of three standard infantry regiments. In Mahaska County, state officials assigned 475 recruits to the 33rd Infantry and 175 to the 40th Infantry.

With the exception of one company of Holland natives from Pella, U.S. natives comprised the 33rd Infantry. Members of the 33rd trained in Oskaloosa, while Mahaska Democrats assigned to the 40th Infantry joined the other Democrat volunteers training in Iowa City. In Council Bluffs, 150 recruits from Pottawattamie County (including Charles Musser) destined for the 29th Infantry trained along with other recruits from southwestern Iowa. Fort Dodge recruits joined volunteers from other north-central frontier counties in the camp of the 32nd Infantry.[15]

Iowa's 21,000 recruits included some inexperienced officers who would prove their talent in 1863 and 1864. Oskaloosa's Samuel Rice, the former state attorney general, was among the state's best new commanders. He had been assigned as colonel of the 33rd Infantry. In Council Bluffs, the 29th Infantry trained under the watchful eyes of Thomas Hart Benton, Jr., a Tennessee native and nephew of the famous Missouri senator. Delaware County's Salue Van Anda, the major of the 21st Infantry, rose quickly through the ranks. Another noteworthy civilian officer was Sylvester Hill, a Muscatine merchant assigned to lead the 35th Infantry. Hugo Campbell, a Muscatine sergeant in the ninety-day regiment in 1861, earned promotion to major of the 18th Infantry, the same regiment that included Corporal Simeon Stevens of Oskaloosa.

As a whole, Iowa's 1862 recruiting class differed in several respects from the men who enlisted in 1861. In addition to being older on average, the second-year recruits were typically wealthier and more likely to vote Republican. They also tended to come from households associated with evangelical Protestant denominations. Although religion alone cannot explain the motivation of Iowa's latest recruits, the denominational profile reflected strong evangelical roots. Few German atheists enrolled in 1862, but thousands of Calvinists and Methodists did. The appeal for temperance men attracted enough recruits to fill an entire regiment. Led by a Wesleyan minister appointed its colonel, the 24th Infantry came to be known as the Methodist Regiment.

The Initial Impact of Iowa's 1862 Recruits

Iowa's draft-averse recruits entered training camp at a time when Union commanders desperately needed additional troops. In Tennessee, Rebel cavalry destroyed miles of railroad track behind Union lines that summer and fall. To protect Nashville and guard the railroads, General Grant dispersed the mass of bluecoats encamped near Corinth, Mississippi, leaving only a modest force to defend the railroad junction. In hopes of filling the void, Grant redeployed New West units stationed in Missouri to Tennessee.

Unfortunately, the shifting of forces from west to east invited roving bands of pro-Confederate insurgents in Missouri to infiltrate neighborhoods there in the late summer. In central Arkansas, meanwhile, Confederate commanders prepared to lead 20,000 Rebel troops, including legions of gray-clad conscripts, north toward the Missouri border.

The Union Army's reassignment of regiments to western Tennessee placed considerable burdens on Samuel Curtis, the top Union commander in the New West. From his office in St. Louis, the former Iowa member of Congress faced the immense challenge of patrolling a huge expanse of territory where anti-Federal guerrilla bands roamed at will. Local dissidents received a boost when Missouri Confederates, captured earlier in Tennessee, returned home on parole.

Adding fuel to the insurgent fires already burning, some well-educated sons of dispossessed planter-class families joined ranks with the hundreds of lower-class guerrillas in 1862. The lethal combination of ex-prisoners, itinerant planters, and uneducated hoodlums terrified local unionists and confounded state administrators who had been left with fewer military resources with which to contain the marauders.[16]

In the midst of the chaos that was Civil War Missouri, the status of Springfield became critical. Home to the largest Union military warehouse in southwestern Missouri, the city attracted the attention of guerrilla forces in Missouri and Rebel cavalry operating out of Arkansas. As more Union regiments exited Missouri for western Tennessee, the novice bluecoats assigned to the Springfield area found themselves outnumbered and facing increasing pressure from pro-Confederate forces.

The 18th Iowa, Simeon Stevens's regiment, encamped near Springfield along with the 19th Iowa and 20th Iowa, which had just arrived from Keokuk. The actions of all three of these newborn regiments during the fall and winter of 1862–63 served notice on the Confederate states that Iowa's newest citizen-soldiers possessed a high level of physical ability and mental determination. Also meriting distinction was the 17th Iowa, an infantry brigade organized in April and assigned to defend the Union staging area at Corinth.

Developments in the Springfield district culminated in the Battle of Prairie Grove, a bloody engagement in northwestern Arkansas in December 1862. At this site, Union forces moving south from Springfield clashed with a large Rebel army advancing northward with the intention of seizing Springfield, Jefferson City, and ultimately St. Louis. Thanks to the bold actions of the Iowans stationed at Springfield, the Rebels beat a hasty retreat south after the battle without having reached the Missouri-Arkansas border.

General Samuel Curtis was not present to lead his troops at Prairie Grove, but he did earn much of the credit for the campaign's success. At his headquarters in St. Louis, Curtis received warning of an impending Rebel offensive in September, soon enough to rush some reinforcements to the area. The task was a tall one, as Arkansas state administrators formed forty new Rebel regiments plus twelve batteries of artillery in the Little Rock area. The relocation of 1,000 former members of the Missouri State Guard from the state of Mississippi added considerable strength to the Confederate forces in Arkansas, as did the arrival of several thousand new Rebel volunteers from Missouri. The majority of the new Confederate Army consisted of conscripted Arkansas residents.

Despite their draft status, they would perform relatively well in the battle that lay ahead.[17]

To resist the 20,000-man army gathering near Little Rock, General Curtis had only a few thousand Union infantry at Springfield, mostly new recruits. Of the several Union regiments that had fought at Pea Ridge in March, only one infantry unit was still deployed in the Springfield area. The general had two other 1861 infantry regiments available, but neither unit had much battle experience.

The task of defending Springfield thus fell on the shoulders of a small number of infantry regiments recruited in 1862 and sent south after minimal training. Three green Hawkeye regiments (the 18th Iowa, 19th Iowa, and 20th Iowa) represented the core of the bluecoats defending Springfield. Newly formed regiments from Wisconsin and Illinois also deployed to southwestern Missouri. A regiment of mounted Arkansas unionists provided timely reconnaissance for the Prairie Grove campaign in the hilly, sparsely settled Ozarks. To bolster his chances of defeating the much larger Rebel army advancing northwest from Little Rock, Curtis sought the assistance of a modest-sized army of bluecoats forming in southeastern Kansas and led by Kansan James Blunt.

The fate of Springfield depended on the Iowans' ability to coordinate their movements with the bluecoat units in southeastern Kansas. General Blunt's force consisted of five newly composed regiments made up largely of displaced Missourians, plus two veteran cavalry regiments from Ohio and Wisconsin. He also recruited three regiments of Oklahoma Indians. Rather than deploy his hybrid army of Union soldiers near Springfield, Blunt marched into northwestern Arkansas without Curtis's blessing and without realizing the size of the advancing Rebel army.[18]

When he learned of Blunt's move, Curtis quickly ordered his Springfield units south in early December. Although he would have preferred a battle location near Springfield, time was of the essence. In hopes of saving Blunt's army from total destruction, the Springfield units set out on a forced march of 120 miles through mountainous terrain. Most of the men who survived the forced march arrived in time to join Blunt's modest force before the Rebels had isolated and destroyed the Kansans.

Prairie Grove, like Wilson's Creek and Pea Ridge before it, pitted New West Rebels against New West unionists for the most part. Fortunately for the Union cause, the modest number of Great Lakes units at Prairie Grove included several batteries of artillery. Union cannon performed a critical role in the battle by holding back the numerically superior Confederate infantry after Union infantry attacks failed. The artillery held the Rebels in check long enough to permit Blunt to reinforce the bloodied Springfield units.

The morning after the battle at Prairie Grove, Rebels abandoned the field and headed south toward the Arkansas River. Despite their numerical superiority, the aggressive Union frontal attacks the day before combined with the artillery power convinced the Confederate commanders not to risk a second day of battle against the combined forces of Blunt and Frank Herron, the Iowan who led the four-day forced march from Springfield to Prairie Grove.

After the Confederate retreat commenced, the 20,000-man Rebel army disintegrated into 6,000 demoralized troops, effectively neutralizing Confederate authority in Arkansas, at least for the time being. With Union forces now in control of Fort Smith on the Oklahoma border and Grant's army in possession of Arkansas Post and Helena in the southeastern corner of the state, Confederate forces in Arkansas could not block Union efforts to capture Vicksburg.

Although they won the day, Union forces at Prairie Grove suffered tremendous casualties. The citizen-soldiers experienced severe casualties even before the guns started firing. On their forced march south from Springfield, hundreds fell out of the ranks exhausted. Without proper shoes, Herron's men had to walk on a road covered with a mix of "ice, snow, slush, and mud leavened with sharp, flinty rocks," undergoing an "epic of human endurance," according to historian William Shea. The footsore and hungry bluecoats survived the march and then charged directly at the Confederate units defending a hill overlooking the river valley.[19]

No regiment incurred greater casualties than the 19th Iowa, which included 90 volunteers from Lee County. Of the 350 soldiers in the regiment who made it to the battlefield, 190 were wounded during the assault on the ridge, a casualty rate of 55 percent. The 20th Iowa suffered almost as many casualties as the 19th Iowa. The 18th Iowa Regiment, assigned to protect Springfield, did not participate in the Battle of Prairie Grove, although they did contribute in major fashion one month later.

The soldiers of the 18th Iowa, Simeon Stevens's regiment, earned a battlefield commendation for their role in defending Springfield from Rebel cavalry raiders in January 1863. Assigned to bolster local militia forces guarding this critical staging center, the soldiers of the 18th Iowa led the defensive stand on January 8, when Confederate marauders launched a surprise attack.

Rebel horsemen outnumbered the Missouri militia units at Springfield, and the 18th Iowa represented the only Federal unit deployed there. In this desperate situation, the several companies of Iowans assigned to defend the town square teamed up with Missouri militiamen and turned back the attack by determined Rebels who advanced toward the main square on foot. The next day, rather than renew their attack, the Rebel marauders mounted their steeds and slipped away, never to reappear in the vicinity of Springfield.[20]

The soldiers of Corporal Stevens's regiment suffered more from the unsanitary camp conditions at Springfield than they did from Confederate bullets. After departing Iowa in August 1862 with 877 soldiers, fewer than 500 answered the drum roll on January 8, 1863. Every company in the regiment had been depleted by disease. One disabled soldier was Corporal Stevens, who became severely ill with the measles. Before the Confederate attack, military authorities shipped the patriarch of the Stevens family to a hospital in St. Louis, where he died two months later.[21]

The Battle of Corinth

Historian Peter Cozzens commends the performance of the Union soldiers assigned to defend the railroad junction at Corinth in October 1862. This two-day battle, fought under miserable conditions, witnessed some of the most intense fighting of the entire war. After a newly formed Iowa regiment led the charge that cleared the town of Confederates at the end of day two, the Rebel army, reduced to two-thirds strength by battle casualties, fled west for the safety of Vicksburg, never again to return.

No state had more regiments deployed at Corinth than Iowa, and every Hawkeye regiment contributed to the victory. Twelve of the forty-five Union infantry regiments guarding Corinth represented the state, and the Iowans used their experience at Shiloh to their advantage. Ben Stevens of

Oskaloosa had survived the summer of 1862 in western Tennessee despite terribly dry weather. He also survived the Battle of Corinth, as did most members of the 15th Iowa, although the Union victory exacted a large toll on other Iowa units.

Over the summer months before the battle, Union forces guarding Corinth incurred a 35 percent casualty rate from disease and heat exhaustion. Potable water was difficult to obtain there even during rainy years, and 1862 happened to be one of the driest on record. It was so hot on July 18 that Colonel Hare stopped the daily drill exercise after four men experienced heatstroke. Despite the high temperatures, officers assigned soldiers to picket duty for twenty-four hours at a time.

The Rebels' surprise attack on Corinth was led by Earl Van Dorn, the commander responsible for the dishonorable defeat at Pea Ridge. Once his troops had recaptured the vital railroad junction at Corinth from the bluecoats, Van Dorn intended to drive his 22,000 Western Confederates north over the Ohio River, invade the Old Northwest, and eventually capture St. Louis.[22] Unfortunately for him, the list of Iowa regiments stationed in Corinth included the 2nd Infantry and 7th Infantry, the veterans of Shiloh's "Hornet's Nest." Also guarding the junction was Marcellus Crocker's all-Hawkeye brigade made up of four regiments recruited in 1861, including the 11th Iowa (led by Muscatine's recruits) and the 15th Iowa, Ben Stevens's unit from Oskaloosa. Crocker's regiments marched together for the remainder of the war, earning a reputation as one of the most reliable Union Army brigades.[23]

The Battle of Iuka foreshadowed the intensity of the upcoming brawl at Corinth. Four Iowa regiments figured prominently in the brief but bloody encounter at this railroad town east of Corinth. Iowans made up 45 percent of the Union casualty list at Iuka. Two weeks later, after the Union survivors marched back to Corinth through several inches of loose dirt, Van Dorn struck that town from the west. On day one of the Battle of Corinth, the enthusiastic Rebels successfully captured the outer perimeter defense line three miles from the railroad junction. The Confederate battle plan on day two targeted the Union center and the Union right flank, ground held by veterans of the Hornet's Nest and Iuka. After General Sterling Price's Rebels broke through the Union defense line at Battery Phillips,

2,000 Confederate fighters headed toward the railroad junction in the middle of town, one mile to the south of the battery. With Rebel soldiers seemingly in control of the town, Union commander General William Rosecrans convinced himself the battle was lost.

As so often occurred in the Western theater of operations, the outcome of Corinth hinged on the response of the Union troops forced to flee the initial Rebel attack. After retreating from Battery Phillips, the Shiloh veterans rallied and then counter-attacked on their own initiative to recapture the artillery reserve. We "[drove] the enemy back down the slope with terrible slaughter," recalled one private in the 2nd Iowa. The heroes of Fort Donelson captured thirty-one prisoners and one Rebel battle flag. About the same time that Battery Phillips returned to Union hands one mile north of town, troops from Illinois who were guarding the railroad junction temporarily halted the scattered Rebel forces as they approached the Tishomingo Hotel, the headquarters of General Rosecrans.[24]

At this juncture of the battle, the momentum might have swung in either direction. Two nearly simultaneous events tipped the balance in favor of the bluecoats. On the north side of Corinth, the 17th Iowa intervened in dramatic fashion. Meanwhile, the 5th Minnesota charged into town from the west. Remarkably, neither unit had much combat experience, yet the green recruits rose to the challenge with the outcome of the battle on the line.

As the 5th Minnesota marched into the town from the west, the Iowans fired upon Confederates from a low ridge overlooking the streets on the northern edge of town. After several well-directed volleys, the 17th Iowa charged downhill into the streets of Corinth. Notwithstanding the appalling heat of the day, they captured the colors of a Mississippi regiment and took many prisoners, inciting the battle-worn Union regiments nearby to rally. As bluecoats flooded into town from several directions at once, the Rebel ranks completely disintegrated. In a matter of minutes, several hundred Iowans and Minnesotans reversed the momentum of the battle from a Confederate triumph into a decisive Union victory.[25]

The Confederate assaults on the second day at Corinth, writes Cozzens, "stand among the fiercest of the war and among the few in which the fighting became hand to hand."[26] Led by tough New West veterans from

Texas, Missouri, and Arkansas, Van Dorn's Rebels propelled themselves forward toward the Union defensive line, convinced that a Confederate victory would end the war once and for all. Unable to achieve a dramatic Union defeat, groups of demoralized Confederates surrendered rather than fight their way back through town to the woods north of Corinth.

Two days of heavy fighting exacted a huge toll in casualties on both sides. Crocker's brigade had the good luck of being on the quiet sector on day two, yet Iowans still made up more than one-fifth of the 2,500 Union casualties at Corinth. The 2nd Infantry suffered 40 percent casualties, 150 men down over the course of two days, many of them Lee County soldiers. The valiant regiment that had survived the Battle of Shiloh relatively intact never fully recovered from its battle losses during the summer and fall. With most of its original officers killed or disabled, command of the 2nd Iowa devolved upon James B. Weaver, a Bloomfield lawyer who had entered the service in 1861 as a first lieutenant.[27]

With so many experienced regiments depleted, Federal commanders in the West welcomed the waves of new recruits, which were not slow in coming. Around New Year's Day, several green Iowa regiments received their baptism of fire, first at Chickasaw Bluffs and then at Arkansas Post.[28] General Grant brigaded green regiments with veteran units as much as possible in 1863, a practice that aided the inexperienced troops during their first encounters against Confederate forces.

Several Iowa regiments recruited in 1862 marched with Colonel Williamson's Pea Ridge veterans in a second all-Iowa brigade. In the Vicksburg sector, Federal officials brigaded the 21st Iowa (including the Delaware County recruits) with a regiment of Wisconsin veterans. Muscatine's new regiment (the 35th Infantry) marched with the 12th Iowa, Abner Dunham's unit.

Back at home, families contemplated the death lists as they struggled to sustain themselves through the cold winter of 1862–63. When winter turned to spring, the absence of 22,000 adult males on top of the 20,000 volunteers of 1861 greatly reduced the number of Iowans available to perform labor at home. Mary Alice Vermilion, a resident of south-central Iowa, remarked on the changing appearance of the countryside in May 1863:

As I came through Iowa [traveling back from Indiana,] I couldn't help noticing the many old, white-haired men, and little boys—some hardly as tall as their plow handles—that were working in the fields. I knew . . . where all the young men were. But the farming is going on better than you would think. They have to work harder, but I have heard no one complain yet. Some say their girls must go into the fields.[29]

Women, young boys, and older men would have the bear the brunt of the home-front work for some time. Two more years would pass before the soldiers who survived the war returned home.

CHAPTER EIGHT

1863: Triumph in Mississippi and Arkansas

—————•————

The monumental events of 1863 generated a wide range of emotions. How Americans acted and reacted varied depending upon their political beliefs and family circumstances. For unionists like Abner Dunham, the year began on a profoundly negative note. Nothing but bad news seemed to come from the war front, and at home Iowans organized peace rallies. He wondered if the United States would ever be reunited. Having spent seven months of captivity in Confederate prisoner of war camps in 1862, the Delaware County bachelor struggled to recover from the physical and psychological effects of incarceration.

Winter saw thousands of Iowans attending peace rallies at home. Some of those in attendance argued on behalf of accepting secession. Others insisted that reunification would follow a decision by the president to withdraw all Union military forces from the South. For soldiers like Dunham, the first argument was treasonous and the second ill-advised. As winter turned to spring, his outlook improved. General Grant's activity near Vicksburg energized him, and his optimism turned to euphoria on the Fourth of July, the day that witnessed three major Union military victories.

For Iowa soldiers stationed in the South, death from disease continued to be a frequent occurrence. In March, Ben Stevens learned of the death of his father. Despite the tragic circumstances, the young Oskaloosa artisan never questioned his own decision to remain in the army. In fact, he turned over a new leaf and embraced the cause of African American enlistment as the key to winning the war.

The experience of 1863 also transformed Charles Musser. When the year began, he was homesick. During the inactive spring months, he openly regretted his decision to enlist. Confined to a filthy army camp in Helena, Arkansas, he gradually came to embrace a military solution to the war and welcome the prospect of emancipation. When the Rebels attacked Helena on July 4, the battle experience opened the eyes of the Pottawattamie County farmboy and made him realize he must either desert from the army or adopt a prowar attitude. He chose continued enlistment, a position from which he never retreated. Even when Charles learned that his older brother had been fighting as a Rebel soldier against Union forces in Mississippi, his commitment to the war effort remained strong.

In Muscatine, Alexander Clark celebrated the first of January along with other abolitionists by rejoicing at the news that Lincoln had carried out his earlier vow to proclaim emancipation. Their euphoria quickly dissipated, however, when state administrators refused to pursue radical policies. Black Iowans grew increasingly frustrated at the unwillingness of white Iowans to organize an African American regiment. Rather than pursue equal rights legislation, state party leaders adopted a conservative platform and settled on a nonradical unionist for governor. Not until November 1863, when Federal officials commissioned the 60th U.S. Regiment of Colored Troops, did Alexander Clark come to believe the full rights of citizenship would be granted to nonwhites.

Cyrus Carpenter spent a frustrating twelve months in Tennessee working for Iowa general Grenville Dodge. Anxious to go back to Fort Dodge and wed the woman he had promised to marry in 1859, he continually saw his furloughs canceled as the ebb and flow of warfare pushed and pulled the quartermaster in different directions. By the end of the year, gloom and frustration undermined his morale. Rather than abandon his assignment, Carpenter proved himself a very capable administrator in 1863, performing tedious work in an ethical manner that several years later gained partisan rewards back home.

The task of organizing supplies exposed Carpenter, a moral idealist, to some of the most amoral aspects of war administration. He saw generals in need of supplies use their political connections to obtain goods and equipment assigned to other units. He saw sick animals and inferior military equipment arrive at his warehouse, paid for in full by the U.S. Treasury Department. He saw profiteers hover around the staging areas looking to buy rejected supplies and resell them to an army quartermaster in another district. Near the war front, soldiers and nonsoldiers alike stole civilians' personal property. Food produced by local farmers was confiscated without compensation. Annie Wittenmyer's year was one of high peaks and low valleys. Barriers rooted in sexism continued to plague her and her colleagues during 1863. Between furious bouts of letter writing, she engaged in a series of activities near the front lines that would have made for a splendid movie. When a regimental surgeon invited her to visit his hospital near the Vicksburg battlefield, Wittenmyer swam a horse across a canal in order to examine the facility. Shocked by the hospital's unsanitary condition, she immediately dispatched a report to General Grant, who closed the hospital in short order and transferred the patients to a health care facility twenty-five miles upstream.

In April, Wittenmyer accepted an invitation from General and Mrs. Grant to sit with them and observe the U.S. Navy boats pass under the guns at Vicksburg. August found her stationed in Helena, Arkansas, where she grew disgusted with the putrid conditions of the hospital there. Thinking always of the welfare of the soldiers, she boarded a steamboat in Helena bound for Memphis and arrived for an unscheduled appointment with the army regional medical director. After two days of badgering, the Memphis director eventually agreed to her demand to close the facility. Four steamboats dispatched to the Arkansas port removed 2,000 sick and wounded soldiers to sanitary facilities upriver.[1]

The Political Transformation of Women War Workers

Wittenmyer's successes were not typical of her work or that of other women working on behalf of the soldiers. Despite her popularity among top-ranking generals and ordinary soldiers, male doctors in charge of poorly managed hospitals refused to accept her advice and services. Back in Iowa, female charity leaders found themselves increasingly marginalized. Clergymen appointed to the Iowa Army Sanitation Commission (IASC) board conspired to accuse Wittenmyer of violating commission guidelines by selling donated goods to Catholic nuns in Arkansas.

Angry at the treatment of women volunteers, Wittenmyer and her allies in the LSAS network maneuvered to ensure that the collection and distribution system remained in the hands of local society leaders. When the IASC board pushed harder, they unilaterally elected their own governing board, notwithstanding the preferences of Governor Kirkwood and Senator Harlan. Unilateral action failed to resolve the governing dispute. When her opponents within the LSAS organization successfully transformed the governing dispute into a debate over a proposed alliance with the U.S. Sanitary Commission (USSC), Wittenmyer eventually lost control over the distribution system.

Events in Missouri and Illinois, the two closest neighboring states, influenced the outcome of the sanitary dispute in the Hawkeye state. In Illinois, LSAS leaders ducked fairly quickly under the umbrella of the USSC, which had established a distribution office in Chicago. Historian Judith Giesberg attributes the result in Illinois to the actions of assertive women like Mary Bickerdyke, an LSAS leader who worked cooperatively with the all-male USSC board in exchange for a certain measure of autonomy.[2]

In contrast, Missouri's sanitary leaders continued to operate as the Western Sanitary Commission (WSC), which was headquartered in St. Louis. For the duration of the war, the WSC resisted efforts by the USSC Chicago office to compel a merger. Fearful of losing their autonomy, St. Louis managers obtained large amounts of money, recruited hundreds of volunteers, and maintained high standards of service. The USSC and the WSC each recruited women nurses and hospital cooks, so neither organization could be characterized as profemale or antifemale.[3]

In Iowa, LSAS leaders like Wittenmyer associated a USSC merger with the loss of autonomy. Although operating through St. Louis was not ideal, she preferred the semi-independence it provided. By 1863, she had experienced considerable success coordinating the distribution of goods through St. Louis, where she and WSC leaders developed a cooperative relationship. Despite the influence of progressive women leaders in Illinois who advocated on behalf of the USSC, joining the USCC meant losing control of the existing transfer system through Keokuk.

Rather than letting it slip from her grasp, Wittenmyer sought out allies within the Iowa LSAS in hopes of blocking IASC attempts to force a Chicago merger. Conflict engendered bitterness, so much so that she considered joining the U.S. Christian Commission (CC) rather than merge with the USSC. Although the CC got its start later than the USSC, by 1863 it operated independent hospital facilities in several Ohio River valley states.

When male IASC board members debated whether to merge with the

WSC, join the USSC, or continue to operate independently, the USSC merger proposal won out. Several board members with business connections in Chicago pushed hard to achieve the outcome. The secretary of the IASC, a minister from Davenport, argued that a merger with the Chicago branch would centralize distribution of donated goods. When Wittenmyer opposed the merger, IASC board members formed an alliance with dissenting LSAS leaders who favored the merger.

In many Iowa towns, including Keokuk, women found themselves on opposite sides of the distribution debate. Reasonable people could disagree over the proposal to merge with the USSC, but a perception of prejudice against women raised the level of hostility. "I went to Muscatine to Mrs. Wittenmyer's convention," the secretary of the IASC noted in his diary. "Found it packed and at her Command . . . From Feminine Conventions Good Lord deliver me."[4] As the debate continued, Wittenmyer's personality contributed at times to polarize the debate among women. Although she was usually tactful and rarely rude in public, prominent women who supported the USSC merger characterized her and her disciples as a group of "strong-minded women," a term that had a negative connotation in 1863.

In retrospect, an observer is struck by the commonalities between the opposing groups. Not only did each faction zealously support the war effort, but each group was led by devout evangelical Protestants who opposed the sale of liquor. Teetotal Methodists in Wittenmyer's faction questioned the motives of teetotal Methodists in the other faction.

The disagreement became very personal at times. IASC board members accused Wittenmyer of sloppy bookkeeping practices, while her advocates accused USSC proponents of attempting to remove women entirely from their work with the sanitary commission. When the debate reached its peak, Wittenmyer and her allies argued that a USSC merger would result in the complete loss of women's power. One of them accused the IASC of opposing a "woman's right to dispense alms." The polarizing rhetoric precluded conciliation and encouraged an all-or-nothing attitude on both sides. Wittenmyer and her allies remained confident of success. "Believe me," one supporter wrote to her, "the whole movement against you . . . will fall to the ground."[5]

Wittenmyer responded to her critics by writing hundreds of letters in 1863 in an effort to ensure the safe passage of goods to the donor's intended destination. "Which railroad cars are being used to ship goods to Cairo?"

she wrote in one letter. "Please confirm the goods were received by the soldiers" in another letter. "Please find enclosed a bill of shipment of a box of goods." From an army camp near Vicksburg, she wrote: "Is Jerome Beach Company A 25th Iowa dead or alive in the St. Louis hospital? Search thoroughly and report immediately whether dead or alive and where."[6]

Around the state in 1863, different towns sided with different factions. LSAS leaders in Muscatine stuck with Wittenmyer and rejected the USSC merger plan. The chapter in Oskaloosa contemplated supporting the USSC merger. So did the Council Bluffs LSAS. However, their votes against Wittenmyer were an exception to the general pattern of support.

When the majority of LSAS chapters continued to support the status quo and oppose the USSC merger, IASC board members appealed to Governor Kirkwood to intervene and force a merger with the USSC. He preferred not to intervene directly. As the conflict became more polarized, he quietly endorsed the USSC merger and conspired behind the scenes with the Harlan family—by now longtime opponents of Wittenmyer's network. He also encouraged LSAS members to convene a statewide leadership assembly in hopes that the pro-USSC faction would outnumber anti-USSC delegates and vote in favor of the merger once and for all time.

Kirkwood might have gone further in an effort to achieve the desired outcome, but he did not. No doubt, some IASC board members pressured him to revise the system of LSAS democratic governance in order to minimize Wittenmyer's influence. Kirkwood declined, however, to place the state LSAS network under the auspices of the IASC. He also declined to change the voting rules. Men who attended the LSAS convention in 1862 could not vote. When some IASC board members proposed that men as well women be permitted to vote, Kirkwood refused. Such a measure would almost certainly have benefited the anti-Wittenmyer faction, but as long as Kirkwood remained governor, a majority vote of women LSAS delegates would determine the outcome of the controversy. The pro-USSC faction, unable to rein in Wittenmyer's faction through procedural changes, looked to other means to resolve the matter in their favor.

The Capture of Vicksburg

Of the many Rebel citadels erected along the Mississippi River, none proved more difficult to capture than Vicksburg. Situated near a hairpin turn in the river, on a high bluff, its location offered Confederate forces defending the port several natural advantages. Home to some 5,000 residents when the war began, the port saw the defeat of a series of waterborne attacks starting in the spring of 1862. Deep-draft U.S. Navy vessels steaming upstream from New Orleans became easy targets for the Rebel cannoneers stationed on the tall hills. Shallow-draft navy gunboats heading downstream from Memphis found it impossible to negotiate the hairpin turn and later return upstream. When Memphis transport ships attempted to dock upstream from Vicksburg by steaming through one of the several meandering streams north of the port, Rebel soldiers blocked their advance by felling giant trees miles before the ships could reach the foot of the bluffs.

When the War Department attempted a direct army-navy attack on the citadel in December 1862, the combined effort failed miserably. Commanders expected that the cliffs north of the port would be undefended, but Rebel soldiers were waiting there in force, having recently turned back General Grant's attempt to descend upon Vicksburg overland from the vicinity of Corinth. Faced by a line of cannon atop the bluffs, thousands of exposed Union infantry headed straight for the foot of the cliffs, only to suffer hundreds of casualties. Not a single regiment reached the foot of the cliffs.

The War Department poured more resources into the area during the late winter. Miles of tents lined the west bank of the Mississippi River north and south of the hairpin curve. With each passing month, however, the fort walls rose higher around Vicksburg and additional obstacles protected the vulnerable eastern (landward) side of the citadel. By April, the outer (eastern) wall of fortifications ran for eight miles from north to south. Along the river bluff, the line of Rebel cannon stretched for miles north and south of the port.

The final capture of the citadel in July 1863 came about after Grant approached Vicksburg overland from the south, a dangerously risky gambit. With the Rebel artillery still in command of the bluffs, the Union troops operating south of Vicksburg had no direct supply line. Once ashore on the east bank of the Mississippi River, the 35,000 soldiers in Grant's three army corps had to march through hostile territory without regular supplies of food and ammunition. Everything depended upon the ability of the Western soldiers to utilize local resources effectively and survive the heat and humidity. The overland campaign lasted three full weeks before a direct supply line was reestablished. After regular army supplies arrived, six more weeks passed before the citadel surrendered on July 4.

During the Vicksburg campaign, one Iowa recruit in the 22nd Infantry described the sultry conditions as having an "enervating effect." "The entire system—mental, physical and nervous—is weakened and prostrated to a degree that I never felt, nor even had any idea of before," the Iowan noted. "This is not the case with me alone, but every one here even the strongest and most [healthy] feel this way to a greater or lesser extent." By the time Vicksburg finally surrendered, 1,800 Iowa soldiers had died or been discharged for wounds, heat exhaustion, or other disability.[7]

Over the three-week period that preceded the siege, Grant's soldiers covered two hundred miles and fought seven separate battles. All told, twenty-six Hawkeye infantry regiments fought at Vicksburg, fifteen of them newly recruited units. Only Illinois boasted more regiments in this campaign. During the battles fought near Vicksburg, Iowa generals commanded units involved in some of the heaviest fighting. Grant's division commanders included Iowans Marcellus Crocker and James M. Tuttle. Two others, Jacob Lauman and Frank Herron, arrived in the late spring of 1863 after the siege began, each in command of a division of fresh troops.[8]

Iowa's top-ranking general, Grenville Dodge, spent much of 1863 away from Vicksburg. Now in charge of an entire corps, he rebuilt the railroad network in Tennessee with the assistance of Iowa regiments, including the 2nd Infantry and 7th Infantry. The 2nd Iowa Cavalry, commanded by a Muscatine resident, participated in a scorched-earth campaign in northeastern Mississippi, a venture that successfully destroyed valuable resources while distracting the Confederate commander in Vicksburg.

As a result of their troop strength, Iowans seemed to be everywhere during the Vicksburg campaign. In the early spring months, they built plank roads and bridges through the swamps, hauled huge cypress trees out of shallow waterways, shoveled mud to form canals, burned inland Rebel supply bases, and destroyed railroad tracks. On the Louisiana shore, Crocker's Iowa Brigade (later known as the Old Iowa Brigade) protected the all-important Union supply route. After Grant made the bold decision in late April to transport his infantry from the Louisiana side across the river to a point forty miles south of Vicksburg, Hawkeye regiments secured Grant's bridgehead on the east side of the river. Once the bridgehead was established, Iowa units expanded Grant's zone of control, neutralized the Confederate forces that attempted to counter-attack, and isolated the Vicksburg garrison.

As Grant tightened his grip on Vicksburg, Iowa soldiers scoured the countryside for supplies and dug trenches in the hills around the city while under enemy fire. When Rebel forces launched a surprise attack on African American soldiers from Louisiana protecting a staging area upstream, Iowans passing upriver on a steamboat disembarked and fought side by side with the new recruits.

On the several Vicksburg battlefields, Hawkeye units performed exceptionally. They led the charge that captured the Mississippi capital of Jackson. They saved Grant's army at Champion Hill, a battle that sealed the fate of the Confederacy, some historians say. They pierced the Rebel line guarding the Big Black River Bridge, the last obstacle before Vicksburg. During Grant's second attempt to storm the Vicksburg fortress on May 22, two Iowa regiments nearly breached the Rebel defensive position at the Railroad Redoubt.

Remarkably, it was the citizen-soldiers recruited in the late summer of 1862 who decided the fate of the Union offensive. The 1862 volunteers brought a much-needed enthusiasm for combat, which blossomed under aggressive commanders like Grant. Despite their lack of military experience, the recruits fought toe to toe against the Confederacy's best Western soldiers.

Two battles in particular stand out as exemplary. At Champion Hill, the 17th Iowa—the heroes of Corinth—arrived in the nick of time to rally the wavering Union regiments trying to defend Grant's headquarters. When the battle-worn Iowa soldiers in the area recognized the newly arrived 17th Regiment, they threw their caps into the air and shouted "Iowa, Iowa, Iowa!" The inspired bluecoats formed an assault line and advanced toward the stubborn Confederates defending the hill near the Champion family's farm. Along with the 10th Missouri, the 17th Iowa pressed the advance one full mile, all the way to the crossroads, picking up exhausted but jubilant bluecoats along the way.[9]

The day following this triumph, the 21st Iowa (which included a company of Delaware County soldiers) led a spectacular charge against Rebels dug in behind fortifications guarding the railroad bridge over the Big Black River. As the 1,500 charging Union soldiers approached the cotton-bale parapets, nervous Rebels began to flee. More defenders ran as the Iowans prepared to fire a volley. "The Rebels [at the point of attack] rose, almost *en masse*, from the rifle-pits and fled for the bridges [a half-mile in the rear]," recalled Major Van Anda of the 21st Iowa. "Those who remained [held] up bunches of cotton on their guns in token of surrender."[10]

Once inside the Confederate works, the Iowans turned and fired on the gray-clad defenders manning the fortifications farther down the line. Within a few moments, the entire Rebel line broke in retreat, and the Rebel commander reluctantly ordered his men back to Vicksburg, twenty miles away. To honor their heroism under fire, Grant assigned a regiment of Iowans to escort the 1,751 Rebel prisoners upstream to Memphis.

Skulking—evading battle—did not occur on a large scale among the new regiments. At Champion Hill, Rebel troops forced two inexperienced Hawkeye regiments to retreat nearly one mile, yet the Iowans organized a counter-attack rather than hide out for the remainder of the battle. As a result of the troops' ability to endure intense combat, the back-to-back victories at Champion Hill and Big Black River exacted a heavy toll on the green Iowa units that did most of the heavy fighting. The terribly hot weather further reduced their ranks. The 21st Iowa, which had left the state nearly 1,000 men strong, by July 10 had only 158 members present for duty.[11]

Abner Dunham, back on duty after his stint in a Confederate prison, survived the Vicksburg ordeal. Despite the rain, hot weather, lack of potable water, food shortages, and all of the hard marching, the Delaware County farmboy thrilled at the challenge of the military venture. "I never saw such a grander sight in my life," he wrote as he observed from a distance the attack on Jackson. The corporal had a keen sense of the generals' strategy and listened carefully when Grant and Sherman discussed their next moves in his presence.[12]

While on the march in search of food, men in Dunham's regiment resorted to vandalism. Despite strict orders against pillaging, the hard-bitten Iowa veterans of Shiloh—those recently released from Confederate prison camps—took particular delight in wrecking opulent plantation homes and burning commercial buildings in Jackson. Dunham's letters home do not indicate whether he himself participated in the vandalism, although the destruction was extensive. Dunham's brigade, commanded by a Prussian-trained Iowan from Burlington, was fortunate to avoid casualties during Sherman's two unsuccessful assaults on the Vicksburg fortifications, May 19 and May 22.

Following the failed Union attack of May 22, Abner composed a letter home. Notwithstanding the scale of the catastrophe, he remained optimistic on May 23:

> In the charge yesterday the slaughter was awful. Fortunately for me our Brigade is held in reserve and did not get a man hurt . . . Our troops are in good spirits and are confident of success. We have taken about 10,000 prisoners since our expedition was commenced. There was several days that we were very short of food but now we have plenty . . . During our march our feet got very sore but we all stood it finely. I stood it as well as any one in the crowd. Am well now.[13]

During the six-week siege, Abner's unit remained deployed near Vicksburg. The Iowans took their turn relieving Union regiments in the front trench line closest to the fortress. By July 4, those who had survived the weather and the Rebel sharpshooters were in dire need of a furlough.

News of Vicksburg's July 4 surrender ignited hundreds of neighborhood celebrations back in Iowa. "I was washing the dishes when I heard a church bell ringing," wrote one Mount Pleasant housewife to her husband in Sherman's corps. "In a few minutes every bell in town was ringing, the flags were flying, cannon roaring and men and boys shouting, horses and cowbells were making all the noise they could." Vicksburg's capture, coupled with the capture of Port Hudson, Mississippi, several weeks later, meant that Union forces had split the rebellious slave republic into two portions.[14]

The Battle of Helena

The same day that 23,000 starving Confederates surrendered at Vicksburg, three untested Iowa regiments received their baptism of fire defending the port of Helena, Arkansas. Confederate forces in central Arkansas attacked the port, 250 miles upstream from Vicksburg, in hopes of cutting a link in the tenuous Union supply line that enabled General Grant to sustain pressure on the citadel's defenders.

The enthusiastic Rebels who assaulted Helena's outer defense line outnumbered the Union troops nearly two to one. Notwithstanding the numerical disadvantage, Helena remained in Union hands, in large part because of the fortitude of the Iowans stationed there. Although overshadowed by Gettysburg and Vicksburg, the two other major Union victories on July 4, the bluecoats' success in defending Helena represented a major step on the path to liberating Arkansas.

Helena became vulnerable to Rebel attack when Grant diverted thousands of Federal troops downstream to Vicksburg. As of July 1, eight regiments guarded the Arkansas port, only one of which had any previous battle experience. The 4,100 citizen-soldiers defending the mudhole included Charles Musser of the 29th Iowa and the Mahaska County volunteers in the 33rd Iowa. With General Sterling Price leading the attack, Rebel forces confidently expected to capture the port and then invade Missouri following a victory at Helena. A few weeks before launching the surprise attack, Arkansas state officials recalled thousands of conscripts to the ranks and welcomed hundreds of volunteers from Missouri into the Confederate Army.[15]

In the early morning hours of the Fourth of July, 7,600 Rebels emerged out of the woods and attacked the line of Union fortifications on the hills surrounding the river port. Iowans fought in every sector of the Union battle line at Helena. In the northern sector, two Hawkeye regiments successfully defended Battery A and Battery B, yielding not an inch of turf to the 1,750 veteran Rebel cavalrymen who dismounted and advanced toward them. In the center, Rebel infantry targeted Battery C and Battery D, ground defended by Samuel Rice's brigade, which included the 33rd Iowa. The popular Oskaloosa lawyer had won a promotion from regimental colonel to brigade commander before the battle.[16]

One member of the 33rd Iowa recalled after the war how the novice soldiers coped with the threat of death in this, their first major encounter. "We acted and felt apparently just as though we had been in a hard battle every day of our lives," A. F. Sperry wrote in 1866. "Up in the breast-works, men shoot at Rebels as though aiming at buffalo or deer. Laughing and chatting were abundant as ever."[17]

Skulking did not occur on a large scale. Just as at Prairie Grove, Corinth, Port Gibson, Champion Hill, and Big Black River, the novice soldiers hung together. Some of the Iowans assigned to the Helena hospital before the battle left their beds, intent on joining the engagement. Charles Musser, writing home after the battle, noted that General Prentiss happened to be out of town when the Rebels launched their assault. "There was no commander, no officer here that day" remarked the twenty-two-year-old. "Every man fought. Every man was as good as a Brigadier General."[18] Here was another example of the Iowans' commitment to democracy making them good soldiers.

No regiment incurred more casualties than the 33rd Iowa, whose battle flag, planted in the trench between Battery C and Battery D, sported twenty-seven bullet holes when the firing finally stopped. It was here, in the center, where the Rebel attackers came closest to victory after uprooting a Missouri Union regiment and capturing Battery C. In the struggle for Battery D, the 33rd Iowa rallied and dispersed the anxious Confederates. Union artillery fire knocked down hundreds of Rebels charging up Graveyard Hill, and the Iowans trapped several hundred prisoners as the bluecoats moved forward to recapture the guns of Battery C.

By the time the dazed Rebel trumpeter sounded the order to retreat, Price had suffered 1,600 casualties, 22 percent of his entire force. By comparison, Union adjutants counted only 240 casualties. The jubilation that followed Price's retreat reached a crescendo when news arrived of Vicksburg's surrender.[19]

Charles Musser's positive reaction to the victory represented a remarkable turnaround. Four months earlier, the young farm laborer from Pottawattamie County had lamented his decision to enlist. Writing to a cousin contemplating enrollment, he advised him not to join up. Homesick and dejected over the direction of the war, Musser wrote home complaining about Republicans (the "War Party"), the deep mud, the multitude of former slaves ("contrabands"), the weather, and the high death rate from disease. "It is really discouraging the way the war is going on," he wrote before the battle, "but we hope it will all soon be over." [20]

Musser's religious training compelled him to question the morality of war. The Democrats who composed a majority of his company contributed to Musser's political disillusionment during the late winter. "The boys are getting so that they do not care much for anything . . . They are in for peace in any way or form," Charles wrote home.[21]

One low point came on March 20, when Charles announced, "I hope this unholy war will soon end and stop this horrible slaughter of so many men. What will we gain if the war continues one year longer?" In late June, a few days before Price's Rebels attacked Helena, Musser looked around the port and regarded the multitude of dead Union soldiers felled by disease. "I counted two hundred and eighty graves, and some of them had as high [as] three corpses in them."[22]

Military success suddenly revived Musser's spirits. When the firing started on July 4, the twenty-two-year-old held the picket line near Battery A. He counted four separate charges against his position. "We just mowed them down like grass," he remarked in a letter home. "In the hottest of the fight, some of the rebs yelled out 'by goddamned them must be Iowa boys.' And then we yelled out, 'Iowa, Iowa for ever.'"[23]

Despite the "unearthly yells" of the charging Rebels, Musser felt a great sense of accomplishment when the troopers beat a hasty retreat back to Little Rock. The victory at Helena, combined with the surrender at Vicksburg, transformed his whole attitude about enlisting in 1862. "Rebellion is knocked in a cocked hat in the west," he wrote afterwards. "I would not have missed [the battle] for six months wages . . . I have escaped without a scratch."[24]

After the battle, Musser divided his world into two camps. His list of "enemies" included guerrillas, regular army Rebels, and peace Democrats ("Copperheads") back home. When an acquaintance in Iowa wrote to him and advised him not to fight, he told his parents he would never again correspond with such a "traitor." In September, word reached Charles that his older brother living in Missouri had enlisted in the Confederate Army in 1862. "I am sorry that I have to fight against a brother, but fate so ordered it and I cannot help it."[25]

Perhaps even more remarkable, he now saw escaped slaves as his allies. "The arming of Negroes for soldiers is now considered by all or a large majority of the boys as a necessity, and they go in strong for it," Musser explained to his parents. On one expedition into the countryside in June, his regiment employed four freedmen as guides. Slaves found along their route marched back to Helena "as recruits for our black regiment," he noted. "For my part, I say arm every nigger of them and let them fight, for they need not force . . . to make them fight. I know they will fight and like demons, too." The knowledge that they would be killed or returned to slavery if taken prisoner convinced Musser that he could rely upon them in battle.[26]

Just as Charles Musser experienced a metamorphosis, the confluence of events in Mississippi transformed the attitudes of Ben Stevens and Abner Dunham as well. During the Vicksburg campaign, local slaves served as invaluable guides, directing the bluecoated columns through dense foliage. Union military success led to loud celebrations among the people held in bondage on local plantations. On May 6, Abner Dunham recorded in his diary that "one old negro today . . . prayed the lord to bless every one of us."[27]

Even the most racist soldiers changed their opinion about slavery after being exposed to the inhumane practices of slaveowners. Cyrus Boyd, a sergeant in the 15th Iowa, recorded how one fellow in his unit "exclaimed in the fervent patriotism of his feeling" after learning that one master had fathered three slave daughters. "By G—d I'll fight till hell freezes over," the Iowan exclaimed to Boyd, "and then I'll cut the ice and fight on." Boyd, like many other young farm laborers from south-central Iowa, came to believe that a moral imperative underlay their military mission.[28]

Oskaloosa's Ben Stevens took matters one step further. Convinced that arming former slaves would expedite an end to the bloody conflict, the twenty-three-year-old resigned from the 15th Iowa to accept a position as officer in the 10th Louisiana Volunteers of African Descent, later the 48th U.S. Colored Troops. "I have recruited one hundred and thirty-three good [African American volunteer soldiers]," he wrote to his mother on August 12, "which filled up our Regiment to the required number. There are a great many [black] Regiments organizing in this Department at this time. The work is progressing beyond description." Although the carpenter's son still would not embrace equal rights for nonwhites, he willingly accepted the opportunity to train ex-slaves as the most direct means to facilitate reunion.[29]

A Black Regiment for the Hawkeye State

Alexander Clark spent much of the summer of 1863 traveling around the upper Midwest imploring African Americans to enlist. His efforts produced some volunteers, but at other times he experienced setbacks. Many whites changed their minds about black enlistment during 1863, but obstacles still frustrated him. Blacks who enlisted were not promised the opportunity to vote following the war. Thousands of Missouri blacks wanted to enlist, but white officials there would only accept into the ranks those previously certified as freemen.

When War Department policy reduced black soldiers' pay and prohibited the appointment of black officers, some African Americans in Iowa

FIGURE 10. An undated print of Alexander Clark, Iowa's leading spokesman for African Americans before, during, and after the war. His parents had been slaves in Pennsylvania, and at the age of seventeen he relocated by himself from Cincinnati, Ohio, to Muscatine. When he died in 1890, he was serving as U.S. ambassador to Liberia. *Photo courtesy of Musser Public Library, Muscatine.*

urged young men not to sign up until equal rights and equal pay were guaranteed. Clark himself intended to enlist, but the camp surgeon disqualified the longtime Muscatine businessman on account of an old leg injury. Despite the rejection and all of the racism, Clark continued to push forward on black enlistment in order to prove that he and his brethren deserved equal citizenship.

Momentum in favor of creating an African American regiment in Iowa came to a head in August 1863 when state officials designated Keokuk as the rendezvous point. That city's proximity to Missouri presented Clark and other recruiters with an opportunity to circumvent the Missouri governor's freemen-only policy by luring escaped slaves across the border and enlisting them in Iowa.

War Department rules required that whites be appointed as officers, and a sufficient number of Keokuk civilians accepted the invitation to lead the First Regiment of Iowa African Infantry, later the 60th U.S. Colored Troops. In September, Clark traveled to St. Paul, Minnesota, to recruit former slaves brought up to Fort Snelling the previous year by army officials. As an inducement, Clark gave each one the $2 fee he received for signing them up. Although not as many Fort Snelling men signed up as Clark had hoped, hundreds of former Missouri slaves made the passage across the Des Moines River to enlist at Keokuk.

By the end of October, 650 black men were training at the army camp in Keokuk. More would join them after the regiment transferred to St. Louis. While the men endured the hazards of training camp, black women in Keokuk and Muscatine stitched together an American flag emblazoned "1st Colored Regiment of Iowa."[30]

For Clark, the penultimate moment took place at Benton Barracks in St. Louis, where he traveled with the regiment despite not being able to serve in it himself. "We left Keokuk last week on three boats," he wrote to his hometown newspaper on November 16, "and arrived here all safe." He continued, "Our regiment numbers over 800 and will soon be full. All must feel proud of our noble little State for giving one colored regiment to help put down this unholy rebellion." He added, "I should like to have been mustered in as Sergeant Major of the regiment, but it is as it is, and I am satisfied, feeling proud of my country and myself."

"I am proud," Clark proclaimed to his home community, "that I recruited 50 men for the regiment at my own expense and won the esteem and respect of all of the field and line officers of the regiment, as well as the men." Four days later, with all ten companies drawn up in formation, he presented the regimental flag and addressed the unit he had spent more than a year trying to organize. The "regiment received the ensign with evident gratification and lively enthusiasm," noted the *Muscatine Journal*.[31]

One question still remained. Despite all of Clark's work, Iowa's black recruits were not guaranteed an opportunity to display their courage on the battlefield. Several prominent whites predicted the unit would be relegated to noncombat work, a role frequently assigned to African American units during the war. Indeed, when the War Department had announced Keokuk as the training site, the original plan called for assigning the black troops to patrol along the Iowa-Missouri border rather than fight regular Rebel units in the Deep South. Many Iowans, including General Samuel Rice, still doubted the ex-slaves' military prowess. Some state officials promoted black enlistment only as a means to reduce the number of new white recruits required to meet the state's enrollment quota. Clark, as he presented the regiment its flag in St. Louis, worried the unit would never see action on the war front.

The Invasion of Central Arkansas

Successfully defending Helena was one thing, but liberating the entire state of Arkansas was quite another task. In the contest to establish a permanent unionist government in Little Rock, no Union jurisdiction played a more prominent role than Iowa. Several of its regiments, including the state's lone African American regiment, remained stationed in Arkansas until 1865. Five white infantry regiments recruited in 1862 spent the duration of the war here, as did the 1st Iowa Cavalry, 3rd Iowa Cavalry, and 3rd Iowa Artillery Battery.

Several other Iowa infantry regiments deployed temporarily to Arkansas between 1863 and 1865. Iowans from practically every district in the state, including Keokuk, Muscatine, Fort Dodge, Oskaloosa, Council Bluffs, and Delaware County, marched through the backwoods of Arkansas at some point during the war.

Two of Annie Wittenmyer's brothers fought in Arkansas with the 1st Iowa Cavalry. Charles Musser spent more than two and half years in Arkansas before his discharge in 1865. Members of the Stevens family never deployed in Arkansas, but Mahaska County was well represented, with the 33rd Iowa and 40th Iowa assigned to the state. The 32nd Infantry, a regiment recruited from Iowa's sparsely settled frontier counties, made a name for itself as part of a cavalry brigade. The Muscatine recruits in the 35th Infantry, the regiment that logged more miles than any other unit during the war, spent considerable time chasing Rebels from one corner of the state to another.

Led by Union general Frederick Steele, the campaign to capture the Arkansas state capital began in the late summer. Unfortunately, rather than approach Little Rock via the Arkansas River valley, where potable water was available, Federal military planners selected an overland route through flat, waterless prairie. Hundreds of soldiers already ill from disease lay stranded in the hospital in Helena, and many more men dropped by the wayside as the blue column marched westward into central Arkansas.

By the time the survivors reached the Arkansas River near the state capital, a line of graves marked their route. Temporary hospitals in DeValls Bluff and Clarendon overflowed with soldiers too sick to march. At one point, the 750-man roster of the 40th Iowa showed only 219 men fit for duty. In spite of the miserable conditions, few members of the 40th Iowa deserted or faked illness in order to return home.[32]

As the thin line of bluecoats approached Little Rock, several feats of determination encouraged Confederate general Price to abandon the city. The 1st Iowa Cavalry broke through Rebel roadblocks at several key points on the road from Helena. Three miles southeast of Little Rock, the Iowa horsemen dismounted and acted as skirmishers pressing in on the main Confederate picket line.

As General Steele's infantry neared the Arkansas capital, the 40th Iowa Infantry led the Union assault across the river south of the capital city, dashing across the pontoon bridge in perfect order and advancing one-half mile to a tree line to secure the bridgehead. When Rebel counter-attacks on the Federal vanguard failed to intimidate Steele, Price chose to flee toward southwestern Arkansas rather than risk Union forces laying siege to his forces in Little Rock. A few hours after Price's last regiment departed, Iowa cavalrymen led the liberators into the capital city.[33]

The most challenging work started after the capture of Little Rock. The Federals had arrived there without their clothing kits or camp tents and with very little meat. With no direct railroad connection and low water on the Arkansas River, Union soldiers had only local resources at their disposal until a river-borne supply network could be established. That took three weeks. Little Rock had barely 3,000 residents when the war began, and many of the town's merchants left the capital with Price's retreating army. Left behind were hundreds of sick Rebel troops, whose presence forced the 10,000-plus bluecoats to sleep out of doors on the cold ground.

During the three-week interlude before their supply line caught up with them, Union soldiers survived by foraging for vegetables and fruit from farms in the district and cutting wood for fuel and makeshift dwellings. Their letters home mention a diet of Irish potatoes, sweet potatoes, cucumbers, pumpkins, and other squash varieties.

Finding enough fodder for the 12,000 horses and mules became a never-ending task. Federal troops collected hay in the countryside and made use of local grain mills to meet the demand for foodstuffs. After raiding farms in the area surrounding Little Rock, bluecoats butchered cows, hogs, and fowl, and milled recently harvested grain. To avoid dysentery, they devised a system for drawing potable water from the wells in town rather than drink the river water.[34]

Finally, the Union clothing kits arrived from Helena, along with some hard wheat crackers. The Federal troops spent the late fall months building sturdy wooden barracks on the outskirts of the capital city, complete with stoves and brick chimneys. As they settled down for the winter, the intoxicating spirit of liberation lifted the morale of the cold and hungry soldiers at Little Rock. Despite the constant shortages of critical supplies, Iowans wrote home expressing satisfaction with the war's progress. In the wake of this campaign, hundreds of white and black Arkansans came forward to enlist in the Union Army. The local economy also improved. An upbeat Charles Musser sent a glowing description home to his father on the family farm near Council Bluffs.

Interracial fraternization occurred on several different levels. In the hostile countryside, ex-slaves served as excellent scouts. One Iowa captain hired a former slave as a cook for his company. The captain, in turn, socialized with the African American community and attended a black church service in Little Rock conducted by a former slave.[35]

These and other examples of interracial cooperation reflected the Iowans' new willingness to fight alongside black soldiers. Four regiments of black Arkansans were organized in 1863, and by the end of the war a total of 5,526 black Arkansans served in the Union Army. When the president appointed a white unionist to serve as governor in the spring of 1864, a battalion of African American soldiers escorted him to the inauguration podium in Little Rock.[36]

Miles away from the state capital city, soldiers of both races spent the remainder of 1863 enduring the day-to-day drudgery of counter-insurgency warfare. Historians Gregory Urwin and Cathy Kunzinger Urwin point out the far-reaching impact of the work performed off the battlefield and the contributions made by ordinary Union troops in transforming Arkansas into a Union state free from the oppression of slaveowners. By vigorously policing suspect neighborhoods, the 33rd Iowa Regiment "applied the sustained pressure that did as much in breaking the South's will to resist as the war's big battles."[37]

The Resolution of the Sanitary Commission Dispute

The year 1863 ended on a bittersweet note for Annie Wittenmyer. Shortly before Thanksgiving, the state installed a new governing board to oversee sanitary commission activities in Iowa. The all-male board established in 1861 no longer operated. However, Wittenmyer lost her bid to become a board member and executive officer. Her allies not only failed to gain access to the new governing board, but a majority of the newly appointed board members endorsed the plan to merge with the U.S. Sanitary Commission (USSC).

The setback came as a shock to Wittenmyer supporters, who six weeks earlier had nominated their heroine to preside over all sanitary affairs in the state. But as of late November, she no longer controlled sanitation policy. To her credit, she did not immediately leave her position as agent for the IASC despite the sudden turn of events. However, by mid-1864, she reluctantly resigned her IASC agency commission and joined the U.S. Christian Commission (CC).

The merger issue remained contentious for as long as it did because of the highly polarized environment. Two sanitation conventions met during the fall of 1863, the first in Muscatine in October and the second in Des Moines in November. Wittenmyer supporters chose the former city because it was a town where local LSAS leaders backed the Keokuk system of routing goods through St. Louis rather than Chicago. Flyers announcing the "Loyal Women's Convention" attracted more than 250 women, 90 percent of them Wittenmyer supporters.

Their decision in Muscatine to choose Wittenmyer as their president energized their opponents to convene a second convention in short order. Held in Des Moines, a location more difficult to reach than Muscatine for most Iowa residents, the November convention attracted a majority of women who favored the Chicago plan—that is, a merger with the USSC.

The debate at both convention sites over the proposed merger with the USSC aroused strong passions. One promerger delegate argued that the Chicago plan would "save our people much labor and perhaps [avoid the] loss of some of their sanitary supplies." A Wittenmyer delegate who spoke out in favor of an independent state organization pointed to the prior achievements of Iowa women who supported the status quo. "Illinois should not meddle with us, especially when it is a well known fact that Illinois tried to rob Iowa soldiers of the honors won on battle-fields," exclaimed the delegate.[38]

When the male secretary of the Iowa commission rose to speak at the Muscatine convention, some of the women delegates moved to deny him the podium since he did not have voting rights. Wittenmyer, rather than preclude him from speaking on procedural grounds, moved that the secretary be permitted to respond but reserved the right to give the first reply. After the chairman explained that his "engagements" with the USSC compelled him to reject Wittenmyer's argument, she spoke up. According to the convention minutes, she "earnestly appealed to him in the name of God and humanity, to lay aside all personal feeling and unite in a State Organization that would consolidate our sanitary interests, and prevent further confusion."[39]

One month later at the Des Moines convention, Senator Harlan moderated the debate. Closely affiliated with the USSC, he spoke of remaining neutral, but everyone in attendance knew which side he stood on. "The morning session was somewhat spicy," wrote one Chicago journalist in attendance, with "rival parties throwing out scouts and sustaining picket lines to find the position of the enemy and guard against attack."[40]

Mary Livermore, an Illinois USSC agent, traveled all the way from Chicago to Des Moines to advocate on behalf of the merger with her organization. When Mrs. Harlan proposed replacing the 1861 constitution of the state sanitary commission with a new system, Wittenmyer delegates opposed the proposal, arguing that they had already enacted a new constitution at the Muscatine conference one month previously.

Wittenmyer's presence in Des Moines tended to polarize the discussion. In the middle of the debate, one delegate rose to describe her as a "noble daughter" who "has vindicated by her conduct the right of [a] woman to live, and labor, and suffer in her country's cause."[41]

Another Wittenmyer ally rose to defend the right of women to participate in sanitary work. "If your house is on fire, your children in danger, do you stop to ask whether a man's or a woman's hand passed the bucket of water?" Invoking the Christian Bible, the advocate pointed out that "the Great Jehovah himself has given his sanction to woman's work." She continued, "We are glad that Iowa has daughters as well as sons in this war ... We delight in her noble daughters who have not hesitated to leave their quiet peaceful homes for the harrowing scenes and exhausting cares of the hospital."[42]

When the debate finally ended in Des Moines, a majority of the delegates voted to ratify a new constitution for the state sanitary commission. They acknowledged the critical role women had played in supplying the troops, and in lieu of an all-male board, conciliators chose a mixed board, including women as well as men. The new constitution did not preclude Wittenmyer from taking the helm as long as she could collect a majority of votes. In the final count, however, a majority of delegates selected a state judge from Davenport as president and nominated a woman associated with the anti-Wittenmyer faction to the governing board. Although she remained an IASC agent, she now had to answer to the governing board. Not only had Wittenmyer failed to earn enough votes to gain a seat on the commission board, but one of the women selected for the board had opposed her in the contest for president at Muscatine six weeks earlier.

Compounding this defeat, delegates voted to locate the commission headquarters in Davenport, the only Iowa port with a direct rail link to

Chicago. As this decision hinted, board members would ultimately resolve the distribution issue in favor of the USSC merger. Although Wittenmyer did not abandon her opposition to the USSC merger, she did agree to transfer the Muscatine convention's authority to the new commission.[43]

The outcome of the Des Moines convention, as disappointing as it was for Wittenmyer, did not discourage her from continuing to assist the state's soldiers. In January 1864, the legislature invited her to speak in Des Moines on behalf of the proposed state orphans' home. She spoke for two hours and received a thunderous ovation.

Wittenmyer's continued opposition to the USSC merger, however, precipitated political retribution. In February 1864, a group of anti-Wittenmyer legislators in Des Moines proposed amending the 1862 statute in order to remove her name as one of Iowa's two official sanitary agents. The anti-Wittenmyer bill never came to a vote, in part because dozens of local LSAS chapters flooded the legislature with petitions on her behalf. The petition sent from Muscatine contained more than 300 signatures.

Despite this show of support, in June, a few weeks after the state convention approved routing supplies exclusively through Chicago, Wittenmyer resigned as a state agent and joined the Christian Commission. The CC agreed to promote her hospital diet kitchen plan, and Wittenmyer spent the final twelve months of the war managing the CC's diet kitchens from its headquarters in Louisville, Kentucky.[44]

The Gubernatorial Election of 1863

Partisan politics did not shape the debate for govenor within the state sanitary commission. The anti-USSC faction and the pro-USSC faction each endorsed Republican candidates for office. In fact, Wittenmyer had appealed to patriotism in her bid to establish a female-led organization. The Muscatine Loyal Women's Convention had taken place the weekend before state elections in mid-October. Inside the meeting hall, Wittenmyer's allies rallied for prowar Union candidates while promoting the independence of local LSAS chapters.

But partisanship persisted elsewhere. Nearly 140,000 white males went to the polls that month to select Samuel Kirkwood's successor. When the governor declined to run for a third term, Iowa Democrats and

Republicans each selected an army officer to head their ticket. War Democrat James M. Tuttle outranked William M. Stone, the Republican candidate, but continuous allegations of the disloyalty of Tuttle's party plagued the Democrat's chances from the beginning of the campaign. In the army camps down south, 85 percent of Iowa soldiers eligible to vote would stand in line for the Republican candidate for governor.

During the summer of 1863, state Democrats approved a party platform that opposed the Emancipation Proclamation and advocated a peace convention. The convention's demand for peaceful reconciliation offended Democratic soldiers, independent soldiers, and Republican soldiers alike. As the political dialogue in the army camps devolved into polarized notions of patriots and traitors, loyalty came to mean Republicanism and the endorsement of emancipation.

General Tuttle defied his party's platform and approved emancipation as a necessary war measure. But the Democratic candidate still collected only 15 percent of all ballots cast by soldiers in uniform. "Bully for Iowa," Charles Musser wrote home, "Copperheadism is about 'played out' in our State." The 29th Infantry voted for Stone over Tuttle, 360 to 77. Musser, who was on picket duty when the state election results arrived, heard a shout "sweep the field like an avalanche from the mountainside" and observed his comrades express their "patriotic feelings" for a considerable period of time.[45]

The army voting results did not assure Republican control of the governor's chair. Back in the Hawkeye state, war Democrats and peace Democrats cast their ballots for Tuttle, and the war hero's prospects appeared fairly bright, at least initially. Lincoln's Emancipation Proclamation had not caused the grand uprising of slaves that many had predicted. However, the increasing presence of former Missouri slaves in Iowa seemed to confirm Democratic claims that a flood of former slaves was about to descend upon the state. The prospect of forced enlistment—real conscription, not just a threat—also worried conservative voters.

Following a dirty campaign marked by highly inflammatory rhetoric, 10,000 more voters turned out for the 1863 gubernatorial election than had cast a ballot in the 1860 Lincoln-Douglas presidential contest.[46] Across the state, the Republican gubernatorial candidate, Stone, garnered 56.4 percent of all civilian votes.

It was not all about support for the Republican Party. Intra-party turmoil contributed to Tuttle's problems at the polls, as 5,000 peace Democrats deliberately refused to vote for him. Even more impressive than Stone's margin of victory was the trickle-down effect on the fall 1863 legislative elections. In the southern interior districts, voters selected Republican legislators in all but one county, Van Buren. When the General Assembly met in January 1864, the party of Lincoln controlled an astonishing 41 of 45 seats in the Senate and 89 of 95 seats in the House. One antiwar Democrat described his party as "powerless and dead" in Iowa.[47]

Prowar Iowans inspired by Colonel Stone's election expected that the war would end in 1864. In anticipation of a swift Confederate surrender, a unified General Assembly funded several new projects, including an asylum for war orphans. Annie Wittenmyer and her alliance of women leaders rejoiced at the legislators' contribution. Unfortunately, the celebration was premature. Rather than surrender in 1864, Confederate military leaders renewed their commitment to independence. Iowans would have to wait another year to find out how many orphans would need to be cared for when the war finally ended.

CHAPTER NINE

1864: A Heightened Level of Violence

To the surprise of many Iowans, the war did not end in 1864. Instead of peace breaking out, the intensity of the violence escalated in nearly every military theater. In the New West, insurgent activity spiraled out of control during the summer. The social order in Missouri disintegrated further as guerrilla bands renewed raids on Union households. General Price's Rebel cavalry entered southeastern Missouri from Arkansas intent on capturing St. Louis. With no Union soldiers able to intervene, Price's force sped toward the Missouri River.

For the residents of Iowa, the distinction between home front and war front blurred in 1864. After Confederate horsemen invaded Missouri, Iowans feared the marauders would strike into the Hawkeye state. In Iowa's southernmost counties, adult men not serving in the army hastily formed militia groups.

Other factors also blurred the line. As the three-year enlistment periods reached expiration, thousands of soldiers recruited in 1861 returned home to Iowa, some temporarily and some permanently. While large groups of soldiers circulated between home and camp, more civilians ventured south to observe the army camps and work in hospitals. In December 1863, a new facility to house Rebel prisoners of war opened its doors on the Federally owned portion of Rock Island near Davenport. Dozens of local men applied for guard work at the Rock Island prison, and hundreds more volunteered to garrison Federal staging areas farther south.[1]

On the front lines, Confederate resilience challenged the psychological endurance of Union soldiers who had thought the war was nearly won. The military campaigns that year stood out as among the most physically demanding of the war. In northwestern Georgia, Union soldiers experienced three months of continuous warfare during the sultry summer months. Trench warfare, a different style of fighting, tested the mettle of the citizen-soldiers, as did the weather conditions. The combination of heat, insects, and mud drove many soldiers to the brink of exhaustion.

"It rains every day terrible rains," wrote Cyrus Carpenter to his wife on June 21, "and 50,000 men have to lie right in the trenches. If they stick their heads up six inches they will be shot off." He noted, "Yesterday, fully one half of the men were lying in the mud and water in some instances their whole body submerged and had been so for hours."[2]

Carpenter had finally married his sweetheart in Fort Dodge just before the Georgia campaign. After the ceremony, he hurried back to join General Sherman. The combat he observed that year would be the most horrific to date. One lieutenant in the Old Iowa Brigade stationed near Atlanta described the carnage to his father. "I have never seen dead men lay so thick since the War began as they did on the 22nd and 28th days of July" on the battlefields near Atlanta. "In many places they lay in piles. In burying them we put as many as 40 of them in one grave."[3]

After Atlanta fell into Union hands, Confederate commanders further intensified the violence by threatening to massacre Union prisoners. When Rebel general John B. Hood surrounded a Georgia town defended by a single regiment of white Iowans in October, he sent a note to the colonel demanding "an immediate and unconditional surrender of the post and garrison under your command." He promised, "should this be acceded to, all white officers and soldiers will be paroled within a few days. If the place is carried by assault, no prisoners will be taken."[4] Rebel threats against white Union soldiers rarely resulted in the mass execution of prisoners, but African American prisoners were routinely executed.

Iowans at home and in the army responded in constructive ways to the challenges set before them. Tens of thousands of ordinary taxpayers facilitated new enlistments by paying bounties to recruits and financially supporting their families. In some communities, employers continued paying wages to the families of employees who enlisted. In part because of support back home, thousands more Iowans signed up for three years of service, and a majority of the 1861 recruits reenlisted. The veterans of 1861 served as role models to the newly enlisted soldiers during the fall campaigns.

In November 1864, as winter approached, fifteen regiments of Iowa infantry marched three hundred miles with General Sherman to the

Atlantic Ocean, relying entirely on the countryside for their food. The list of Iowans who marched to the sea included Will Turner (Annie Wittenmyer's brother), Cyrus Carpenter, and Stephen Stevens (the younger brother of Ben Stevens).

Abner Dunham's regiment finished out the year in high fashion at Nashville after marching hundreds of miles through Mississippi and Tennessee. "I wish you could be here to see perhaps the most beautiful sight you ever saw," he wrote home on the eve of the Nashville battle. "Every hill and vale is lighted up by the camp fires . . . Our batteries have opened again and fairly make the earth quake.[5] Meanwhile, in Louisiana, Ben Stevens captained his company of African American soldiers during much of 1864. Charles Musser spent the entire year in Arkansas along with many other Union soldiers, white and black.

The Red River Campaign

The bulk of Iowa regiments not in Georgia deployed in Arkansas and Louisiana in 1864. That spring, President Lincoln's overambitious campaign to invade Texas exacted a heavy toll on the Hawkeye state. More than 4,000 Iowa soldiers participated in the Red River campaign, either in the group marching northwest from Baton Rouge under General Nathaniel Banks or in the group marching south from Little Rock under General Frederick Steele. Lincoln intended for the two forces to combine near Shreveport, Louisiana, at which point they were expected to strike west along the Red River on a joint expedition into Texas. The rendezvous never took place, leaving each expedition exposed to the elements and to hundreds of mounted Confederate soldiers.

Lincoln's expedition into the semi-wilderness nearly came to a disastrous conclusion. Notwithstanding the substantial commitment of resources by the War Department, Banks was fortunate to return to Baton Rouge with the bulk of his army and navy intact. Defeated by Confederate forces in two battles, he retreated south before Steele's Union troops, marching south from Little Rock, had reached the Louisiana-Arkansas border. When the Rebel army commander sensed an opportunity to bag Steele's entire army before it could make its way back to Little Rock, the combat focus shifted from Louisiana to Arkansas.

One of the Iowans penned up in the town of Camden in south-central Arkansas was Charles Musser. He and his Iowa colleagues spent a miserable month nearly surrounded by a larger Rebel army. Although they managed to avoid capture at Camden, they trudged one hundred miles through the rain and mud with virtually no food, back to the security of Little Rock.

All told, ten Iowa infantry regiments participated in the Red River campaign, four under Steele and six under Banks. Soldiers from Pottawattamie County (including Musser's 29th Iowa) and Mahaska County (the 33rd Iowa and 40th Iowa) marched south with Steele while volunteers from Delaware, Muscatine, and Webster counties marched north with Banks toward the rendezvous point of Shreveport.

Historian Michael Forsyth assigns credit for the salvation of General Banks's army to General Steele and his 10,000 bluecoats in Arkansas. Had the Confederates continued to pursue Banks downstream, Forsyth argues, a complete Union catastrophe might have occurred. Instead, Confederate commander Kirby Smith became bogged down near Camden after heading north to intercept Steele. Rather than retreat to Little Rock at his first opportunity, the Union commander chose to fortify Camden. Instead of returning to Louisiana and catching Banks in a vulnerable position, Rebel general Smith kept his entire force in Arkansas, intent on destroying Steele, but in the end most of the Union soldiers made it back to Little Rock.[6]

When Smith's four divisions of Texans and Louisianans joined Sterling Price's two divisions of Arkansans and Missourians near Camden, the Confederates realized a significant advantage in numbers. With 14,000 Rebel infantry and cavalry on hand, Union control of central Arkansas hung in the balance. English-speaking white troops, German-speaking troops, and black troops made up Steele's modest force, and the Rebels' aggressiveness tested the bluecoats' ability to work collectively. As Union supplies dwindled, the Confederate threat challenged their resourcefulness.

Rather than surrender, the Union troops inflicted a severe drubbing on Smith's Rebels at Jenkins' Ferry on the road back to Little Rock. The Union victory at the ferry, where Union engineers installed a makeshift pontoon bridge, came despite the Rebels' numerical advantage. When the pursuers launched their first assault, nearly half of Steele's army had already crossed the swollen Saline River. The Union infantry guarding the ferry cooperated to beat back the charging Texans, Arkansans, and Missourians, inflicting more than 1,000 Rebel casualties and ensuring their safe return to Little Rock.

The Battle of Jenkins' Ferry stands out as one of the bloodiest encounters of the war. Four thousand bluecoats stood between the Rebels and the lifeline of the pontoon bridge, nine infantry regiments in all. The rear guard included three Iowa regiments (the 29th, 33rd, and 40th), three German regiments from Wisconsin and Illinois, an Indiana regiment, a black regiment organized in Kansas, and an all-white regiment of Arkansas unionists.

Fortunately for Steele, the topography of the river valley created obstacles for the attacking graybacks. Charles Musser, along with his comrades in the 29th Iowa, stood in line near the bridge when the attack began. "So heavy was the musketry that we could not hear one another speak at four feet distance," he wrote afterward. "The roar of the battle was awful . . . Charge after charge was made on both sides in gallant style, and the ground was strewn with dead, wounded, and dying." But the Union troops did not give up. "We drove the enemy about half mile off the field and held our ground until we had orders to cross the [Saline] River, for it was rising very fast and would soon cover the [pontoon] bridge. When we got to it, it was covered two feet on one side with water."[7]

Colonel Thomas Hart Benton, the commander of the 29th Iowa, "proved himself as cool and brave as a lion," recalled the surgeon of the regiment. "His roan horse was shot under him. He dismounted, cool as a cucumber, and had the saddle and bridle removed and sent to the rear. The enemy, finding our line as immovable as a rock, brought up two pieces of artillery and opened at two or three hundred yards." Samuel Rice, the brigade commander, "intimated that he wanted that battery," related the surgeon. "Colonel Benton waved his sword and on went the boys with a yell . . . In ten minutes the struggle was over and the guns were hauled within our lines by about one hundred men detailed for that purpose."[8]

From start to finish, the battle lasted five hours. To Charles Musser, it seemed like eight, "the hardest fighting ever done in Arkansas," he wrote. Despite the intensity of the combat, the 29th Iowa's surgeon noticed only one soldier skulking. The volunteer soldiers "forgot cold, hunger and wet," noted the surgeon. Several of the wounded men who had withdrawn from the firing line to seek medical treatment eagerly returned to the battle after having their wounds dressed.[9]

Because the Iowans performed much of the dirty work at Jenkins' Ferry, the casualty lists saddened hundreds of families in Mahaska and Pottawattamie counties. Musser's regiment lost 117 killed, wounded, or captured, more than one-quarter of those engaged. The greatest single loss was Samuel Rice. Several weeks after the battle, the Oskaloosa lawyer died from an infected foot wound he sustained during the battle. His loss, after he had seemed to be everywhere on the Union defense line, was mourned by many soldiers in Steele's army. Rice, wrote Charles Musser, "is one of the bravest men I ever saw."[10]

The soldiers who survived the Camden expedition did not sense victory upon returning to Little Rock. Despite their triumph over bad weather, hunger, and a ferocious enemy pursuit, the Red River campaign was not to their taste. They had not volunteered to fight in 1862 for the purpose of surviving a retreat. Some talked of a "gigantic failure" or even a "terrible defeat." "This spring's campaign," wrote Charles Musser, "has been a disastrous affair for us. We have lost over 2000 men, 8 pieces of artillery, 600 wagons, and 2400 mules besides an immense amount of camp and Garrison Equipage."[11]

In several respects, the failure of the Red River expedition did set back the Union cause in the New West. But the hard work of Steele's men ultimately contributed to the final victory. Historian Michael Forsyth argues that the suffering the men endured did not come in vain, though they failed to realize it at the time. For having diverted Rebel attention away from Banks, "the soldiers and leaders of [Steele's army] deserve great credit as their tiny force had done much to win the Civil War and preserve the Union," argues Forsyth.[12]

New Enlistments, Reenlistments, and Conscription

In the late winter, the War Department demanded an additional levy of 6,000 soldiers from Iowa. Two new cavalry regiments were organized in order to entice new recruits, and once again the state met its quota without having to implement a draft. The list of winter volunteers included young

Stephen Stevens of Oskaloosa, who chose to march in the 15th Iowa, his older brother Ben's original unit.

Reenlistments by soldiers who had volunteered in 1861 contributed to satisfy the Federal quota. Of the two Turner brothers who had joined the 1st Iowa Cavalry in 1861, the oldest reenlisted while the youngest mustered out after completing the three-year term of service. In Company A of the 2nd Iowa Infantry, twenty-one of the forty-nine Lee County men still alive and in uniform in 1864 elected to reenlist as their anniversary date approached.

Reenlistment rates varied from unit to unit. In Abner Dunham's company of the 12th Iowa, twenty-five of the thirty-two men still in uniform reenlisted despite the high number of casualties their unit had suffered. "Excitement here runs high in regard to re-enlisting," wrote Abner from Tennessee in December 1863. The twenty-four-year-old initially hesitated because his parents in Delaware County were urging him to return home following the expiration of the three-year term. Despite his parent's wishes, Abner reenrolled.

The Old Iowa Brigade, which included Muscatine, Keokuk, and Oskaloosa troops, also achieved a high rate of reenlistment. Union general James B. McPherson's personal appeal resonated with the soldiers in the 11th, 13th, 15th, and 16th regiments, most of whom opted for the thirty-day furlough granted to early reenlistees. The Hawkeyes took pride in achieving the designation of "veteran company," "veteran regiment," and "veteran brigade."[13]

Iowa recruiters achieved success in other ways in 1864. More than 4,000 Iowans signed up for 100 days' service in the spring. The 100-day units did not reduce the number of three-year recruits required by the War Department, but when Governor Stone offered Federal officials five 100-day units, the gift was not turned down. The 100-day enlistment period appealed to Iowans who were unwilling to commit to three years of service. A number of the soldiers in the 100-day units had signed up in 1861 and received a disability discharge in 1862 or 1863. Three of Iowa's 100-day regiments served in Tennessee and one served in Arkansas, while the fifth unit guarded Confederate prisoners on Rock Island.

But by the fall of 1864, the state had to institute a draft at last. Iowa's all-volunteer army ended when 1,900 unfilled three-year positions forced state officials to resort to conscription. In July, the War Department had demanded a total of 10,000 new three-year commitments, 8,100 of which were filled by volunteers.

Considering the state's high volunteer rate during the three previous years, it was remarkable that so many additional Iowans enlisted voluntarily. Iowa might have met the 10,000-volunteer goal had Congress not reduced the Federal bounty from $300 to $100. Ironically, in view of the majority of white Iowans who had opposed African American migration into the state, the lack of ex-slaves in the state further handicapped state officials. In 1863, 440 African American enlistments had contributed to meet the state's Federal quota, but in 1864 very few black men of military age resided in the state.[14]

By late summer 1864, Iowa state officials instructed local administrators to begin the process of registering men of military age. Other Western states, including Missouri and Wisconsin, had already instituted a draft, with mixed results. In Missouri, the fighting quality of the draftees proved far inferior to that of the old volunteer units. Veterans dubbed one conscript unit the "Fortieth Misery" regiment.[15]

In Iowa, the renewed draft threat compelled a substantial number of whites to enlist. So did a new state law requiring every male of military age to serve in a local home guard company if he did not enlist for Federal service. Under state rules, conscription took place only in those districts that failed to satisfy the per capita figure calculated by state and local officials.

One county that failed to meet its quota was Mahaska. As the deadline approached, Mahaska, the home of the Stevens family, came up forty-five men short. Compared to other noncompliant districts, the forty-five-man deficit in Mahaska was relatively modest. Still, the shortfall necessitated implementing a system of posting the names of county men eligible for the draft, selecting names at random, and seeking out the individuals.

Given Iowa's rural makeup and tradition of local control, one might have imagined violence erupting and neighbor-on-neighbor vandalism spiraling out of control. Recent research on draft resistance in Pennsylvania and Indiana reveals the ease with which draft resisters could disrupt and even shut down the conscription process. In some neighborhoods on the East Coast, law and order completely broke down. Death and destruction came to New York City, the Pennsylvania coalfields, and farming communities from central Pennsylvania to Indiana.[16]

Remarkably, every district in the Hawkeye state met its 1864 quota without violence. The civilized implementation of the draft represented a defining moment in Iowa's young history. Despite a tradition of vigilante justice in the state,[17] county officials completed the militia rolls with a minimum of resistance. In Mahaska, officials tracked down every one of the forty-five men selected at random and notified them of their legal obligation to report to training camp by the deadline or go to jail. Once all forty-five men enrolled, county officials proceeded to organize militia units in each township with the men not selected for the draft.

Every county in Iowa completed the militia enrollment process successfully. The collective action of township leaders resulted in the organization of 917 home guard companies across the state in 1864, a total of 86,600 men. As winter neared, almost every Iowa male of military age was either deployed in the South or drilling with his neighbors in compulsory militia exercises.[18]

Peace Democrats deserve a fair share of the credit for the nonviolent resolution of the conscription crisis. Although they strenuously opposed conscription and other federal policies they saw as overzealous and tyrannical, party members in southern Iowa declined to organize a mass resistance to the draft in 1864. They remained unionists at heart—unionists with a fundamentally different opinion about how to reunite the country, but unionists nonetheless.

In Dubuque, a district that peace Democrats controlled, war opponents in charge of the county government went to considerable lengths to recruit volunteers from other counties. A $400 bounty brought in enough nonresidents so that no conscription was necessary. Prompt action by Dubuque peace Democrats thus spared the state the ordeal of having to administer a draft in this heavily Irish city, which had consistently come up short in previous enlistment drives. "The final conflagration never came," notes historian Russ Johnson. "Beyond some isolated brawls, no war-related violence occurred in the city during the war." So many volunteers streamed to high-bounty districts like Dubuque that the low-bounty districts, such as Mahaska County, struggled to meet their quotas.[19]

The Atlanta Campaign

Historians cite the Atlanta campaign as the key event preceding Lincoln's reelection.[20] With Union forces halted in Virginia, many Americans at the time believed that only the capture of Atlanta could rescue the Lincoln administration from failing at the polls. The capture was achieved on September 1, thanks in large part to the performance of the Western soldiers who had captured Vicksburg the year before. In the climactic battle near Atlanta on July 22, the Vicksburg veterans defended Bald Hill against two-thirds of the Rebel army. A few days later, General Sherman maneuvered the Vicksburg veterans, who represented one-quarter of Union forces, to the west of Atlanta, where they repelled another ferocious Rebel charge near Ezra Church. The weeks ahead witnessed several more attempts by Sherman to encircle Atlanta from the west. By late August, ten weeks before the Federal election date, Confederates prepared to abandon the critical railroad junction.

The 10,000 Iowans deployed to Georgia in the spring of 1864 included the Old Iowa Brigade, Williamson's Iowa Brigade, and two of the Hornet's Nest regiments. In terms of their war experience, the Iowans represented a mix of veteran and green troops, but they included not a single conscript. Refitted in the spring of 1864, Iowa's veterans sported new shoes, pants, and jackets. Most Iowa regiments in Sherman's army had organized in 1861, so the timing of the original enlistments determined the proportion of veterans in each unit. The 11th Iowa, formed late in 1861, included every original member who had not yet been killed or discharged, plus a modest number of volunteers who had enrolled after 1862. In contrast, the 2nd Iowa Infantry, organized shortly after Fort Sumter, contained more post-1862 volunteers than reenlisted veterans.

The density of soldiers in the staging area around Chattanooga complicated the task of commissary officers like Cyrus Carpenter. Still working under General Grenville Dodge, he found his work in 1864 more challenging than ever. Dodge's troops, now deployed to Georgia, had a chance to reengage the enemy after a year of policing the byways of Tennessee. Dodge commanded several Iowa infantry regiments (including the 2nd and 7th) in the Atlanta campaign. The Old Iowa Brigade and Williamson's Brigade participated under different corps commanders. The soldiers in the 11th Iowa (part of the Old Iowa Brigade) spent the late winter months foraging through the hinterlands of Mississippi before trudging through the hilly country in northern Alabama on their way to join Sherman. "The roads are very rough and stony, making it hard on our feet," noted one member of the 11th Iowa.[21]

Their task became even more arduous on May 11, when members of the regiment were assigned to herd 1,000 cattle while on the march. "We had a hard day's march, having to cross a large swamp, wade four creeks, and cross one river twice," wrote one soldier, "yet we covered fourteen miles with the cattle, and got into bivouac near Clarenceville at 9:00 p.m." On June 8, the 11th Iowa met up with their comrades in the Old Iowa Brigade north of Atlanta.[22]

Carpenter, who won promotion to lieutenant colonel that spring, attributed much of Sherman's success to the self-reliant habits of his Western veterans. "The mode of living in camp," he remarked in a letter, "has constantly improved since the first doubtful campaigns of this great struggle." The quartermaster described how soldiers found ways to make themselves comfortable when tents and other equipment did not reach the front. They also learned how to stay healthy. Rather than eat raw meat and drink "sickish warm water," savvy veterans split apart old canteens and boiled water in one part while using the other as a frying pan. A soldier now has "sufficient experience to cook his food until done and to avail himself of everything that comes in his way that will protect his health and add to his comforts."[23]

In battle, soldiers no longer favored charging headlong "against the enemy buried behind breastworks," wrote Carpenter. Rather than charge out in the open, the soldier "is always ready to dig his way to the front," he noted. "Now soldiers will frequently carry a spade along with them, on all their marches, besides their other plunder, and will refuse even to allow the quartermaster to haul it for them."[24]

The Vicksburg veterans brought their poise to the Atlanta campaign in addition to their survival skills. Since they had never lost a campaign, these Western soldiers possessed a supreme level of confidence in their ability to whip the Confederacy's best soldiers in battle. Their self-assurance and skills enabled them "to continue fighting in circumstances which they could reasonably have been expected to surrender or flee," notes historian Steven Woodworth.[25]

The mental fortitude of the Vicksburg veterans proved invaluable on July 22, during the successful Union defense of Bald Hill. Several historians point to this battle as the most significant fight of the entire Atlanta campaign. It happened to be the campaign's bloodiest day. But it was not just the high number of Rebel casualties that made this day critical to the outcome of the war. Had the Vicksburg veterans defending Bald Hill not stood firm following an all-night surprise flanking maneuver by the Confederates, the Rebels' strategy would have produced "the most spectacular [Rebel] victory of the war," argues historian Albert Castel. Union general McPherson's death during the first hour of the battle, near the Old Iowa Brigade, presented the Confederates with a golden opportunity to catch the Vicksburg veterans at a vulnerable moment as they grieved the sudden loss of their commander.[26]

When July 22 dawned, unsuspecting Union troops occupied a line of trenches near Bald Hill, several miles east of Atlanta. The trench line faced toward the city in anticipation of a Rebel assault force striking from the railroad center. The southern end of the Union trench line curved back in the shape of a fishhook, three-quarters of a mile southeast of Bald Hill. The hill anchored the left flank of the Union army, but south and east of the fishhook gaps existed in the Union line (fig. 11).

It was these gaps that the 17,000 night-marching Rebels sought to exploit. When shots sounded around noon at the fishhook, Confederate general John B. Hood's best shock troops charged straight for the Old Iowa Brigade, the unit assigned to defend the trenches in the fishhook. Approximately one mile east, two more divisions of Rebels burst out of the woods and attacked three Union brigades commanded by Grenville Dodge. For Sherman's entire force to avoid a total collapse, the citizen-soldiers would have to withstand the series of multidirectional attacks without a West Point general to lead them.[27]

Elliott Rice of Oskaloosa commanded the first of Dodge's three brigades to come under Rebel fire. His men had already endured three months of intensive fighting, "the hardest campaign that we have yet experienced," wrote one Iowa soldier to his wife. In May, Rice's soldiers had led a river crossing, and in June they fought off Rebels attacking through dense woods during the night. In the intervals between the bloody clashes, the Iowans had marched several hundred miles under the hot sun, erected numerous log breastworks, and slogged through muddy roads. In June,

THE BATTLE OF ATLANTA
July 22, 1864   12:30 p.m.

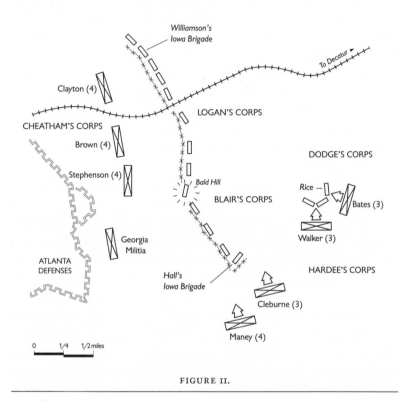

FIGURE II.

they had tolerated eight straight days of rainy weather without tents while constantly exposed to mosquitoes and swarming insects. On July 22, they would have to defend a wooded area without the benefit of defensive fortifications because the Rebel attack caught them marching in an open area to the Union rear. Despite being attacked unexpectedly, they prepared to stop Hood's Rebels cold in their tracks before the surprise flank attack could gain momentum.[28]

The July 22 battle began well for the Union cause as Rice's soldiers repelled three understrength Rebel brigades. Despite the Confederate advantage in numbers and surprise, Rice utilized the natural terrain as best he could when positioning the 2nd Iowa, 7th Iowa, an Indiana regiment, and one Illinois regiment. With no time to prepare trench lines, the Union soldiers fought standing upright, exposed to enemy fire, without dirt fortifications to protect them. The veterans had grown accustomed to fighting behind earthworks, but their exposure to enemy bullets did not faze them as they calmly fired round after round at the Rebels advancing out of the woods.

The bloody repulse effectively knocked one entire Rebel division out of action for the remainder of the day and allowed Dodge's two remaining brigades to concentrate their energy on beating back a second Rebel division. Rice, the brother of Samuel Rice, the hero of the Jenkins' Ferry battle, later wrote that his four regiments stood like "a fence of iron, not a man deserting his colors."[29]

Thanks in part to Rice's leadership, Dodge's three isolated brigades effectively neutralized two of the four Confederate divisions sent on the all-night flanking movement. The next task was to neutralize the two other Rebel divisions marching north along the Flat Shoals Road, a dirt path close to Bald Hill. The Rebel assault on the hill lasted a full eight hours. The spearhead of the Rebel assault fell on the 1,500 soldiers in the Old Iowa Brigade.

The day before the battle, the four Hawkeye regiments had suffered 226 casualties assaulting a line of entrenched Texas sharpshooters north of Bald Hill. Anticipating a Rebel counter-attack after being reassigned to the fish-hook, the vigilant Iowans produced a network of entrenchments designed to withstand attacks from two directions on the morning of July 22.

The Old Iowa Brigade, "one of the best fighting units in the whole Union army," according to Castel, fully expected that more blood would be shed when the sun rose on July 22. They installed wooden obstructions in the form of abatises well in front of their position and placed two cannon from an Illinois artillery battery to shore up the corner of the trench line. Using their axes and hatchets, the Iowans cleared trees fifty yards in front of their trench for maximum fire effectiveness.[30]

Thanks to these efforts, the Rebel attack up the Flat Shoals Road did not catch the Old Iowa Brigade unprepared, but the Union forces soon found themselves under attack from three directions instead of two. Once they realized their predicament, two-thirds of the Iowans followed their regimental commanders and fled west, where they re-formed under the protection of a nearby Union brigade. Having narrowly avoided capture, the surviving Iowans split up into regiments and fought the remainder of the day separated from one another, defending the Union trench line between the fishhook and Bald Hill. When the fourth Rebel division joined the fighting around the hill, the Iowans felt the heat coming from several directions at once.[31]

At this moment, the Iowans in the 15th Regiment occupied a portion of the Union trench line near Bald Hill, about one-quarter mile away from the fishhook. Just as the Iowans prepared to recuperate, they came under attack from opposite directions. Despite the chaos, the Iowans helped to blunt several assault waves and prevent Bald Hill from falling into Rebel hands. By firing in one direction and then turning to meet the attackers coming at them from the opposing direction, the Iowans narrowly avoided capture.

During the brief lulls between the waves of the Rebel assault, the resourceful Iowans ventured forward to retrieve rifles from dead and wounded Confederates, then reloaded the captured rifles in anticipation of the next charge. Through such initiatives, the bluecoats guarding Bald Hill turned back every Rebel assault wave. By the end of the day, the 15th Iowa Regiment had changed positions on the battlefield at least four times and had fired on five different Confederate brigades.

Bullets fired by the 15th Iowa killed or injured hundreds of Rebel soldiers during the course of the afternoon, officers as well as enlisted men. One Arkansas colonel fell dead in front of the 15th Iowa at the fishhook, and in the afternoon's action near Bald Hill, the regiment's haul of prisoners included an Alabama colonel and a lieutenant colonel from Tennessee.[32]

The Muscatine soldiers in the 11th Iowa experienced a different sort of deadly military chaos one-quarter mile away. After Confederates captured the fishhook, a fresh brigade of Tennesseans attempted to advance along the diagonal Union trench line from the fishhook toward Bald Hill. The only Union troops in the area were remnants from the 13th Iowa and 11th Iowa regiments. As the Tennessee bullets flew in several directions at once, the Iowans jumped from one side of the earthworks to the other side seeking shelter. Despite being severely outnumbered, they prevented the Rebels from enveloping a nearby Union brigade that was struggling to defend its ground against a different brigade of Tennesseans.

The several mid-afternoon charges by the Rebels, launched just a few minutes apart, occurred close enough in time to have routed most Civil War troops, notes Woodworth. But on this day, the more numerous Rebels could not "overcome the superb tactical virtuosity" of the Vicksburg veterans. When the Rebels retreated temporarily to the southeast to regroup for another charge, Union leaders formed a new defense line to protect Bald Hill by calling on Dodge to relocate his three Union brigades closer to the hill.[33]

When the last Rebel attack on the hill came at six p.m., Union soldiers faced Rebels charging from two directions, the west and south. Much blood had already been spilled on Bald Hill during the previous thirty-six hours, and in the final daylight hours of July 22, 1,000 more soldiers would be added to the casualty list.[34]

Confederates at no other time during the war fought more desperately than did the soldiers participating in the six p.m. attack on Bald Hill. Several squads of bluecoats from six northwestern states had to fight like tigers to preserve the hill. Union soldiers persevered despite their near exhaustion, lack of reinforcements, and heavy casualties. Nearly all Iowa casualties sustained after six p.m. hit the soldiers in the 11th Iowa, the unit assigned to defend a crude fortification on Bald Hill. Despite incurring nearly a hundred casualties, the 11th Iowa successfully defended the fort in the face of several determined Rebel assaults.

The Union troops fought without reinforcements because General John Logan's soldiers had experienced a crisis of their own near the railroad cut one mile north of the hill during the late afternoon. Rebels marching out from Atlanta along the rail line captured several batteries of Union cannon guarding the railroad cut and then pushed through the breach nearly one-half mile. The task of sealing off the Rebel breakthrough occupied General Logan's total attention.

With the help of Williamson's Iowa Brigade, Union forces counter-attacked, recaptured the cannon, restored the defensive line, and compelled the anxious Rebels to retreat back toward Atlanta. With the Union line north of the Bald Hill once again secure, the Rebels lost their best chance to surround the bluecoats guarding the hill.[35]

When the sun rose the following day, Bald Hill remained in Union hands, but more than one-half of the soldiers in the Old Iowa Brigade were now dead, wounded, or captured. The 15th Iowa, Stephen Stevens's regiment, lost 159 of 380 soldiers in the July 22 fighting, including Stephen, who was captured and taken to Andersonville Prison.[36]

The Iowans' sacrifice did not come in vain. Although the Union position still remained vulnerable, the bleeding Confederate Army had suffered too many casualties to mount another attack. General Patrick Cleburne's formidable Rebel division lost 40 percent of its strength on July 22, including many of its best officers. The same was true for the three other Rebel divisions that had taken part in the nighttime flanking movement.

With his ranks so reduced, General Hood could not "plan a tactical strike with any hope of significant success," historian Gary Ecelbarger points out. Sherman, in turn, came to realize Hood's limitations. With the Confederate commander no longer able to sustain a flanking movement, the capture of Atlanta became a near certainty. When Hood evacuated Atlanta on September 1 rather than face a Union siege, Lincoln's chances for reelection suddenly took on a new life. In New York City, George Templeton Strong, a prominent war bond investor, called Atlanta's capture "the greatest event of the war."[37]

The March through Georgia

Following Hood's decision to strike out north toward Nashville, Sherman elected to divide his army into two groups. In the group that would accompany him to Savannah on the Atlantic coast of Georgia, he placed his most reliable Western troops. No longer able to obtain supplies shipped by railroad, the marchers would have to survive several weeks without extra ammunition or food.

Despite being cut loose from the supply base at Atlanta, the logistical challenge appealed to the frontiersmen-turned-soldiers, who relished the opportunity to display their physical talents and resourcefulness. Iowa's soldiers, like their commanding officer, saw in the hinterlands of Georgia the chance to slide a dagger into the heart of the Confederate States of America. Sherman's maneuver defied conventional military wisdom, but his soldiers were up to the task.

The Georgia campaign was not the first time Iowa soldiers had marched overland beyond their supply line. Nine months before the march on Savannah, Sherman's troops had trekked from Vicksburg to Meridian, Mississippi, near the Alabama border, and back to Vicksburg. Living off the land, thousands of Iowa soldiers endured the journey in splendid style.

On their way out to Meridian, the bluecoats realized the fruits awaiting them in districts not yet exposed to the vandalism of war. The soldiers also realized the strategic advantages of empowering Southern unionists to action. Having bided their time for several years, Southern unionists now stepped forward to assault the Confederate States of America at its power base. In the eyes of Iowa's white soldiers, the mass liberation of white unionists, combined with the mass liberation of African American slaves, inspired them to march even faster.

Seneca Thrall, a doctor assigned to the 13th Regiment of the Old Iowa Brigade, rode through Mississippi with Sherman and left an account of the expedition. Dr. Thrall delighted in the prospect of a southern unionist uprising. "I have seen and conversed with a number of the [white] inhabitants on this trip who are *really* and *truly* union," he wrote. "I have heard the *children* sing union songs composed in the South and they have told me some facts of the manner in which they have been *persecuted*." He noted, "They are *poor, ignorant* creatures and beg us to take them with us."[38]

Many of the white unionists followed the Union legions back to Vicksburg, as did multitudes of former slaves set free by Sherman's incursion. By the time the 13th Iowa returned to Vicksburg, Dr. Thrall estimated that 1,500 to 2,000 ex-slaves trailed the Old Iowa Brigade.

As the Old Iowa Brigade neared Vicksburg and the conclusion of the Meridian campaign, Dr. Thrall proudly boasted of its accomplishments. "We have been out 25 days, have marched 300 miles, and have *not one* man to send forward with the sick or those unable to march." On one day in central Mississippi, the Hawkeyes marched twenty-nine miles to secure a bridgehead. On another occasion, they marched eighteen miles in six hours carrying guns, blankets, sixty rounds of cartridges, and two days' rations.[39]

"Our brigade was selected to send forward because it is considered the best marching brigade in the army," remarked Dr. Thrall. The endurance of the Iowa soldiers "is almost incredible." He added, "For myself, I am about as *dirty* and healthy as the best of them; not an officer in the regt. has a tent or cot, and I do not think there are a dozen tents with the whole army. *All* from Genl. Sherman down are taking it in the rough."[40]

Nine months later in Atlanta, Sherman chose his Vicksburg veterans to lead the March to the Sea. Stamina and resourcefulness would be critical as the 58,000 bluecoats passed through pinewood forests, sand fields, and swampy lowlands without standard army food supplies. Unpredictable weather complicated the topographical challenges, dumping rain and light snow on the dirt paths.

Away from the main roads, small squads of troops foraged with only a modest number of Union cavalry available to protect their flanks. Without artillery support, without reinforcements, and without the opportunity to replenish their ammunition, these isolated units survived by banding together and repelling surprise attacks by mounted Rebels.

Fifteen Hawkeye regiments participated in the March to the Sea, including the Old Iowa Brigade and Williamson's Iowa Brigade. To revitalize the former unit after the bloody fighting at Bald Hill, Sherman assigned an Illinois regiment to join it and appointed William W. Belknap, the colonel of the 15th Iowa, as brigade commander.

Sherman also negotiated a prisoner exchange that set free most of the Iowans captured at the fishhook on July 22. Stephen Stevens of Oskaloosa was one Iowan who survived Andersonville Prison long enough to be exchanged. He returned to the 15th Iowa in time for the march to Savannah.

Cyrus Carpenter and Will Turner also participated. Turner's regiment, the 2nd Iowa Infantry, was now part of John Corse's fourth division of John Logan's XV Corps. Corse, a Burlington merchant who started the war as a major in the 6th Iowa Infantry, had earned promotion to division commander following his brilliant leadership at Allatoona Pass, where one Iowa infantry regiment under his command anchored a defensive line that beat back repeated charges launched by General Hood.

On the march through Georgia, Iowa soldiers maintained supreme confidence in their commander. Carpenter, now managing the logistics for Logan's XV Corps, recognized after the fall of Atlanta that Sherman's "mysterious magnetic influence" had infused "its own enthusiasm into a vast body of men." This army, Carpenter noted, "has perfect confidence in the skill and judgment of its commander."[41]

Despite the difficult terrain and weather conditions, not to mention the constant need to forage for food, the Iowa foot soldiers pressed forward with amazing energy. In December, as Sherman's troops approached the coastline, Corse's division marched at the head of the blue column. Three companies from the 2nd Iowa Infantry crossed a wide river in pontoon boats under heavy fire. The contingent of Hawkeyes from Elliott Rice's brigade established a foothold on the opposite bank and held it long enough for a Missouri engineer battalion to complete a pontoon bridge. To permit the remainder of Rice's brigade to safely cross the river, the Iowans in the advance group expanded the security perimeter, wading through knee-deep swamp water for more than one mile before coming to dry land. Backed by the 7th Iowa Infantry, the 2nd Iowa soldiers at the point of attack overwhelmed a Rebel defensive fortification in their path and seized the nearby railroad.[42]

While walking north up the rail line looking to clear out the last Rebel defenders, Rice's Iowans met up with a line of bluecoats marching toward them. They were members of Williamson's Iowa Brigade who had crossed the river upstream several miles after repairing a fire-damaged bridge with the aid of a canoe.

In Savannah, letters sent home by Iowans gushed enthusiastically over the scale of their success.[43] Jacob Ritner, now a captain in Williamson's Iowa Brigade, described the destruction to his wife back home in Henry County: "We marched on several roads. The army was spread over a strip of country from 40 to 60 miles wide, which was completely cleaned out and ruined. We ate all the hogs, and kept and drove off the cattle. We got hundreds of good horses and mules and Negroes, and did an immense amount of mischief generally. We destroyed the railroad and all its branches from Macon to this point."[44]

Nearly every Iowan who began the march in Atlanta arrived in Savannah winded but alive. Carpenter wore himself out attempting to keep the few supply wagons close to the front columns. Destruction of property, even in the name of military progress, always disheartened him, and he expressed mixed emotions in his letters home.

Turner arrived in Savannah exhausted, both mentally and physically. The army granted Turner's request to be discharged, and Annie Wittenmyer's brother returned to Keokuk to await the return of his sister, who was still hard at work at her Christian Commission office in Louisville. He tried to relax on the Turner family farm while she battled a mountain of hospital administration work. From time to time until the conclusion of the war, she made trips to Union hospitals in eastern Tennessee and on the East Coast.

How long the war would last was anyone's guess in January 1865. Richmond remained in Rebel hands, as did Charleston, Columbia, and Raleigh. Some Union households in Iowa presumed the Confederate States of America would never surrender and called for ending the war with a negotiated resolution. Iowa's soldiers for the most part rejected a negotiated resolution.

Hawkeyes in uniform looked ahead to the year 1865 optimistically. The sacred cause of unionism had driven them to enlist in 1861 or 1862, compelled them to perform at a high level in 1863, and in 1864 inspired them to stay the course. Now they prepared to bring the oldest Southern states to their knees and conclude the holy task of reunion.

In Savannah, Captain Ritner and his colleagues prepared to knock South Carolina out of the war. Notwithstanding rumors of 30,000 Rebels awaiting them there, Ritner expressed supreme confidence in the inevitability of victory. "Have no fears at all for our army, it can't be whipped," the Henry County farmer predicted. "[If] General Sherman thinks we can take Richmond, we can, and will."[45]

CHAPTER TEN

The Radical Legacy

Iowa stood on the brink of a major political revolution in 1865. As the military conflict neared its conclusion, the spirit of victorious unionism sparked a new definition of patriotism among white Union Party members, a definition that included support for black civil rights at home. Radical Republicans in Iowa triumphed in the state legislative elections of 1865, and for years afterward the equal rights momentum continued to define patriotism in the Hawkeye state. By the end of the decade, Iowa's Republican leaders invited Muscatine's Alexander Clark to address their state convention, something unthinkable in 1863. They also selected him to attend the national convention as a representative of Iowa.

The Federal election in 1864 set the stage for the radical transformation of the Hawkeye state. During the late winter, thousands of abolitionists and emancipationists attended their local political caucuses and demanded the nomination of a candidate more radical than Abraham Lincoln. They sought a candidate who favored equal rights legislation in the Deep South. Although the state party and the national party convention renominated Lincoln, Iowans in favor of Federal equal rights legislation refused to concede defeat. Many endorsed the candidate nominated by radical delegates who attended an anti-Lincoln convention in Ohio.

After Lincoln's election, the cause of equal rights in the Deep South won the support of grassroots Republicans. Previously nonradical voters also came to support equal rights in Iowa. The list of converts included Ben Stevens, William Turner, Charles Musser, and Cyrus Carpenter. Sympathy for black civil rights faded in other states, but a majority of Iowa voters in 1868 granted African Americans and other nonwhites equal rights under state law.

Equal rights also received the support of Annie Wittenmyer and other women leaders in Iowa. When she spoke to veterans' groups after the war,

Wittenmyer acknowledged the contributions made by African American soldiers as well as white soldiers. Although she herself could not vote, her actions helped sustain the radical enthusiasm. The groundswell of support became so powerful that the new generation of Iowa radicals took the giant step of embracing black civil rights as a complete package of rights rather than as a voting rights bill only.

Local Caucus Outcomes

Iowa was not predestined to become a radical state in 1864. Most Iowans simply wanted the nation reunited. Those who believed radical legislation would achieve that result demanded that Congress enact radical legislation targeted at the slave states. Iowans who wanted slavery eradicated in the Deep South did not necessarily favor repealing racist state laws at home. Notwithstanding the grassroots support for radical Republican candidates in many neighborhoods, the racist laws in place in the state in 1864 might have remained in place beyond Lincoln's reelection.

Had Iowans alone determined the nominees for president and vice president in 1864, the names Lincoln and McClellan would not have appeared on the respective Republican and Democratic ballots. Iowa peace Democrats who attended the state party convention bitterly opposed General George McClellan, the eventual nominee. Clement Vallandigham of Ohio was one Democratic candidate whose name was bandied about as a candidate to head their party's ticket.[1]

In Republican circles, Iowans frustrated with Lincoln endorsed Salmon Chase, the most radical member of the president's cabinet. When Chase withdrew his name from consideration, some Iowans endorsed John C. Fremont, the favorite of radicals in Missouri, or Horace Greeley, the longtime antislavery newspaper editor in New York City. After a splinter group of radicals held a national convention in May and nominated Fremont for president, the faction of anti-Lincoln Republicans in Iowa rallied around Fremont. They campaigned against Lincoln until Fremont withdrew from the race in early September.[2]

Several issues turned Iowa voters against Lincoln, at least initially. Union military forces in Virginia and Louisiana sustained a series of bloody defeats in the spring of 1864. Household economic challenges added fuel to the intra-party debates. Iowa farmers, many barely able to subsist, groaned under the weight of additional taxes to support the war effort. Conscription added another element of stress to the political tension on the home front. When President Lincoln raised the army enlistment levels in 1864, state officials insisted that families already sponsoring one or more men of military age contribute additional volunteers.

In the army camps down South, support for the president deteriorated in the spring and summer. Before the Union Army's capture of Atlanta, many Hawkeye soldiers feared Lincoln would lose the election. "Abraham is getting very unpopular among the soldiers," wrote a dejected Charles Musser in Little Rock. "I can tell you [that] the politics is awfully mixed in this army ... The Republican Party is split, the Democratic Party is split, the Abolition Party is split. It is a regular conglomeration of all sorts of political opinions, but I believe the Democratic Party will win this time."[3]

Every political faction in Iowa experienced a metamorphosis during the months leading up to the presidential election. The state Democratic Party nearly dissolved into two organizations, with groups of war Democrats holding separate meetings from groups of peace Democrats. Republicans who supported Lincoln, meanwhile, rebranded their organization as the "Union Party" and deliberately sought to nominate ex-Democrats as candidates for office. As the election date approached, many war Democrats deserted their party's candidate even though a war Democrat, George McClellan, had won their party's nomination.

In the end, the Democratic Party did not win the election as Musser had predicted. Republican Party stalwarts reluctantly renominated Lincoln, and following the capture of Atlanta the prospects of a victory for the president's party suddenly appeared bright. Union armies made little military progress between September 1 and November 1, but war supporters in Iowa still turned out for Lincoln in droves. His victory plus a quick succession of postelection military victories galvanized the resolve of Iowans to ensure the death of slavery and the triumph of equal rights legislation, both at home and in the Deep South.

The Threat of Rebel Invasion

The passions aroused by the perceived threat to the Hawkeye state contributed to promote equal rights legislation in Iowa. The killing of innocent civilians in Lawrence, Kansas, by proslavery Missouri guerrillas in 1863 heightened fears that the renegades would launch similar strikes north into Iowa. In the summer of 1864, when Iowans learned that Confederate general Price's cavalry had invaded Missouri from Arkansas, farmers gathered in villages across southern Iowa to perform militia drills. Price's horsemen eventually retreated back to Arkansas without crossing the Iowa border, but the Rebel cavalry did get as far north as Kansas City.

Incursions by small groups of Missouri vigilantes during the fall of 1864 revived fears that a Lawrence-like murder spree was about to take place in Iowa. Guerrillas roaming north of Kansas City crossed the state line and burned down the Fremont County Courthouse in southwestern Iowa. In southeastern Iowa, vigilantes rode into Davis County and kidnapped Union soldiers home on leave. The insurgents failed to disrupt the state's war economy, but the psychological impact of the small raids proved substantial. Governor Stone, rather than calm unsteady nerves, increased the tension by announcing in August that "refugees from Rebel armies, guerrillas, and bushwackers" were migrating into Iowa "every day."[4]

The perceived external threats disturbed Iowa's southern border counties more than any other region in the state. Rumors of fifth column activity by Rebel agents in southern Iowa circulated, and fearful citizens transcribed the rumors and sent them on to state officials in Des Moines as facts. War supporters reported that Sons of Liberty lodges had replaced the Knights of the Golden Circle as the preferred organization of Copperhead dissenters. Republican spies who purportedly attended secret meetings accused the Sons of operating a network of pro-Confederate militia companies.

Governor Stone, rather than question the truthfulness of the rumors, issued statements that confirmed the wildest reports. "On the first day of August," he announced, "there were over 30,000 members of this secret order enrolled in this State, bound together by oaths which, if obeyed, renders every one of them an active traitor to the Union, and an abetter of civil strife in our state."[5]

The perceived danger to the home front transformed the political debate on the eve of the Federal election. Convinced that hundreds of Rebel agents had relocated to southern Iowa, where Sons of Liberty lodges supposedly trained members to take up arms on behalf of the Rebel cause, state administrators issued a series of decrees to discourage suspect militia units from acting independently. Anticipating resistance to his edicts,

Stone threatened that any nonconforming militiamen would be treated as Confederates. "Companies which disregard [my orders] will not be recognized or treated for any purpose as portions of the State militia," the governor proclaimed in September. "If the conflicts which they seem now desirous of inviting be forced upon us . . . there will be no blank cartridges used or shots thrown away."[6]

In hopes of avoiding an all-out battle between rival militia companies, the adjutant general removed several questionable officers who had been elected by unit members. Militia captains and lieutenants not removed by the adjutant general were required to take a public loyalty oath. Officers deemed loyal received orders from Governor Stone to "stop and detain suspected persons, and unless they can give satisfactory account of themselves they must be refused permission to remain in the state."[7]

The Presidential Contest

The fifth column hysteria drew southern Iowa voters to embrace Lincoln. When Democrats attempted to counter Stone's exaggerations, a dirty political environment became even dirtier. The rumors induced marginal voters to stand in the ballot line. About 10,000 more voters turned out in 1864 than had stood in line for the hotly contested race in 1860 between Lincoln and Douglas, adding up to more than 90 percent of all eligible voters in Iowa.

The level of internal distrust rose to its highest point in mid-September, the same time the race for president evolved into a two-way contest between Lincoln and McClellan. John C. Fremont's decision to drop out of the presidential race simplified Republican campaign strategy and improved the Union Party's chances for carrying Iowa's electoral votes. Iowa's Republican leaders had been pursuing a conservative campaign strategy designed to appeal to war Democrats and independent voters rather than radical voters. The end of Fremont's candidacy did not compel the state's Republicans to change course and pursue a more radical plan of action. Rather than talk up black civil rights, party leaders continued to pound the drum of patriotism.

Republican notions of loyalty and treason ultimately persuaded many independents and Democrats to stand in line for Lincoln. By characterizing the draft and other events as home security issues, Governor Stone capitalized on the paranoia that prevailed in many parts of the state. When hundreds of draft-age males in Iowa contemplated moving to the sparsely settled Great Plains to avoid conscription, a majority of state voters supported the governor's efforts to prevent a mass migration. The deaths of two draft officials in Poweshiek County in late September further undermined the cause of McClellan, the Democratic candidate. Independent Iowa voters who perceived the murderers to be Democrat draft dodgers expressed their outrage by standing in line at the polls with the Republican voters.

The ballot count confirmed the wisdom of the conservative Republican strategy. McClellan collected about 50,000 votes in Iowa—6,000 fewer than Douglas in 1860—while Lincoln drew almost 90,000, nearly 20,000 more than he had polled in 1860. In choosing a candidate for the Iowa Supreme Court, Republicans selected C. C. Cole, the attorney who had run for Congress as a Democrat in 1860. Despite Cole's former party affiliation, few longtime Republicans shied away from the war Democrat. Cole received virtually the same number of votes as every other candidate listed on the state Union Party ticket.[8]

But Iowans were not all of one mind. Hubert Wubben's research indicates that voters in Catholic immigrant neighborhoods rejected Republican appeals to patriotism more consistently than did native-born Democratic voters. In Dubuque County, 66 percent of voters backed McClellan. Fortunately for Republicans, counties with a large proportion of U.S. natives showed very different results. The defection of native-born Democrats from their party had a remarkable trickle-down effect on local elections.

William B. Allison, the Republican representative from Dubuque, faced the prospect of defeat if he failed to muster enough votes from native-born Democrats. In the final tally, he carried a majority of ballots in the Dubuque congressional district as a result of crossover votes cast in counties outside of the port city. Radical Republican Josiah Grinnell also benefited from his party's attempts to woo conservative unionists. Despite the preponderance of Douglas Democrats in his district, in the final count the former Underground Railroad stationmaster defeated his Democratic rival by 3,500 votes, 58 percent to 42 percent. In Mahaska County, only four of seventeen townships cast a majority of ballots for Democratic candidates that year.[9]

Ballots cast in other regions of the state followed a similar pattern. Lincoln did not lose a single county he had won in 1860 and added several traditionally Democratic districts to his column. For the first time in presidential election history, Lee County voted against the Democratic nominee. Votes cast by independents and crossover Democrats combined with traditional Republican strength to produce Lincoln majorities in fifty-six of the sixty-two counties that cast 500 or more ballots for president. In the rural southern tier of Iowa, the region where Douglas had drawn so many votes in 1860, the defection of Democrats in 1864 propelled Lincoln to victory in every county but Appanoose. Even without the votes cast by soldiers, Republican candidates would have triumphed among the stay-at-home male adults.

In the army camps, Lincoln earned 91 percent of the ballots cast by Iowa soldiers. The survivors of the Atlanta campaign polled for the administration, as did Iowa soldiers deployed in other states. The president collected overwhelming support from Iowa soldiers stationed in Virginia, Mississippi, Tennessee, Arkansas, Louisiana, and Missouri, and the territories of Dakota, Colorado, and Montana.

While some companies (including Charles Musser's unit) split between McClellan and Lincoln, only the 40th Iowa Infantry cast a majority of its votes for the Democratic challenger. "The soldiers as a class are 'true as steel,'" wrote one pro-Lincoln member of the 22nd Iowa Regiment, "and will show at the coming election that they can fight for their country with *ballots* as valiantly as they do with *bullets*." He went on, "It is absolutely impossible for a *true* soldier to be a copperhead. We *all* hate them, despise them, yes even loathe them *ten thousand times* more than the armed traitors who oppose us in the field."[10]

Compared to states east of the Mississippi River, the level of support for Lincoln was impressive. In the Northeast, the president failed to earn a majority of votes in three states and nearly lost New York and Connecticut. Yet in the Hawkeye state, he secured nearly two-thirds of all ballots cast. Rather than experience a decline in support in Iowa from 1860 to 1864, the president increased his margin of victory from 14,500 to 39,000.

The Emergence of Radical Patriotism

In Washington, the list of congressional bills designed to empower former slaves included the Wade-Davis military bill, the Freedman's Bureau creation act, and an amendment to the U.S. Constitution abolishing slavery (later the Thirteenth Amendment). All three provisions were critical to postwar Reconstruction in the Deep South. After the conclusion of the war, administrators in the Freedmen's Bureau sought to ensure the citizenship rights of recently freed slaves. The Wade-Davis bill established a legal foundation for a Federal military presence in the former Confederate states.

As of mid-1864, these and other radical measures were stalled in Congress. The detractors included some moderate Republican leaders from Iowa. Although the preconvention caucuses at home inspired thousands of radical Republican voters to participate, Iowans elected in 1862 contributed to block Federal legislation aimed at assisting slaves and former slaves.

Iowans in Washington hesitated to back radical measures in part because Republican moderates back home were appealing to war Democrats for their votes. Persuading Democrats to cross the line and join the Republican camp meant downplaying emancipation as a war aim and opposing black civil rights. Within Iowa's six-member delegation, only Representative Grinnell consistently voted with the radical faction in 1864. When he proposed to insert a black voting rights provision into the Wade-Davis bill, his five Iowa colleagues in the U.S. House declined to follow suit. In the U.S. Senate, the new spirit of Western radicalism failed to rub off on Grimes and Harlan. The upper chamber now contained eight radical senators from the New West or Far West, but the two Iowans remained in the moderate faction. Senator Grimes voted against the proposed Freedmen's Bureau when it was first introduced. A less radical version of the Wade-Davis bill eventually passed both houses, with the state's two senators endorsing the final bill, along with four of its six representatives.[11]

Events in the state legislature further discouraged Iowa radicals at home. When radicals proposed granting equal voting rights to black men in Iowa, a majority of Republican legislators refused to do so. The 1864 General Assembly did repeal the 1851 black exclusion law. Legislators also approved a resolution endorsing the Thirteenth Amendment to the U.S. Constitution banning slavery. But black civil rights seemed far out of reach.

Even the emerging women's movement failed to energize moderate Republicans on equality issues. Annie Wittenmyer was one of many women leaders wary of alienating conservative unionists opposed to emancipation. She preferred to avoid racial issues when LSAS leaders met in Muscatine in October 1863. Instead of endorsing black rights, her delegates enacted a series of prowar resolutions that echoed the conservative Iowa Republican Party platform. Not a single African American delegate attended the Muscatine convention in October 1863. The all-white body of female delegates called for restoring the "tender relations of a common brotherhood" among the states and repeated common Republican campaign themes that marginalized the civil rights issues so important to radicals. The word *slavery* was not even mentioned in the stated goals of the Muscatine Loyal Women's Convention.[12]

To the benefit of radicals everywhere, events in Iowa in 1865 transformed the definition of patriotism. The emergence of radical patriotism coincided with General Sherman's march through Georgia and the Carolinas, a triumphant military campaign in which Iowa soldiers played a prominent role. The military campaigns in Arkansas, Louisiana, Mississippi, and Tennessee also contributed to redefine patriotism. When the army veterans returned to Iowa, they brought a new perspective on black civil rights. To their surprise, they encountered many local leaders who had likewise undergone an epiphany.

The military campaigns in the lower Mississippi River basin proved particularly enlightening to racist Iowans. To sustain the war effort, white Iowa soldiers in Arkansas, Louisiana, Mississippi, and Tennessee worked side by side with African American refugees and troops throughout 1864. The Confederate practice of murdering captured black soldiers made an impact on white troops as well as former slaves. Although the policy was not applied to captured white soldiers, the Rebel practice of killing black prisoners aroused the passions of all Union soldiers, white as well as black.

In response, white soldiers from Iowa threatened a "no prisoners" practice of their own. "I say give the Rebels no quarter," wrote Charles Musser from Little Rock on May 11, 1864. "The feeling is the same through out the army in the west," he noted. "*We will retaliate.* No prisoner will ever

FIGURE 12. Soldiers from the 19th Iowa Infantry posing in New Orleans upon their release from a Confederate prison camp in 1864. They were fortunate to survive long enough to be exchanged for a similar number of Rebel prisoners of war released from Union prisons. Many Iowa soldiers died in prison, and the soldiers pictured here endured ten months of captivity. The Confederate practice of killing African American prisoners of war in 1864 compelled Federal officials to refuse to exchange white prisoners. After the war, many Union soldiers demanded that harsh penalties be imposed upon the Confederate administrators responsible for the barbaric condition of prisoner of war camps.
Reprinted by permission of the State Historical Society of Iowa, Des Moines.

be taken by me, and I ask not to be shown any quarter by a prisoner-murdering traitor." Lieutenant William Blain of the 40th Iowa wrote, "It would not surprise me in the least, if this war would ultimately be one of extermination."[13]

African American units seemed to be everywhere as Union armies repelled Confederate offensives in the Mississippi River basin during 1864 and 1865. In Arkansas, Iowa's lone black regiment (now marching as the 60th U.S. Colored Troops) patrolled the eastern region of the state in concert with white units. "Oh, we're the bully soldiers of the First of Iowa," the African Americans called out as they patrolled the Arkansas backwaters. "We can hit a Rebel further than a white man ever saw."[14]

In Little Rock, black units guarded the Arkansas capital along with

Charles Musser's white unit. Abner Dunham, stationed in Mississippi, marched alongside black regiments in pursuit of renegade Rebel cavalry. At the Battle of Nashville, he watched as black troops bravely rushed toward entrenched Confederate infantry. Even though the first wave suffered appalling casualties, more waves of black troops continued the charge. In Vicksburg, Ben Stevens and his black regiment, the 48th U.S. Colored Troops, shared garrison duties with white regiments in the vicinity.

The March through the Carolinas

General Sherman's capture of Savannah, Columbia, and Raleigh influenced postwar race relations back in Iowa. Fifteen Iowa regiments accompanied him through the Carolinas, and the nature of the overland campaign brought Iowans in close contact with slaves in the cradle of the Confederacy. During the three-month campaign, the jubilant reaction of freed slaves influenced many Iowa soldiers in a positive way. "Upon entering [Columbia], crowds of negroes greeted us with the most extravagant expressions of joy," wrote one captain to his family. "As we neared the center of the scene, one which will never be forgotten by those who beheld it, thousands of the colored race were congregated in the streets through which we marched, all in perfect ecstasy of delight."[15]

During the initial weeks of the campaign, the Iowans' hatred of South Carolina secessionists propelled them forward to Columbia. In Mississippi and Georgia, Sherman's men had been careful not to torch the homes of ordinary citizens, but that practice changed once they set foot in South Carolina. "The instigators and abettors of Rebellion get their reward," wrote one lieutenant in the 15th Iowa. Over a span of five weeks, until they crossed the North Carolina border, every residential dwelling in their path was put to the torch.[16]

"Oh! the horrors of war!" exclaimed Captain Ritner in a letter to his wife from North Carolina. "Hundreds of families are left without a mouthful of anything to eat—not even a chicken or pig, cow, or anything." Several days after flames engulfed Columbia, the state capital, one Iowa lieutenant reflected on the massive destruction without regret. "South Carolina, the nation-state of John C. Calhoun, the hot-bed of treason, the first state to rebel, the most defiant aider and abettor of the Rebellion, pays this small price for her crimes."[17]

Politically based anger motivated the Iowans through physical and logistical challenges even more daunting than the March to the Sea. In an effort to protect their capital, South Carolinians flooded entire lowland areas that had been drained decades earlier to grow cotton and rice. Rebel cavalry patrols tracked down Union Army foragers and hanged small squads of bluecoat prisoners as a warning to others. The invading troops who avoided capture found fewer farms to plunder. At this time, in the dead of winter, fall vegetables had already been harvested. Rice paddies posed an obstacle to marching and offered little in the way of immediate sustenance.

The shortage of food did not deter the Iowans. Nor did the Rebel practice of executing foragers. Nor did the swampy lands they had to march through. To reach South Carolina's capital, Union soldiers corduroyed more than 100 miles of wetland roads with tree trunks and tree limbs so that army mules pulling the artillery and wagons might keep pace with the infantry. During the first week of the campaign, the Old Iowa Brigade forded thirty-four separate channels of water "waist deep generally and in many points still deeper," noted General Belknap.[18]

The hazards required teamwork to overcome, and the officers worked alongside privates and noncommissioned officers to accomplish the tasks. On the road to Columbia, rank did not matter when it came to physical work. Officers willingly trudged through the wetlands, a habit that perpetuated the enlisted men's self-perception of invincibility. Sherman's legend grew as stories circulated of the commander wading through waist-deep water. At one point, Illinois soldiers witnessed General Logan working "nearly all night, tugging at the ropes like a Trojan, covered with mud from head to feet." Although they covered less ground each day than they had on the Georgia march, the bluecoats made steady progress toward Columbia. After only a few weeks, the Vicksburg veterans caught sight of the city and prepared to take personal revenge on the capital city of treason.[19]

The opportunity to fly the national flag over the Columbia statehouse generated fierce competition among the Iowa troops at the head of the converging blue columns. Union commanders selected Stone's Brigade (formerly Williamson's) to enter the city and formally accept the surrender of the town. As part of General John Logan's corps, Stone's men advanced on Columbia from the northeast. Approaching the town from the south came the Old Iowa Brigade, the lead unit in General Frank Blair's corps.

Very few Iowans in either brigade had slept much over the last three days, and the Iowans had not eaten a decent meal in weeks. Nevertheless, the chance to plant the national flag atop the capitol building presented the Iowans in both brigades with an opportunity they could not resist. Proceeding against orders, using boats that leaked water, a squad of soldiers from the Old Iowa Brigade crossed the fast-flowing Congaree River intent on raising their regiment's flag over the South Carolina capitol. Nearby, a squad of Illinois soldiers crossed in another boat with similar designs.

On the north end of town, soldiers from Stone's Brigade waded through chest-deep water carrying their rifles and cartridge boxes above their heads and scaling a steep riverbank to establish a bridgehead. Columbia's mayor, after learning of the Union bridgehead, approached the Iowans under a white flag. Almost as soon as Colonel Stone accepted the mayor's surrender, a squad from his 31st Iowa headed straight for the capitol building with their regimental flag.

The colonel followed them in short order. Stone arrived at the capitol only to find that a squad of men from the Old Iowa Brigade had already hauled down the giant Palmetto state flag, which had flown atop the flagpole for five years, and replaced it with the 13th Regiment's Stars and Stripes. Undaunted, he removed the 13th Regiment's Stars and Stripes battle flag and replaced it with the national flag of the 31st Regiment.[20]

General Corse, the Burlington merchant in charge of a full division under Sherman, took the time to calculate the military damage inflicted by his troops near the state capital. In just two days, soldiers in his division had burned 600 bales of cotton and destroyed nine miles of railroad track, along with several boxcars, bridges, sawmills, barracks, culverts, and water tanks. Goods captured and converted to army uses during the two-day period included sixty-five mules, eight horses, two thousand pounds of meal and flour, and "a large quantity of salt meat, cattle, sheep, etc."[21]

Back home in Iowa, peace Democrats recognized the capture of Columbia as an ideal opportunity to restore the Union without demanding a formal surrender. The Confederate high command did not propose such an arrangement, but in the minds of the peace Democrats in Iowa, a negotiated peace would most likely improve postwar relations and accelerate the process toward reunion. That approach did not fly with the state's citizen-soldiers in the Carolinas, who rejected any consideration of negotiation. Nothing short of unconditional surrender was acceptable.

Captain Ritner expressed extreme confidence that Sherman was on the verge of forcing a final surrender. In a March 14 letter home, the Mount Pleasant Republican sensed his men were on the verge of dealing a death blow to the rebellion. "The great satisfaction," he told his wife, "is that we are cleaning out the Confederacy."[22] He looked forward to the long march to Virginia and taking their scorched-earth campaign to Richmond: "I am quite well and hearty—so are all the men. The health and spirits of the army never was better. It is wonderful what men can stand when they get used to it. I believe that we can go any place or do anything we please. We wade swamps and creeks waist deep, march through mud and rain, day and night, sleep out on the wet ground with clothes and blankets wet through and through, eat nothing but 'slap jacks' and meat—yet no one gets sick or discouraged."[23]

Ritner did get to see Richmond, but not before the Union troops in Virginia managed to capture the Confederate capital. A few days after thinning Rebel forces guarding Richmond finally yielded, General Robert E. Lee surrendered what remained of his army. Jefferson Davis and his Confederate cabinet members avoided capture initially, but their attempts to sustain the rebellion quickly faded after Lee's surrender. Once Davis was captured in Georgia, all that remained was to determine what role Federal troops and Federal administrators would perform during Reconstruction.

By the time Sherman's troops reached Richmond, the Rebel capital had taken on a ghostly appearance as a result of the destruction that followed the evacuation of General Lee's army. They proceeded on to Washington, where the War Department recognized their role in forcing Lee's surrender. Banners bearing the slogans "Welcome to Our Western Boys" and "Hail to Sherman's Army" fluttered over the streets during the triumphal grand review parade in Washington on May 24. The parades lasted for two days, with Sherman's troops marching by themselves on day two.

Sherman's troops made quite an impression on the audience in the nation's capital, which included Annie Wittenmyer and several diet kitchen nurses. Also present in the stands was Cyrus Carpenter. In his diary, he expressed his pride for the performance of the Western soldiers who marched through Washington one day after the Eastern soldiers' parade. "[Sherman's] army is on its toes," Carpenter noted. "I never saw better marching than was done by that army. Everybody admits they exceeded the Army of the Potomac. Every man in the army feels like a major general tonight."[24]

From Radical Impulse to Radical Revolution

On April 15, the day of Lincoln's assassination, Sherman's troops were encamped near Raleigh, North Carolina's state capital. Had it not been for the timely intervention of Sherman and other top Union commanders, Iowa's enlisted men would have torched the city in retaliation for the actions of John Wilkes Booth. A desire to retaliate also infected war supporters back home. When some dissenters in Iowa joked in public after learning of Lincoln's assassination, many Iowans demanded retribution against anyone who condoned his death. They also demanded retribution against the Deep South. "Revenge is my motto," wrote U.S. Marshal Peter Melendy to Henry Perkins, editor of *Cedar Falls Gazette*. "Would to God that the hot wrath of the people might swing every man that rejoices in this calamity."[25]

Many war Democrats felt likewise. Despite their long-held animosity against the Illinoisan, Democratic newspaper editors across the state condemned local critics who praised the assassination. The official platform of the Iowa Democratic Party that year declared the assassination of President Lincoln "an act of unmitigated barbarism, and one that should be held in utter abhorrence by every good citizen." The legacy of the assassination, which would linger for years, was another factor in changing the direction of state Republican policy on black civil rights.

In Des Moines, a growing number of state legislators supported Federal legislation designed to remove proslavery influences in the defeated Southern states in the spring of 1865. As part of what would come to be called Reconstruction, many Iowans demanded the permanent disenfranchisement of ex-Rebels and Rebel sympathizers. In February, two months before the conclusion of the military conflict, some moderate Iowa Republicans moved to support Federal laws restricting the political rights of former slavemasters. They also proposed to elevate black men residing in the Deep South to full citizenship.

Following the assassination of the president, many Iowa Republican newspaper editors endorsed black male suffrage in the Deep South as a means to punish Confederate leaders. When the "blood" of the president, wrote the editor of the Keokuk *Gate City*, "swells the red current of the righteous atonement for the blood drawn by the lash from an oppressed race, the people cannot fail to believe that the negro has rights which God designs to compel white men to respect."[26]

The goal of ensuring black civil rights in the Deep South revived interest in a state equal rights law. By the time state Republican delegates gathered for the annual party convention in June, the radical star was on the rise.

The Republican Party's June 1865 state convention produced a platform with several radical provisions. In addition to endorsing the enfranchisement of male ex-slaves in the former Confederate states, party delegates adopted for the first time an equal rights plank for nonwhite male residents of Iowa. The radical momentum did not end there. In selecting its nominees for state office, delegates chose longtime radicals for lieutenant governor and school superintendent. William Stone won renomination for governor over the radical faction's nominee, but he and the majority of convention delegates pledged to defend black civil rights as the cornerstone of the party of Lincoln. Although Republicans differed over the definition of black civil rights, a majority in attendance agreed that voting rights should be granted to African American war veterans.

The unlikely heroes who broke ranks and joined the radical delegates included a curious mixture of conservatives and moderates. Some previously cautious delegates switched their votes after hearing Hiram Price address the convention. In his speech, the Davenport member of Congress pointed out that black ex-soldiers could not vote, yet peace Democrats could continue to cast ballots against Union Party candidates. Moving beyond his pragmatic argument, Price condemned the hypocrisy of white privilege. The ethical fortitude of the speech moved many conservatives and moderates to break with party tradition and vote to end the racial double standard.[27]

In nineteenth-century America, ulterior motives and behind-the-scenes scheming often influenced votes on party platform resolutions.

Two historians, Bob Dykstra and Robert Cook, each conclude that jus-tice prevailed in Iowa for the right reasons. Despite warnings from the inner circle of moderate party kingpins, a critical mass of minor figures in the party voted their conscience. The list of converts included some con-servative Republicans from southern Iowa: Governor Stone and former governor Kirkwood converted, for example. Altruism motivated several ex-Democrats to approve the black rights provision, including Gen-eral Crocker, Lieutenant Governor Bateman, and Judge C. C. Cole. So many delegates turned radical that the final convention vote in favor of equal rights for blacks exceeded the nay votes by more than a two-to-one margin.[28]

Democrats predictably expressed outrage. Privately, several prominent Iowa Republicans expressed opposition to the party's 1865 state platform as well. Iowa's representatives and senators also objected. Although they endorsed voting rights for blacks in the former slave states, black civil rights at home was another matter, they insisted. Among the state's rep-resentatives in Washington, only Representative Price argued on behalf of equal rights in Iowa. Grimes and Harlan, along with Supreme Court Justice Samuel Miller, feared a popular backlash against the party on a scale that would propel Democrats into office. Even Representative Grinnell reverted to his practical habits and dismissed calls for idealism at home.

In every other state in the Northwest with the exception of Minnesota, party pragmatists defeated calls for black civil rights. The Hawkeye state would have continued its double standard of white racism had the party's top circle of leaders had their way. Radicals still made up a minority of the state party delegates in 1865, and the process for amending the state constitution required two consecutive majority votes in both chambers of the state legislature, plus a majority vote in a special statewide referendum. Even if legislators passed a black civil rights measure in 1866 and again in 1868, a popular referendum on the measure could not be held until 1868 at the earliest. By the time the next party convention was held, party kingpins expected that the majority of delegates would reject a black voting rights plank.

Alexander Clark saw in the 1865 Republican platform an opportunity for which he had been waiting his whole lifetime. "Strike for freedom whilst it is day!" proclaimed one poster he produced as a means to persuade local blacks to attend a State Colored Convention. At the convention, Clark and his allies designed a plan to expand membership in the state organization by including the former soldiers of the 60th U.S. Colored Troops. When the regiment returned to Davenport in the fall, Clark circulated an equal rights petition to the several hundred African American soldiers in attendance. Addressed to "the people of Iowa," the petition insisted that "he who is worthy to be trusted with the musket can and ought to be trusted with the ballot."[29]

Clark reasoned that the value of the military victory could not be realized until justice appeared in the form of equal rights. "We wish we could truthfully address you as 'fellow citizens,'" he explained, but those words could not be spoken until the state's racist laws were erased and replaced with wording that reflected what the black soldiers' military service had demonstrated. "Being men, we claim to be of that number comprehended in the Declaration of Independence, and who are entitled, not only to life, but to equal rights and the pursuit and securing of happiness—in the choice of those who are to rule over us." Before breaking camp, the black veterans signed off on a series of resolutions pledging to refrain from alcohol, to pursue "education, industry, and thrift," and to take political action to secure their rights.[30]

To Clark's delight, Republican candidates prevailed at the polls in 1865 notwithstanding the fears of party leaders. To the surprise of many whites, ordinary voters responded affirmatively to the Republicans' endorsement of equal rights. They did so despite the selection of Colonel Thomas Hart Benton, Jr., to oppose Stone's reelection bid. The colonel of Charles Musser's regiment, Benton ran for governor on the "Anti-Negro Suffrage" ticket, a fusion party made up of Democrats and conservative Republican ex-soldiers who opposed black civil rights.

Stone drew 16,000 fewer votes than he had collected in 1863, yet the incumbent governor still came out ahead of Benton. In southern Iowa, loyalty to the Union proved a particularly strong motivating factor. In Iowa's thirty-one southernmost counties, the Republican candidate for governor carried a majority of ballots in all but four districts six months after Lee's surrender. Remarkably, the two radicals on the Republican ticket (Gue and Faville) garnered more votes across the state than did Stone.[31]

Soldiers' Impact on State Politics

Iowa soldiers who survived the war returned home radicalized by Lincoln's assassination and their positive interactions with former slaves. The 1865 legislative election involved relatively few ex-soldiers competing for seats in the General Assembly, but that changed substantially in 1867. That year, a wave of veterans ran for the legislature, primarily as Republicans. Nearly every Republican candidate for state office in 1867 carried a military title. After Iowa voters selected Republican candidates for the legislature by an overwhelming margin, the fate of Clark's civil rights measure lay in the hands of the veterans.

When the 1868 General Assembly convened, the constitutional amendment process had already been launched. Legislators in the 1866 session had enacted a bill that called on voters to remove the word *white* from the state constitution, the measure preferred by Iowa's most radical Republicans. The proposal barely managed to win approval in both chambers because of its sweeping language. Some Republicans preferred granting only voting rights, not all civil rights, to Iowa's black residents. Governor Stone had proposed to dilute the civil rights plank further by limiting the black franchise to former soldiers. Fortunately, legislators in 1866 rejected the diluted language in favor of the original bill. As long as the 1868 legislature approved the proposal without changes and a majority of Iowa voters then approved, every native-born or naturalized male Iowan twenty-one years and older would be able to serve on juries and participate in the militia as well as vote, regardless of his race.

Passage was far from certain. Iowa Democrats saw in this development an opportunity to catapult themselves back into power. Some former Democrats had drifted back to the Democratic Party between 1865 and 1867. Wary of a backlash, some Republican Party leaders contemplated diluting or rescinding the equal rights amendment. Rather than dilute the measure, the majority of party leaders determined to define support for the original black rights amendment as a test of party loyalty.

Events in Washington contributed to reinforce the zeal for black civil rights at home. A long period of sustained controversy over President Andrew Johnson's Reconstruction policies galvanized the commitment of Iowa's representatives and senators to support radical causes.

The timing of Lincoln's death contributed to the postwar efforts to impeach President Johnson. Assassinated before the capture of Jefferson Davis, Lincoln never took the opportunity to outline the details of a postwar Reconstruction plan in the former Rebel states. As Republicans in Congress debated the details with President Johnson, the Union Party became bitterly divided between radical and nonradical factions.

Most Iowa Republicans reacted angrily when Johnson, Lincoln's vice president and a former Tennessee senator, espoused a lenient version of Reconstruction. His decision to reject a series of radical legislative measures further polarized the contentious environment in Washington. Most of Iowa's moderate Republicans in Congress sided with the radicals against Johnson's conservative faction rather than linger in the middle. When Northeastern radicals moved to impeach President Johnson, it was Iowa representative James F. Wilson who drafted the charges, in his capacity as chair of the House Judiciary Committee.

The first signs of the radical transformation appeared in 1866 and 1867. Iowa's representatives now embraced the Freedmen's Bureau Act, the version vetoed by President Johnson. The act became the law of the land, thanks in part to a unified group of Iowans in Congress. Meanwhile, Senator Grimes, a member of the Joint Committee on Reconstruction, operated within the coalition of radicals who sought to force Southern officials to recognize the citizenship rights of recently freed slaves.

The list of protective laws endorsed by the Joint Committee on Reconstruction included an amendment to the Constitution affording due process of law and prohibiting government agents from denying citizens their rights. The measure, which became the Fourteenth Amendment to the Constitution, was crafted in part by Senator Grimes. The proposed amendment passed the House of Representatives with five of Iowa's six representatives voting in favor.[32]

Radical patriotism quickly became a cornerstone of party dogma. Despite the precedent set by some rebellious ex-soldiers who bolted the party in the summer of 1865, the vast majority of veterans elected to office in Iowa after 1865 embraced the radical course. Never again would a group of ex-soldiers attempt to skirt the party line and ally with Democrats on the principle of opposing black rights at home. After state Republican leaders accommodated the grievances of ex-soldiers who aspired to run for office at home, the high percentage of soldier-legislators in 1868 voted in favor of removing the word *white* from the state constitution.

The postwar record of Cyrus Carpenter exemplifies the political contributions of ex-soldiers. Upon his return to Fort Dodge, he ran for his party's nomination to the elected position of Register of the State Land Office in 1866. Despite his lack of sympathy for slaves during his service in the military, he now allied himself with the radical faction, the same group that included Grenville Dodge, his former commander in Tennessee. Backed by Dodge, Carpenter won his party's nomination.

According to historian Mildred Throne, Carpenter's commitment to black equal rights was sincere. "Before we will ever have permanent peace," he wrote to his brother in California, "we must do impartial justice to all men and all races looking to our Government for protection . . . Some may call this fanaticism and hair-brained radicalism, but I am sure it meets the approval of my heart and judgment and I believe it to be approved of God."[33]

Defining party loyalty based on one's vote for or against the black civil rights amendment had far-reaching consequences. When Josiah Grinnell sought the Republican Party's nomination for governor in 1867, party delegates rejected the well-regarded member of Congress in favor of Samuel Merrill, a former colonel who had supported the black rights plank at the 1865 party convention. The presence of a large number of ex-soldiers at the 1867 Republican convention contributed to Merrill's nomination and ensured that the civil rights amendment would go to the voters in 1868.[34]

At the polls in 1867, Democratic efforts to play the race card failed to persuade most conservative voters to betray the party of Lincoln. Even in the traditionally Democratic neighborhoods in southern Iowa, Republican candidates won a majority of votes. Buoyed by this support from conservative voters, they stormed to victory across the state. Colonel Merrill defeated his Democratic challenger by a landslide, and the Republicans maintained their dominant position in the state legislature, winning all but five seats in the state House of Representatives. When the legislature convened in early 1868, lawmakers wasted little time approving the same equal rights provision approved in 1866.

Alexander Clark never assumed that a majority of white voters would follow suit. In designing his campaign strategy, he chose to emphasize the moral imperative behind equal rights. One year before the statewide referendum, the longtime Muscatine businessman filed a lawsuit against his local school district. School board policy forced every African American child, including Alexander's twelve-year-old daughter, into a single facility, and Clark saw the lawsuit as an opportunity to emphasize the hypocrisy of racially segregated public schools.

In February 1868, shortly before the state Supreme Court invalidated segregated schools in Iowa, Clark met with thirty other black Iowa leaders to formulate a plan for persuading ordinary white voters to approve the equal rights amendment. He and his colleagues drafted a long statement in favor of equal rights, a document that resembled the petition he had drafted in 1865 for the soldiers of the 60th U.S. Colored Troops.

The petition to white voters reflected the world-class intellect of its self-educated author. "The tendency toward an enlarged freedom . . . distinguishes our age," wrote the forty-two-year-old. Suffrage movements were flourishing in England, Ireland, and on the European continent, he pointed out, and in America "the name of Radicalism impresses us with the firm conviction that our claims to universal suffrage and impartial justice at home and abroad will soon be secured to all." A student of the Enlightenment, Clark drew on Jean-Jacques Rousseau's social contract theory to make his argument. He also cited the legacy of 1776. "Without suffrage," he insisted, "we are forced into strict subjection to a government whose councils are to us foreign, and are called by our own countrymen to witness a violence upon the primary principles of a republican government as gross and outrageous as that which justly stirred patriot Americans to throw overboard the tea from English bottoms in a Boston harbor and to wage war for Independence."

Yet he also underscored African Americans' patriotism: "In spite of all the wrongs which we have long and silently endured in this our native country, we would yet exclaim with a full heart 'O, America! with all thy faults, we love thee still.'" And he noted the limits of the civil rights that the Iowa amendment would guarantee: "Our demands are not excessive. We ask not for social equality with the white man, as is often claimed by the shallow demagogue," but only the right to vote, the right to serve on juries, and the right to serve in the state militia.[35]

The timing of the referendum helped propel the radical cause forward.

Rather than select a separate date, Republican leaders set the referendum to occur simultaneously with the 1868 presidential vote, when voters would be asked to choose between the Union war hero Ulysses S. Grant and New York Democrat Horatio Seymour.

In Mahaska County, a Republican newspaper editor argued that supporting General Grant's bid for president was "not a true honest, *Republican*, vote" unless the voter also moved to strike the word *white* from the state constitution. Word of Grant's approval of the radical measure echoed across the state. In the final count, Grant collected a whopping 62 percent of all ballots cast in Iowa, a ratio that compelled the Republican editor of the Oskaloosa paper to proclaim Iowa "the Star of the West." And the equal rights amendment passed as well: "Negro Suffrage Carries," read the headline in the *Oskaloosa Herald*, "A loyal Black Man as good as a White Rebel, in Noble Young Iowa."[36]

The timing of the vote was critical in this victory. In nine other Northern states, voters turned out for Grant but on other occasions voted down black civil rights measures sponsored by radical Republicans. In Wisconsin, a referendum bill similar to Iowa's failed in 1867 after party bosses there refused to endorse the cause of black suffrage. In Iowa, neighborhoods that turned out for the Democratic presidential nominee rejected the amendment, while pro-Grant districts approved.

Although not every Grant supporter dropped a "yes" ballot in favor of black civil rights, 56.5 percent of all Hawkeye voters in 1868 approved removing the word *white* from the state constitution and thereby opened the way for nonwhites to vote and serve on juries, for example. The correlation proved remarkably consistent from county to county across the state. More than 90 percent of Iowa voters who supported Grant also endorsed the black rights amendments.[37]

The achievement of equal rights under the law diverted Clark's career path. Elated by the outcome of the referendum, he sold his barbershop to another aspiring African American and pursued his prewar interests in real estate and homebuilding. Daughter Susan Clark graduated from Muscatine High School in 1871, the first African American in Iowa to receive a high school diploma. Her younger brother Alex Junior enrolled in the University of Iowa law school following his high school graduation. After receiving his degree, he relocated to Oskaloosa, where he joined a growing black community and practiced law for more than four decades.

Shortly after the 1868 Iowa referendum passed, the elder Clark set his sights on persuading Congress to enact national equal rights legislation. After delivering a series of thunderous speeches at the state Republican Party conventions, he attended the 1872 national party convention as a voting delegate. In the nation's capital, he caucused with Frederick Douglass and other prominent national leaders promoting Federal equal rights legislation. President Grant offered him the position of ambassador to Haiti.

Clark did have international political ambitions. But rather than accept President Grant's offer to serve as ambassador to Haiti at this point in his life, he toured the Mississippi River basin speaking on behalf of the Republican Party. As a representative of the black Masons and the AME church, he later visited England, France, and Switzerland. In 1889, he accepted President Harrison's offer to serve as U.S. ambassador to Liberia.

Sadly, the man known as the "Colored Orator of the West" ultimately lost his battle to preserve the radical memory of the Civil War. Before traveling to Liberia, he spent much of his time in Illinois, where Republicans struggled to enact state legislation promoting equal rights. Illinois never measured up to the Hawkeye state's achievement. Even in Iowa, the state once known as the "Bright Radical Star," the war's meaning for white Civil War veterans gradually changed as the nation approached the turn of the century.

Epilogue

---·◆·---

Every Iowa resident who survived the Civil War experienced a renaissance. Economically and politically, the postwar period was very different from the prewar period. The day-to-day routine on an Iowa farm in 1866 still resembled the day-to-day routine in 1860, but rural social life had been transformed. An Iowan who emerged in 1866 from a five-year hibernation would have been shocked by the magnitude of the changes. Prominent community members at the start of the conflict gained or lost standing within their neighborhoods by 1865.

Alexander Clark, Annie Wittenmyer, and Cyrus Carpenter became well-known national figures because of the Civil War. But for the war, the three might have remained locally known figures. For decades after 1865, the war's legacy influenced social activity and career choices, particularly for the ex-soldiers. Ordinary soldiers in 1865 became extraordinary civilians. Ben Stevens, after four years of service in the U.S. Army, sought out a new profession and moved to St. Louis. Abner Dunham pursued a career in public administration. Charles Musser returned to his family's farm in the Council Bluffs area and eventually relocated to Nebraska. His three years of army service forever endowed him with economic and social privileges not enjoyed by neighbors who never enlisted.

Soldiers who returned to Iowa benefited economically from the state's newfound progressive reputation. Tens of thousands of migrants selected the state after 1865, in part because of Iowa's reputation as staunchly pro-Union.

The "Bright Radical Star," the state's new nickname, also attracted Eastern venture capitalists. They risked huge sums building rail lines across the state. With Omaha as the starting point for the Pacific Railroad, three major national rail lines connected Chicago to Omaha through Iowa by 1875, and within a few years dozens of spur lines integrated rural

[237]

communities into the regional traffic system. Railroad development accelerated the rate at which Iowa's land was converted to farming.

Between 1860 and 1900, the number of farms soared from 61,000 to 229,000, and the state's total population more than tripled, from 674,000 to 2,232,000. Economically, Iowa eclipsed Missouri. By 1900, 30 million acres of Iowa land, representing 85 percent of all acres in the state, had been improved for agriculture, an eightfold increase in forty years. In addition to corn production, Iowa led the nation in number of hogs and horses in 1900 and placed second behind Texas in number of cattle.[1]

Politically, Iowa's role in quashing the Confederate rebellion catapulted it into the top circle of influence in the nation's capital. In 1860 it had been a frontier state with only two U.S. House seats, yet by the end of the conflict Iowa's Republican Party leaders enjoyed considerable Federal political power. An Iowan sat on the U.S. Supreme Court and in the president's cabinet. Iowans figured prominently in the Grand Army of the Republic (GAR), a veterans' organization and major political power. In 1882, eleven Iowans sat in the U.S. House of Representatives. Although no Iowan won the presidency, Republicans in the White House appointed dozens of Iowans to major posts: two Iowans served as secretary of war, two as secretary of the interior, and two as secretary of agriculture.

Community Healing

A public health catastrophe brought on by the war occurred amid the postwar economic boom. Many Iowa veterans experienced psychological maladies, physical disabilities, or both, and the postwar migration more than doubled the number of Union war veterans in the state.

For some army veterans, daily manual labor enabled them to cope with their most terrifying war memories. The routine of daily chores, often performed collectively, helped heal torn social relationships as well. Four years of war had ripped apart the social fabric of nearly every community in Iowa, but with so much land in the state undeveloped in 1865, the task of converting the raw landscape helped to reunite polarized communities.

Postwar pension records confirm the scale of the war's physical toll on Union soldiers. The task of caring for the thousands of invalids—plus the many widows and orphans—proved enormous. Private charity alone failed to cope with the scale of the humanitarian crisis, but legislators in Des Moines initially balked at allocating money. As time went on, Iowa's elected officials became more willing to earmark tax revenues for veterans' services. In Washington, the state's representatives pushed hard for bills granting pensions to veterans struggling with war-related injuries. By the end of the nineteenth century, Charles Musser and Annie Wittenmyer were receiving monthly pension checks.

From today's perspective, Iowans failed to meet the many humanitarian challenges of the postwar years. By 1900, thousands of chronically ill veterans languished on the street and in county homes for the indigent. From the perspective of Iowans in 1900, however, most postwar welfare needs had been successfully addressed. War orphans had been housed, fed, and trained. Disabled veterans received pensions, and a state-funded Home for Soldiers operated near Marshalltown for indigent veterans. In every county, monuments to the fallen soldiers had been erected.

FIGURE 13. The Iowa Soldiers' Home in Marshalltown, photographed in 1895. The postwar migration boom brought thousands of Union veterans to Iowa from other states, many of whom became destitute. When Federal officials declined to build a hospital in Iowa to assist needy ex-soldiers, state legislators in the 1880s allocated funds to build the Marshalltown facility. *Reprinted by permission of the State Historical Society of Iowa, Des Moines.*

To contemporaries, these accomplishments reflected a high level of civility and progress. In retrospect, though, much more tax money should have been allocated to care for chronically ill veterans. Although the Soldiers' Home did represent a major achievement for the relatively young state, Iowa's expanded tax base would have allowed for additional spending on health care. A second state-funded home was never constructed, even though the Marshalltown facility quickly filled to capacity.[2]

Popular notions of charity explain Iowans' reluctance. In an era when welfare-to-work programs exemplified progressive solutions for poverty, the soldiers at the home were not considered patients. Legislators designed the institution on the assumption that the residents would generate enough capital through collective enterprise to cover the operating costs. Just as the county poor farm in Marshall County required every indigent resident there to work, every inmate at the Soldiers' Home was expected to work, with an added martial flair. Veterans reported for reveille each morning in their military uniforms and then proceeded to the garden, machine shop, or wood shop. When administrators judged that the veterans had been rehabilitated, they were discharged involuntarily.

It soon became evident that many veterans in the home required daily nursing care and could not generate income. But rather than support the veterans in need of ongoing medical treatment, facility rules continued to require every veteran to contribute his share of work or leave the facility.[3]

The vast majority of the 13,000 Iowa soldiers who died during the war had farmed in 1860. Many of the survivors returned to farming but found sustained outdoor work difficult, particularly as they reached middle age. Three years of army service in frontier Arkansas compromised Charles Musser's health. He reported severe rheumatism as early as 1884, and in 1890 a family doctor submitted an affidavit to the Federal pension commission declaring Charles to be 75 percent disabled. His 1891 petition for veterans' benefits listed arthritis, heart disease, lung disease, hemorrhoids, kidney disease, and bladder disease. When his arthritis was at its worst, Charles remained cooped up in his home for weeks at a time.

Before his health deteriorated, Musser led an active life. A lifelong member of the GAR, he consistently voted Republican, although his family had been independent before the war. Following his marriage in 1867, he farmed in Pottawattamie County in order to be close to his mother, who was still caring for several young daughters. His father, John, died in 1868, and Charles's older brother, a Confederate war veteran, never reconciled with the family. Charles served as a township officer, an elected position, and in 1880, as a census-taker.[4]

Musser's wife gave birth to ten children during their long marriage. Keeping his children, wife, and younger sisters fed and clothed posed a considerable challenge to the Civil War veteran. Eventually, the Mussers joined the streams of Iowans who relocated to Nebraska in 1884, by which time Charles's sisters had all reached maturity. In 1910, deteriorating health compelled Charles to give up his second Nebraska farm and move into a house in town. Fortunately, his wife and children were available to care for him. He spent the last years of his life at a nursing home in Colorado Springs before dying at ninety-three in 1934.[5]

Many veterans elected to pursue less physically demanding work than farming. Ben Stevens left Iowa in the late 1860s for St. Louis, where the four-year war veteran married and settled in a fashionable home. The former Oskaloosa plasterer ran an accounting operation that managed the wealth of elite businessmen, privileged work that enabled him to hire several live-in servants to care for his family.[6]

Abner Dunham ultimately pursued public service in lieu of farming or business. County sheriff was his first office. While farming his parents' 80-acre homestead in Delaware County, he ran for the position in the early 1870s and was elected to hold the office twice. Family connections and his war record helped him win it. The Dunham name was well regarded in the county where Abner's father Ferdinand served as superintendent of county schools, an officer in the County Agriculture Society, and supervisor on the county board.[7]

The younger Dunham solidified his political standing by remaining affiliated with the Republican Party and participating in the GAR. In the late 1880s, he served as a private secretary to Representative David Henderson, the future speaker of the House, who gained recognition by promoting the Shiloh Battlefield Park bill. In 1894, Delaware County voters elected Abner Dunham to the office of county recorder, a position he filled for ten years. At the time of his death in 1910, his four surviving children had become prominent citizens in South Dakota and Iowa.[8]

Wittenmyer's Postwar Experience

For Annie Wittenmyer, the declining health of disabled war veterans demanded immediate remedy. So did the orphan crisis. She believed that women must assume a prominent role in the postwar relief work. In 1866, she accepted the position of matron of the state's largest war orphanage, in Davenport. Fundraising on behalf of the Methodist Women's Home Missionary Society occupied much of her time during the late 1860s. This activity opened new doors for her, and between 1874 and her death in 1900, she co-founded several prominent women's organizations and served for many years as their chief executive.

Elected as the first president of the national Women's Christian Temperance Union (WCTU) in 1874, Wittenmyer with her colleagues built the group into a formidable power by establishing neighborhood chapters, just as they had done with soldiers' aid societies during the war. Women had helped to defeat secessionism, so she believed they could help to eliminate alcohol, another vice perpetuated by men. To this end, she committed much of her energy for several years. She urged her colleagues to make the same sacrifice. "Give your self, with a single aim, and with all your might, to the work you have undertaken."[9]

Historian Glenda Riley argues that Wittenmyer's war experience directly influenced her commitment to the antiliquor crusade. Traveling from camp to camp, she observed firsthand the ill effects of alcohol consumption on officers, doctors, and ordinary soldiers. After the war, alcohol-based patent medicines became popular among women, a development she feared would inhibit them from fulfilling their role as the moral guardians of society.[10]

Annie Wittenmyer's involvement in democratic efforts to improve veterans' services began in the early 1880s. The last fifteen years of her career found her in the company of other women with close connections to the GAR. Of the GAR's two major auxiliary women's organizations established in the early 1880s, she embraced the Women's Relief Corps (WRC), the group with the least restrictive membership criteria. WRC rules permitted any woman to join who had supported the cause of unionism in any manner without regard to whether their male relatives had served in the military.

Elected national president of the WRC in 1889, Wittenmyer led an effort to build a nursing home in Ohio for needy army nurses and war widows. During the last decade of her life, she championed the cause of female veterans, successfully lobbying Congress in 1892 to broaden the pension coverage to include Union Army nurses who had served at least six months during the war. After the bill's passage, Wittenmyer assisted hundreds of women in verifying their work history so they could obtain the modest $12-per-month pension.[11]

WRC and WCTU chapters flowered across the Iowa landscape during the 1880s. Both organizations created leadership opportunities for thousands of Iowa women. Historian Brian Donovan notes that the WRC chapters, in tandem with the GAR, "acted as a kind of community social club, organizing Fourth of July parades, ice cream socials, and Decoration Day ceremonies." WRC leaders often drove local efforts to build war memorials. The Soldiers and Sailors Monument in Des Moines, erected in 1894, was designed by a woman from Mount Pleasant.[12]

News of Wittenmyer's death in 1900 inspired a flood of memorials from aging veterans. George Perkins, a longtime newspaper editor in Sioux City, recalled his first encounter with her in a hospital in Helena, Arkansas. "I was taken violently ill," he remembered, at a time when "our camp was utterly destitute of hospital supplies . . . It was in the winter season and the rain fell almost incessantly . . . In this situation, Mrs. Wittenmyer found me," Perkins noted. "She was just spying out the ground. She talked with me in such a cheery way, and when she left she said that in a few days they would have me in better shape . . . I was weak at the time, and I may as well confess that I instantly began to moisten with tears. Of course, this is only one small incident in the army work of Annie Wittenmyer; but it is enough to enshrine her in my sacred memory."[13]

Black Civil Rights as a War Legacy

Nationally, the lessons of the Civil War shifted in the popular imagination as the war became a distant memory. The same was true in postwar Iowa. As in other states, many white Iowans redefined the meaning of the war in racist terms after 1865.[14]

The postwar experiences of Wittenmyer, Clark, and Carpenter demonstrate that some unionist Iowans went to considerable lengths to perpetuate a radical memory of the war. They drew different implications about

FIGURE 14. Elizabeth Fairfax, Clinton (Iowa), circa 1885. After the Civil War, Mrs. Fairfax moved north to Clinton, where she became a member of the local Grand Army of the Republic post. A note on the back of this photograph indicates that Mrs. Fairfax worked as a scout in the Union Army and served as an army nurse, caring for sick and wounded Union soldiers. Like many ex-nurses, she struggled economically as she grew older. Mrs. Fairfax was "well known in Clinton," according to the note on the back of the photograph. "For 24 years she kept a laundry, and wove rag carpets for a living. By industry and economy she purchased and is now the owner of a little homestead. She has raised two children. Now advanced in years and feeble in health, she is no longer able to maintain herself by her former occupation. To secure a living she now peddles for a grocery store, and sells her pictures. She served her country faithfully and is deserving of support." *Reprinted by permission of the State Historical Society of Iowa, Des Moines.*

the meaning of social justice. As Alexander Clark contemplated the war's legacy, he sought to deepen its impact on social inclusion by working to enfranchise other oppressed groups. When some women leaders demanded the right to vote, he coupled women's voting rights with black men's voting rights when he spoke on behalf of enacting new citizenship laws.

State court rulings on behalf of black plaintiffs reinforced Clark's view that civil rights for all was one of the war's legacies. Decisions written by Republican judges after the war reflected positive attitudes toward black citizens, including the Muscatine school board ruling. Justice C. C. Cole, in ordering the Muscatine school board to desegregate its facilities, reasoned that black children should be treated the same as Irish American children and German American children, and should be fully integrated into the classroom alongside white children born in North America.[15]

Five years later, the state Supreme Court prohibited steamboat owners from restricting black passengers to the lower deck. "The doctrines of natural law and Christianity forbid that rights be denied on the ground of race or color," reasoned Justice Beck. The old prejudices are "fast giving way to nobler sentiments, and, it is hoped, will soon be entombed with its parent, slavery."[16]

In 1870, a majority of legislators in Des Moines approved a resolution to eliminate the word *male* from the voting section of the state constitution. They also amended several age-old laws that discriminated against women. Although the voting measure failed during the subsequent legislative session, Iowa came as close as any state before the twentieth century to recognizing the citizenship rights of women.[17] Remarkably, Wittenmyer declined to join her former colleagues in the suffrage movement. Despite the growing enthusiasm for women's suffrage, she never progressed to the point of calling for voting rights. She explained that women did not need the right to vote in order to provide alms.

In the end, emancipation outlasted women's suffrage as a war legacy. Assertive efforts by Alexander Clark and other black Iowans to organize Emancipation Day parades reinforced the antislavery legacy of the war. White citizens joined black citizens in celebrating annual Emancipation Day exercises each June. After the procession arrived at the local fairgrounds, prominent citizens took turns reciting President Lincoln's Emancipation Proclamation. Black leaders addressed the mixed-race audience as they feasted on food and beverages prepared by local black women. After the meal, the singing of hymns, patriotic tunes, and old slave spirituals celebrated the African Americans' claim to equal citizenship.[18]

Historian David Brodnax notes that white speakers on Memorial Day and the Fourth of July often demanded more Federal laws protecting former slaves in the Deep South, at least during the period from 1866 to 1876. In Keokuk, white ex-soldiers in attendance sang marching songs associated with emancipation, such as "John Brown's Body." Clark stoked the fires as best he could. Speaking at the state Colored Citizens Convention in Oskaloosa in 1876, the "Colored Orator of the West" noted that sixty-one former Confederates had recently been elected to Congress from former slave states. "My friends, these things rise up today before the American people decked in the somber habiliments of a hideous nightmare, presenting all the bloody horrors of the past, threatening destruction of the fondest hope for the future."[19]

Support for equal rights declined over the years while unionism gradually superseded slavery as the root cause of the war in the popular imagination among whites. In Iowa, deep-rooted racism eventually watered down the war's civil rights legacy. The gigantic wave of white postwar migration tended to weaken memories of emancipation, as did the Democrats' acceptance of the Thirteenth and Fourteenth Amendments. With the two major parties no longer debating slavery, white Republicans had less incentive to include the rights of African Americans in the public discussion. Speeches made at Fourth of July parades, Memorial Day ceremonies, and soldier reunions reflected the war's changing legacy.

Sectional Healing and Its Impact on the War's Legacy

The gradual disappearance of emancipation as a theme at Iowa patriotic events began with the end of Reconstruction in the Deep South in 1876. When thousands of former Union soldiers celebrated regimental reunions in the 1880s, the topics of pensions, medical care, and war monuments dominated the discussion. The state's former slaves continued to celebrate Emancipation Day, but on Memorial (formerly Decoration) Day, white Iowans focused more and more on unionism. By 1900, white speakers rarely addressed black civil rights, while calls for sectional reconciliation became more pronounced.

White soldiers did not exclude black veterans from attending GAR events. In Washington, black veterans were eligible to apply for the same benefits due white veterans. As time passed, however, white ex-soldiers adopted a more forgiving attitude toward their former enemies in the

FIGURE 15. The 35th Iowa Infantry reunited in Muscatine in 1886. The regiment, made up of Muscatine County and Cedar County recruits, held its first reunion that year. Many of those in attendance no longer lived in Iowa. Membership in the GAR revived in the 1880s, the same decade that witnessed the founding of the Women's Relief Corps and the holding of a flurry of regimental reunions in Iowa. *Photo courtesy of Musser Public Library, Muscatine.*

Deep South, a development that undermined the cause of equal rights. White war veterans, rather than push for integrated schools and businesses, celebrated the war's memory by erecting dozens of costly monuments with patriotic themes.

Forty years after General Lee's surrender, the number of monuments erected by Iowans exceeded one hundred. Designed to endure for centuries, they cost state taxpayers hundreds of thousands of dollars. Following the creation of Federal parks at Shiloh, Chattanooga, Andersonville, and Vicksburg, 160 Iowans toured the parks in 1906 in order to dedicate the state monuments there. Regrettably, none of the 160 Iowans who rode the special train through the Deep South that year were African Americans.[20]

The postwar career of Cyrus Carpenter illustrates how the meaning of "radical" was diluted over time. When he first ran for governor in 1871, his main opponent for the Republican nomination, Henry O'Connor, was a personal friend of Alexander Clark. During the war, O'Connor had worked closely with the radical wing of the party, and after the war the Muscatine lawyer took the lead in sponsoring civil rights legislation in his capacity as state attorney general.

Despite O'Connor's radical record, Carpenter prevailed at the 1871 convention because his political godfathers, Grenville Dodge and William Allison, controlled the majority of delegates. Antirailroad legislation came to define candidate differences that year, and as a result Civil War rhetoric lost much of its meaning. During Carpenter's four years in office, racial issues rarely attracted his attention. He spent much of his time dealing with the challenge posed by the nascent Anti-Monopoly Party.[21]

In 1877, the army veteran arrived in Washington to work for the Treasury Department. Still committed to Reconstruction in the Deep South, Carpenter won election to Congress in 1878 and endured the acrimonious 1879–80 session, the first without a Republican majority in the U.S. House since the Civil War. The prevailing winds had changed, and white Iowans in Washington recognized it. When an alliance of Northern Democrats and Southern members of Congress insisted on removing Federal troops from polling areas in the former Confederate states, Carpenter, like most Iowa Republicans, reluctantly accepted the compromise offered by President Hayes.[22]

Back in Des Moines, Republican leaders decorated the opulent new capitol with lily-white artwork following the end of Reconstruction. Unfortunately, the conspicuous absence of nonwhites in the capitol reflected the lack of racial diversity in postwar Iowa. Despite the state's reputation as a radical enclave in the late 1860s, few blacks settled in Iowa after the war. Ninety-nine percent of Iowa residents in 1900 were Caucasian, either American- or European-born.

Alexander Clark never abandoned hope that all of the states would one day welcome former slaves as equal citizens. To his disappointment, racism became entrenched in his home community and adopted state. Despite court rulings in favor of black civil rights, school boards in many Iowa towns (including Keokuk) continued to operate segregated schools. He also faced personal hostility for agitating for black civil rights. In 1878, a fire that many believed had been set intentionally destroyed his home in Muscatine.[23]

White leaders ultimately failed to improve the status of African Americans. Instead of welcoming ex-slaves, some communities enacted local laws that resembled Jim Crow ordinances in the South. Near the Missouri border, towns barred blacks from entering after sundown. By the turn of the twentieth century, a system of de facto discrimination prevailed. According to NAACP statistics, two black Iowans were lynched around 1900, and at least one other victim nearly died as a result of mob violence.[24]

In Washington, D.C., nationalism ultimately drove Iowa's militant Republicans to reconcile with ex-Confederates. Following the U.S. war against Spain in 1898, most Iowa Republicans agreed that slavery had not caused the Civil War. On the Vicksburg monument tour in 1906, James B. Weaver joined the racist chorus. The former commander of the 2nd Iowa Infantry Regiment, who in 1880 had recruited ex-slaves to his Greenback Party, now directed black Americans to return to Africa.[25]

Although Iowa GAR leaders did not support this idea, they did offer an olive branch to Southern whites by assuring them that they themselves did not support black civil rights. During the 1906 monument tour, Governor Cummins minimized the role played by African American soldiers. In 1917, the old soldiers' reunion at Vicksburg coincided with America's entrance into World War I. Iowa's Governor Harding, looking to unite rather than divide, addressed the all-white audience and expressed conciliation.[26]

The War's Legacy Today

The last fifty years witnessed several contradictory developments. In his speech at the 100th anniversary of the Battle of Gettysburg in 1963, Iowa's governor demanded passage of a Federal Civil Rights Act. One year later, the state's senior Republican senator voted against the very same act.

In the 1990s, curators in Des Moines restored the state's old battle flags and polished up the soldier monuments in anticipation of the war's 150th anniversary. In coffee shops and veterans' halls across the state, meanwhile, white Iowans debating the war's legacy did not always agree. Some argued that slavery was not the primary cause of the war, while others argued to the contrary. Some willingly defended white Southerners' treatment of slaves before the war.

Today's debate over the Civil War's legacy coincides with the renewed national dialogue over states' rights, women's rights, civil rights for African Americans, and immigrant voting rights. Even the topic of secession has taken on a new life. Curiously, the original meaning of unionism has largely vanished. As democracy spread across the globe in the twentieth century, the United States lost its title as the prime example of democratic governance.

As more and more nations embraced the banner of self-government, the distinction between idealistic unionism and blind patriotism blurred in Iowa and elsewhere in the United States. Threats to secede no longer stir the same antagonism as they did in the 1800s. Lost in today's discussion are the unionist ideals that led so many Americans to condemn the Rebel flag as treasonous a hundred years ago.

That the ancestors of many white Iowans arrived in the United States after 1865 diminishes the relevance of the war for many. For those without a family connection to the war, anniversary events may not arouse much interest. Although many Iowans today count Civil War veterans on their family trees, six generations of migration and intermarriage have produced a substantial number of hybrid residents in Iowa. This author is one of thousands of Iowans who have both Confederate Army and Union Army ancestors in his lineage. For some white descendants of Confederate veterans, the legacy of emancipation has become difficult to grasp.

Recent events in Iowa testify to this paradox. A quick search of high school mascots in Iowa in 2015 revealed a small number of consolidated rural districts that adopted the nickname "Rebels" during the late twentieth century. Those who selected the nickname apparently had no intention of referencing the Confederate States of America, yet the obvious connection was lost on them. Similarly, displaying the Rebel flag raises few eyebrows in some quarters of the state. Only sixty years have passed since the Rebel battle flag reemerged in the Deep South as the symbol of racial segregation, yet many white Iowans react with ambivalence when the flag is displayed. Today, the Rebel battle flag, identified by generations of African Americans as a symbol of white racism, is displayed on some vehicles in Iowa.

The flag's association with treason seems to have vanished from the popular imagination. During the same week in 2015 when the South Carolina legislature voted to remove the Confederate flag from the statehouse, one Republican county chair in Iowa prominently displayed three Rebel battle flags on his truck in the Fourth of July parade. The state party leaders quickly denounced the display, but the negative publicity surprised the county chair, who has Confederate Army as well as Union Army ancestors.[27]

Fortunately, one need not look far to discover the original meaning of unionism. By recounting the individual and collective achievements of Iowans during the conflict, we can discern the underlying forces that led to the Civil War. As we look back, let us hope that the optimism of the war's heroes and heroines rekindles in us a willingness to embrace participatory democracy as a means to improve our human condition in the twenty-first century.

Introduction

1. For a good historiography, see Judith Ann Giesberg, *Civil War Sisterhood: The U.S. Sanitary Commission and Women's Politics in Transition* (Boston: Northeastern University Press, 2000), 8–12.

2. Lowell J. Soike, *Necessary Courage: Iowa's Underground Railroad in the Struggle against Slavery* (Iowa City: University of Iowa Press, 2013).

3. Gary W. Gallagher, *The Union War* (Cambridge, Mass.: Harvard University Press, 2011).

4. Robert Cook, *Baptism of Fire: The Republican Party in Iowa 1838–1878* (Ames: Iowa State University Press, 1994).

Chapter One

1. Timothy R. Mahoney, *River Towns in the Great West: The Structure of Provincial Urbanization in the American Midwest, 1820–1870* (Cambridge: Cambridge University Press, 1990), 234–38; 238 (*Keokuk Gate City* quote).

2. Ivan L. Pollock, "State Finances in Iowa during the Civil War," *Iowa Journal of History and Politics* 16 (1918): 53–107; Erling E. Erickson, *Banking in Frontier Iowa, 1836–1865* (Ames: Iowa State University Press, 1971); Sarah Kenyon quoted in Mildred Throne, ed., "Iowa Farm Letters, 1856–65," *Iowa Journal of History* 58 (1960): 78 (quote).

3. Mildred Throne, *Cyrus Clay Carpenter and Iowa Politics, 1854–1898* (Iowa City: State Historical Society, 1974), 53 (quote).

4. Throne, ed., "Iowa Farm Letters," 37–88 (quote pp. 77–78).

5. Bela Vassady, "New Buda: A Colony of Hungarian Forty-Eighters in Iowa," *Annals of Iowa* 51, no. 1 (Summer 1991): 35–36 (quote).

6. Michael A. Ross, *Justice of Shattered Dreams: Samuel Freeman Miller and the Supreme Court during the Civil War Era* (Baton Rouge: Louisiana State University Press, 2003), 43–45.

7. Iowa Secretary of State, *Historical and Comparative Census of Iowa for 1880* (Des Moines, 1883), 428, 523; 1860 Population Census Manuscript, Jackson Township, Lee County; Ross, *Justice of Shattered Dreams*, 22–25.

8. Real Estate Deeds, Lee County Recorder's Office, Keokuk.

9. Ross, *Justice of Shattered Dreams*, 22–45.

10. Real Estate Deeds, Lee County Recorder's Office, Keokuk; 1860 Agricultural Census Manuscripts, Jackson Township, Lee County.

11. John O. Foster, *A Memorial Tribute to Mrs. Annie Wittenmyer* (Pottstown, Pa.: Pottstown Ledger, 1900), 13 (quote).

12. *Historical and Comparative Census of Iowa for 1880*, 552.

13. Real Estate Deeds, Muscatine County Recorder's Office, Muscatine.

14. Iowa Census Board, "The Census Returns of the Different Counties of the State of Iowa, for 1856" (Iowa City, 1857), 318. Hereafter cited as "1856 Iowa State Census."

15. David J. Brodnax, Sr., "'Breathing the Freedom's Air': The African American Struggle for Equal Citizenship in Iowa, 1830–1900" (Ph.D. diss., Northwestern University, 2007), 21–95.

16. Robert R. Dykstra, *Bright Radical Star: Black Freedom and White Supremacy on the Hawkeye Frontier* (Cambridge, Mass.: Harvard University Press, 1993), 14–18, 110–18.

17. *Eighth Census of the United States: 1860* (Washington, D.C., 1864–65).

18. 1860 U.S. Population Census Manuscript, Oskaloosa Township; 1860 U.S. Agricultural Census Manuscript, Oskaloosa Township.

19. Richard N. Ellis, ed., "The Civil War Letters of an Iowa Family," *Annals of Iowa* 39 (1969): 561–85.

20. Real Estate Deeds, Delaware County Recorder's Office, Manchester.

21. 1856 Iowa State Census, Delaware County; 1860 U.S. Agriculture Census Manuscript, Delaware County.

22. Mildred Throne, ed., "Civil War Letters of Abner Dunham, 12th Iowa Infantry," *Iowa Journal of History* 53 (1955): 303–40.

23. Barry Popchock, ed., *Soldier Boy: The Civil War Letters of Charles O. Musser, 29th Iowa* (Iowa City: University of Iowa Press, 1995).

24. 1860 U.S. Population Census Manuscript, Pottawattamie County; 1860 U.S. Agricultural Census Manuscript, Pottawattamie County.

25. *History of Pottawattamie County, Iowa*, vol. 2 (Chicago: Baskin and Co., 1883), 116.

26. Real Estate Deeds, Pottawattamie County Recorder's Office, Council Bluffs.

27. 1860 Population Census Manuscripts, Kane Township, Pottawattamie County; 1860 Agriculture Census Manuscripts, Kane Township, Pottawattamie County.

28. Grimes quoted in William Salter, *James W. Grimes, Governor of Iowa, and United States Senator, 1854–1869* (Burlington, Iowa: Gnahn, Mauro and Wilson, 1892), 136–37.

Chapter Two

1. 1860 U.S. election results by state: http://en.wikipedia.org/wiki/United _States_presidential_election_1860#Results (accessed March 21, 2015).

2. Cook, *Baptism of Fire: The Republican Party in Iowa, 1838–1878*, 116–35.

3. Kenneth Millsap, "The Election of 1860 in Iowa," *Iowa Journal of History* 48 (1950): 105–12; Ross, *Justice of Shattered Dreams*, 57.

4. Foster, *Memorial Tribute to Mrs. Annie Wittenmyer*, 18 (quote).

5. Morton M. Rosenberg, *Iowa on the Eve of the Civil War: A Decade of Frontier Politics* (Norman: University of Oklahoma Press, 1972), 204–6; Robert P. Swierenga, "The Ethnic Voter and the First Lincoln Election," *Civil War History* 11 (1965): 27–43; Charles Wilson Emery, "Iowa Germans in the Election of 1860" (M.A. thesis, State University of Iowa, 1940), 59–67; George H. Daniels, "Immigrant Vote in the 1860 Election: The Case of Iowa," *Mid-America* 44 (1962): 146–62. For Lee County's ethnic voting results, compare Official Abstract of the Vote of Lee County, 1860 (*Des Moines Valley Whig*, November 11, 1860) and nativity data in 1856 Iowa State Census, 235–36.

6. Rosenberg, *Iowa on the Eve of the Civil War*, 215–16; Millsap, "The Election of 1860 in Iowa," 115–16.

7. Rosenberg, *Iowa on the Eve of the Civil War*, 222.

8. The Tama County farmer is Robert Young, quoted in "Peter Wilson

in the Civil War: The Training Period," *Iowa Journal of History and Politics* 40 (1942): 153; John Kenyon quoted in Throne, ed., "Iowa Farm Letters," 81.

9. Judge James Love quoted in *Des Moines Valley Whig*, January 28, 1861.

10. *Des Moines Valley Whig*, January 28, 1861, and February 4, 1861.

11. Belknap, Miller, Sample, and Dixon quoted in *Des Moines Valley Whig*, January 28, 1861, and February 4, 1861.

12. William Clagett, William Howell (Republican newspaper editor), and Daniel F. Miller quoted in *Des Moines Valley Whig*, January 28, 1861.

13. Hubert H. Wubben, *Civil War Iowa and the Copperhead Movement* (Ames: Iowa State University Press, 1980), 27.

14. Cook, *Baptism of Fire*, 130–33.

15. Kenneth E. Colton, ed., "'The Irrepressible Conflict of 1861': The Letters of Samuel Ryan Curtis," *Annals of Iowa* 24 (1942): 33 (quote).

16. Salter, *James W. Grimes*, 134 and 135 (quotes).

17. Salter, *James W. Grimes*, 133–35 (quotes; emphasis in original).

18. Cook, *Baptism of Fire*, 135.

19. Johnson Brigham, *James Harlan* (Iowa City: SHSI, 1913), 150–51.

20. Brigham, *James Harlan*, 152–53 (quote).

21. Brigham, *James Harlan*, 139 and 140 (quotes).

22. Brigham, *James Harlan*, 138–40.

23. Salter, *James W. Grimes*, 132 and 136 (quotes).

24. Salter, *James W. Grimes*, 132, 137 (quotes); Dan E. Clark, *Samuel Jordan Kirkwood* (Iowa City: State Historical Society, 1917), 173 (quote).

25. Colton, "Letters of Samuel Ryan Curtis," 32 (quote); Robert Gray Gunderson, *Old Gentlemen's Convention: The Washington Peace Conference of 1861* (Madison: University of Wisconsin Press, 1961), 56.

26. Salter, *James W. Grimes*, 136–37 (quotes).

27. Colton, "Letters of Samuel Ryan Curtis," 22n22 and 37 (quotes). Curtis spoke these words in opposition to an amendment to a military appropriations bill sponsored by a Virginia representative. The amendment proposed to specify that no army appropriations be used to recover Federal installations seized by seceded states or from states that might secede.

28. Susan-Mary Grant, *North over South: Northern Nationalism and American Identity in the Antebellum Era* (Lawrence: University of Kansas Press, 2000), 153–71.

29. Ronald H. Stone, *Eber: Pioneer in Iowa, 1854–1875* (Iowa City: Campus Pope Bookstore, 2002), 102 (quote) .

30. Earl J. Hess, *The Union Soldier in Battle: Enduring the Ordeal of Combat* (Lawrence: University of Kansas Press, 1997), 94 (quote).

31. Hess, *The Union Soldier in Battle*, 94 (quote).

32. William Garrett Piston and Richard W. Hatcher III, *Wilson's Creek: The Second Battle of the Civil War and the Men Who Fought It* (Chapel Hill: University of North Carolina Press, 2000), 51 (quotes).

33. Herbert S. Fairall, ed., *Manual of Iowa Politics: State and National, Conventions, Platforms, Candidates, and Official Vote of All Parties, from 1838 to 1884* (Iowa City: Republican Publishing, 1884), 57 (quote).

Chapter Three

1. Samuel J. Kirkwood, "Special Session Message," in Benjamin F. Shambaugh, ed., *Messages and Proclamations of the Governors of Iowa*, vol. 2 (Iowa City: Iowa State Historical Society, 1903), 252–63.

2. Mildred Throne, ed., "The Civil War Diary of John Mackley," *Iowa Journal of History* 48 (1950): 144–45 (quote).

3. John E. Briggs, "The Enlistment of Iowa Troops during the Civil War," *Iowa Journal of History and Politics* 15, no. 3 (1917): 323–50; Shambaugh, ed., *Messages and Proclamations*, 412–15; Cyril B. Upham, "Arms and Equipment for the Iowa Troops in the Civil War," *Iowa Journal of History and Politics* 16 (1918): 3–13.

4. Briggs, "Enlistment of Iowa Troops," 328–33.

5. Briggs, "Enlistment of Iowa Troops," 330–32.

6. Kirkwood quoted in Jacob A. Swisher, *Iowa in Times of War* (Iowa City: Iowa State Historical Society, 1943), 77 (emphasis in original); Briggs, "Enlistment of Iowa Troops," 333–37.

7. Upham, "Arms and Equipment," 11 (quote; emphasis in original).

8. Pollock, "State Finances," 53–107.

9. Wubben, *Civil War Iowa*, 33–34.

10. Wubben, *Civil War Iowa*, 27–28; William J. Petersen, *The Story of Iowa*, vol. 1 (Iowa City: SHSI, 1952), 428; S. H. M. Byers, *Iowa in War Times* (Des Moines: Condit and Co., 1888), 27–62; Benjamin F. Gue, *History of Iowa*, vol. 2 (New York: Century History Co., 1903), 55–57.

11. Governor Samuel Kirkwood to Simon Cameron, U.S. Secretary of War, April 18, 1861, quoted in Wubben, *Civil War Iowa*, 30.

12. Pollock, "State Finances," 71, 79; Mark W. Geiger, *Financial Fraud and Guerrilla Violence in Missouri's Civil War, 1861–1865* (New Haven: Yale University Press, 2010), 1–82.

13. Addison A. Stuart, *Iowa's Colonels and Regiments: Being a History of Iowa Regiments in the War of the Rebellion, and Containing a Description of the Battles in Which They Have Fought* (Des Moines: Mills and Co., 1865); Petersen, *Story of Iowa*, vol. 1, 454–70, 482–85; Wubben, *Civil War Iowa*, 226. The pro-Lecompton Constitution Democrat was William Merritt of the 1st Iowa Infantry.

14. Stuart, *Iowa's Colonels and Regiments*. Keokuk's William Worthington of the 5th Iowa Infantry supported John Bell for president in 1860. Former Liberty Party member Hugh Reid headed the 15th Iowa Infantry Regiment. Major W. W. Belknap was a Douglas Democrat.

15. Briggs, "Enlistment of Iowa Troops," 323–92; Swisher, *Iowa in Times of War*, 154–61; *Eighth Census of the United States, 1860*, vol. 1, 36–37, 134–35.

16. For a good summary of the historiography on enlistment motivation, see Kenneth N. Noe, *Reluctant Rebels: The Confederates Who Joined the Army after 1861* (Chapel Hill: University of North Carolina Press, 2010), 3–12.

17. Russell L. Johnson, *Warriors into Workers: The Civil War and the Formation of Urban Industrial Society in a Northern City* (New York: Fordham University Press, 2003), 77.

18. Historians who have examined Civil War motivation tend to focus their research on Confederate enlistment rather than Union enlistment. Because the dynamics of enlistment differed between South and North, the body of research to date is of limited value to the study of Iowa. One other difficulty is the lack of attention devoted to nonvolunteers. Understanding the motives of Iowans who declined to volunteer would help us understand the motivations of those who did enlist.

19. Ellis, "Letters of an Iowa Family," 564 (quote).

20. For the best discussion of Wittenmyer's war activities, see Elizabeth D. Leonard, *Yankee Women: Gender Battles in the Civil War* (New York: W. W. Norton, 1994), 50–103. Although Leonard reiterates the legend of

Wittenmyer's purported widowhood, her feminist historical analysis is otherwise keen.

21. Information on William Wittenmyer's life comes from a variety of sources, including the Lee County Recorder's Office (especially Deeds Book 42, 398–99); 1870 Federal Population Census Manuscript, Lake View, Cook County, Illinois, 21; *Porter County [Indiana] Vidette*, January 23, 1879, 3; and Appanoose County Probate Records, File #1087 (Drake Library, Centerville, Iowa).

22. Jerry Rosholt, *Ole Goes to War: Men from Norway Who Fought in America's Civil War* (Decorah, Iowa: Vesterheim Museum, 2003), 15, 20, 36.

23. Piston and Hatcher, *Wilson's Creek,* 51 (quote).

24. Stuart, *Iowa's Colonels and Regiments.*

25. Kirkwood quoted in Shambaugh, ed., *Messages and Proclamations,* 282–83.

26. Ellis, "Letters of an Iowa Family," 565 (quote).

Chapter Four

1. Lyon quoted in Colton, "Letters of Samuel Ryan Curtis," 56.

2. Piston and Hatcher, *Wilson's Creek,* 171.

3. Piston and Hatcher, *Wilson's Creek.*

4. Paddy Griffith, *Battle Tactics of the Civil War* (New Haven: Yale University Press, 1989), 27; Joseph Allan Frank and George A. Reaves, *"Seeing the Elephant": Raw Recruits at the Battle of Shiloh* (Urbana: University of Illinois Press, 2003), 28; Drew Gilpin Faust, *The Republic of Suffering: Death and the American Civil War* (New York: Vintage Books, 2008), 41 (quote).

5. Piston and Hatcher, *Wilson's Creek,* 47–59, 72–73, 118–20, 125–27.

6. Ellis, "Letters of an Iowa Family," 573 (quote).

7. Max H. Guyer, "The Journal and Letters of Corporal William O. Gulick," *Iowa Journal of History and Politics* 28 (1930): 418–20.

8. Mildred Throne, ed., "A History of Company D, Eleventh Iowa Infantry, 1861–1865," *Iowa Journal of History* 55 (1957): 40; C. Stephen Badgley, ed., *Downing's Civil War Diary* (1916; reedited and reprinted, Badgley Publishing Co., 2010), 47, 60, 91, 109, 127, 139, 229; Hubbart, ed., *The Civil War Letters of Union Private Daniel J. Parvin.*

9. Throne, ed., "Letters of Abner Dunham," 304.

10. Kenneth E. Colton, ed., "With Fremont in Missouri in 1861: Letters of Samuel Ryan Curtis," *Annals of Iowa* 23 (1942): 104–67; 166 (quote).

11. Colton, "With Fremont in Missouri," 166 (quote).

12. Dennis K. Boman, *Lincoln and Citizens' Rights in Civil War Missouri: Balancing Freedom and Security* (Baton Rouge: Louisiana State University Press, 2011), 19–62.

13. Captain Samuel Burdett quoted in Guyer, "Journal and Letters of William O. Gulick," 198 (quote).

14. Guyer, "Journal and Letters of William O. Gulick," 402, 404, 451 (quotes).

15. Guyer, "Journal and Letters of William O. Gulick," 454, 453 (quotes).

16. Guyer, "Journal and Letters of William O. Gulick," 426, 444 (quotes).

17. Guyer, "Journal and Letters of William O. Gulick," 444 (quote), 451.

18. Guyer, "Journal and Letters of William O. Gulick," 428, 446 (quotes).

19. Guyer, "Journal and Letters of William O. Gulick," 425 (quote), 455.

20. Guyer, "Journal and Letters of William O. Gulick," 449, 453–54 (quotes; emphasis in original).

21. Nathaniel Cheairs Hughes, Jr., *The Battle of Belmont: Grant Strikes South* (Chapel Hill: University of North Carolina Press, 1991). Lee County casualties at Belmont were calculated from *Roster and Record of Iowa Soldiers in the War of the Rebellion: Together with Historical Sketches of Volunteer Organizations, 1861–1866*, vol. 1 (Des Moines: E. H. English, 1908–11).

22. Throne, ed., "Letters of Abner Dunham," 305 (quote); Mildred Throne, "Iowans and the Civil War," *Palimpsest* 2 (1969): 69–73.

23. Ellis, "Letters of an Iowa Family," 563–67; 565 (quote).

24. Guyer, "Journal and Letters of William O. Gulick," 221 (quote).

25. *Roster and Record*, vol 1.

26. Ruth A. Gallaher, "Annie Turner Wittenmyer," *Iowa Journal of History and Politics* 29 (1931): 523–27.

27. Mildred Throne, ed., "Diary of W. H. Turner, M.D., 1863," *Iowa Journal of History* 48 (1950): 267–82; letters from Will Turner to Annie Wittenmyer, Wittenmyer War Collection (Iowa State Historical Society, Des Moines).

28. Bloomer quoted in Noah Zaring, "Competition in Benevolence: Civil War Soldiers' Aid in Iowa," *Iowa Heritage Illustrated* 1 (1996): 23.

29. Gallaher, "Annie Turner Wittenmyer," 524–25; 525 (quote).

30. Wittenmyer quoted in Zaring, "Competition in Benevolence," 21.

31. Earl Fullbrook, "Relief Work in Iowa during the Civil War," *Iowa Journal of History and Politics* 16 (1918): 198–211.

32. William L. Shea and Earl J. Hess, *Pea Ridge: Civil War Campaign in the West* (Chapel Hill: University of North Carolina Press, 1992), 1–26.

33. Shea and Hess, *Pea Ridge*, 1–26; Louis E. Gerteis, *The Civil War in Missouri: A Military History* (Columbia: University of Missouri Press, 2012), 139–41.

Chapter Five

1. In this paragraph and those that follow, I have relied primarily upon James J. Hamilton, *The Battle of Fort Donelson* (South Brunswick, N.J.: Yoseloff, 1968); Benjamin F. Cooling, *Forts Henry and Donelson: The Key to the Confederate Heartland* (Knoxville: University of Tennessee Press, 1987); Jack Hurst, *Men of Fire: Grant, Forrest, and the Campaign That Decided the Civil War* (New York: Basic Books, 2007); and Steven E. Woodworth, *Nothing But Victory: The Army of the Tennessee, 1861–1865* (New York: Vintage Books, 2005). Additional information from John T. Bell, *Tramps and Triumphs of the Second Iowa Infantry* (Omaha: Gibson, Miller, and Richardson, 1886).

2. Throne, ed., "Letters of Abner Dunham," 309 (quote).

3. Hamilton, *Battle of Fort Donelson*, 263 (quote).

4. Throne, ed., "Letters of Abner Dunham," 309–10 (quote).

5. Woodworth, *Nothing But Victory*, 119; Cooling, *Forts Henry and Donelson*, 2 (quote).

6. Shea and Hess, *Pea Ridge*, xi.

7. Shea and Hess, *Pea Ridge*, 67; Hess, *The Union Soldier in Battle*, 134–37.

8. Shea and Hess, *Pea Ridge*, 20–61.

9. Shea and Hess, *Pea Ridge*, 23, 50, 169 (quote).

10. Hess, *The Union Soldier in Battle*, 136, 135 (quotes). Hess notes that Union soldiers from the working class enjoyed a "phlegmatic insensitivity to danger" on the battlefield that was "partly the result of preconditioning by exposure to rough life of a man of labor before the war" (135).

11. Shea and Hess, *Pea Ridge*, 284–306.

12. In assessing the role of Iowans at Shiloh, I rely primarily on four works: Larry J. Daniel, *Shiloh: The Battle That Changed the Civil War* (New York: Simon and Schuster, 1997); James L. McDonough, *Shiloh—In Hell before Midnight* (Knoxville: University of Tennessee Press, 1977); Wiley Sword, *Shiloh: Bloody April* (New York: William Morrow, 1974); and O. Edward Cunningham, *Shiloh and the Western Campaign of 1862* (New York: Savas Beatie, 2007). For the order of battle by regiment, I rely primarily on Robert U. Johnson and Clarence C. Buel, *Battles and Leaders of the Civil War*, vol. 1 (New York: Yoseloff, 1956), 537–39.

13. Several historians correctly point out that the "Hornet's Nest" defenders did not inflict the bulk of Confederate casualties on day one. Iowans who survived the "Hornet's Nest" created a mythology after the war that exaggerated the proportion of fallen Rebels who died on this portion of the battlefield. Timothy B. Smith, *The Untold Story of Shiloh: The Battle and the Battlefield* (Knoxville: University of Tennessee Press, 2006).

14. Tuttle quoted in Woodworth, *Nothing But Victory*, 179 (quote).

15. Calculating the number of soldiers in action at any one time is particularly difficult for Shiloh. I rely primarily on the numerical analysis of Mildred Throne, "Iowa at the Battle of Shiloh," *Iowa Journal of History* 55 (1957): 211.

16. Ellis, "Letters of an Iowa Family," 568 and 569 (quotes).

17. Sword, *Shiloh: Bloody April*, 352–56.

18. Throne, "Iowa at the Battle of Shiloh," 245; Daniel, *Shiloh*, 214, 305, 322.

19. Gallaher, "Annie Turner Wittenmyer," 541–42.

20. Lisa Guinn, "Annie Wittenmyer and Nineteenth-century Women's Usefulness," *Annals of Iowa* 74 (Fall 2015): 351–77; 352 (quote).

21. R. J. Bickel, "The Estes House," *Annals of Iowa* 40 (1970): 433–35.

22. Guinn, "Nineteenth-century Women's Usefulness," 361 (Lucinda Corkhill quote).

23. Giesberg, *Civil War Sisterhood*, 80–83. See also Jeanie Attie, *Patriotic*

Toil: Northern Women and the American Civil War (Ithaca: Cornell University Press, 1998).

24. Will Turner to Annie Wittenmyer, June 18, 1862, Wittenmyer War Collection.

25. Mildred Throne, ed., "A Commissary in the Union Army: Letters of C. C. Carpenter," *Iowa Journal of History* 53 (1955): 66, 60–61 (Carpenter quotes).

26. Mildred Throne, ed., "Iowans in Southern Prisons," *Iowa Journal of History* 54 (1956): 67–88; Ted Genoways and Hugh H. Genoways, *Perfect Picture of Hell: Eyewitness Accounts by Civil War Prisoners from the 12th Iowa* (Iowa City: University of Iowa Press, 2001).

Chapter Six

1. Throne, ed., "Letters of C. C. Carpenter," 65 (quote).

2. Geoffrey C. Ward, *The Civil War* (New York: Knopf, 1991), 166.

3. Fairall, *Manual of Iowa Politics*, 58 (quote).

4. Charles F. Larimer, ed., *Love and Valor: Intimate Civil War Letters between Captain Jacob and Emeline Ritner* (Western Spring, Ill.: Sigourney Press, 2000), 35–36 (quote).

5. Iowa Secretary of State, Elections Returns, 1839–90; Wubben, *Civil War Iowa*, 49–50, 57.

6. Wubben, *Civil War Iowa*, 33–34, 57–61.

7. Wubben, *Civil War Iowa*, 33–34, 57–61.

8. Leola Nelson Bergmann, "The Negro in Iowa," *Iowa Journal of History* 46 (1948): 3–90; Wubben, *Civil War Iowa*, 51–92.

9. Fairall, *Manual of Iowa Politics*, 68.

10. Edward Younger, *John A. Kasson* (Iowa City: State Historical Society of Iowa, 1955), 135–38.

11. *Oskaloosa Weekly Times*, August 28, 1862.

12. Wubben, *Civil War Iowa*, 60, 66–69, 86–87. Ironically, it was Federal marshal H. M. Hoxie, the former Republican state party chair, who kidnapped Mahony, the former Democratic state party chair, and sent him swiftly off to prison in Washington, D.C.

13. *Oskaloosa Weekly Times*, September 18, 1862. The last lines of one poem read:

The first abolitionist then, was Satan,
  who crawled up from Hell;
The last is still seen among men,
And goes by the Name of Grinnell!

14. Wubben, *Civil War Iowa*, 66–69, 80.

15. Paul S. Pierce, "Congressional Districting in Iowa," *Iowa Journal of History and Politics* 1 (1903): 342.

16. Larimer, *Love and Valor*, 157.

17. Unnamed Iowa cavalry officer quoted in William L. Shea, *Fields of Blood: The Prairie Grove Campaign* (Chapel Hill: University of North Carolina Press, 2009), 26.

18. Wubben, *Civil War Iowa*, 83–84, 86–87; Younger, *John A. Kasson*, 137.

19. Younger, *John A. Kasson*, 136.

20. Shambaugh, ed., *Messages and Proclamations*, 304–5.

21. Fairall, *Manual of Iowa Politics*, 64 (quote) (provision 10).

22. Cook, *Baptism of Fire*, 142. Hawkeye Methodists in the Northern conference had already issued such a declaration.

23. Evidence from the congressional campaigns of Grinnell, Kasson, and Allison indicates that none of the three candidates publicly supported the proposal to transport freed slaves to Central America following the Emancipation Proclamation. Younger, *John A. Kasson*, 135–38.

24. Salter, *James W. Grimes*, 218 (quote).

25. Frank L. Klement, *The Copperheads in the Middle West* (Chicago: University of Chicago Press, 1960), 37.

26. Wubben, *Civil War Iowa*, 83; Ellis, "Letters of an Iowa Family," 582, 571 (quotes).

27. Mildred Throne, ed., *The Civil War Diary of Cyrus F. Boyd, Fifteenth Iowa Infantry, 1861–1863* (Millwood, N.Y.: Kraus Reprint Co., 1977), 63 (quote).

28. Iowa Secretary of State, Elections Returns, 1839–90.

29. Mahaska County Auditor, Mahaska County Election Book #2, 105.

30. Iowa Secretary of State, Elections Returns, 1839–90; Wubben, *Civil War Iowa*, 86, 211–13.

31. David Brodnax, Sr., "'Will They Fight? Ask the Enemy': Iowa's African American Regiment in the Civil War," *Annals of Iowa* 66 (2007): 266–92; 269 (quote).

32. Carpenter quoted in Wubben, *Civil War Iowa*, 141.

33. Throne, ed., *Diary of Cyrus F. Boyd*, 123 (quotes), 118–19.

34. Fairall, *Manual of Iowa Politics*, 66–67, 67 (quote); Wubben, *Civil War Iowa*, 142.

35. Wubben, *Civil War Iowa*, 93–94.

36. Wubben, *Civil War Iowa*, 125–29; *History of Davis County, Iowa* (Des Moines: State Historical Co., 1882), 555 (quote).

37. Glenn L. Carle, "The First Kansas Colored," *American Heritage* (1992): 79–91. See also Nicole Etcheson, *Bleeding Kansas: Contested Liberty in the Civil War Era* (Lawrence: University Press of Kansas, 2004), 219–45; Mark A. Lause, *Race and Radicalism in the Union Army* (Urbana: University of Illinois Press, 2009); Albert Castel, *A Frontier State at War: Kansas, 1861–1865* (Ithaca: Cornell University Press, 1958), 86–101.

Chapter Seven

1. Shambaugh, ed., *Messages and Proclamations*, 497–505; Briggs, "Enlistment of Iowa Troops," 350–54; W. W. Gist, "The Ages of the Soldiers in the Civil War," *Iowa Journal of History and Politics* 16 (1918): 387–99.

2. Shambaugh, ed., *Messages and Proclamations*, 497–98 (quote).

3. Shambaugh, ed., *Messages and Proclamations*, 497–98 (quote).

4. Shambaugh, ed., *Messages and Proclamations*, 497–505; Briggs, "Enlistment of Iowa Troops," 353–61.

5. J. L. Anderson, "The Vacant Chair on the Farm: Soldier Husbands, Farm Wives, and the Iowa Home Front, 1861–1865," *Annals of Iowa* 66 (2007), 241–65, 265 (quote); Elder, *Love amid the Turmoil*, 85 (quote); Ellis, "Letters of an Iowa Family," 576 (quote).

6. George Mills, ed., "The Sharp Family Civil War Letters," *Annals of Iowa* 34 (1959): 481–532; 494–95 (quotes).

7. Mills, "The Sharp Family Civil War Letters," 502, 503 (quotes).

8. Mathilde Hoffbauer to Julie Junkermann, October 8, 1862, *Letters from Mathilde* (privately published, no date, copy in possession of Kristine Meyer Conlon, Muscatine).

9. Ellis, "Letters of an Iowa Family," 573 (quote).

10. Popchock, *Soldier Boy*, 12, 13 (quotes).

11. Wubben, *Civil War Iowa*, 62; Briggs, "Enlistment of Iowa Troops," 382–84.

12. Briggs, "Enlistment of Iowa Troops," 357–58; Shambaugh, ed., *Messages and Proclamations*, 504–7.

13. Briggs, "Enlistment of Iowa Troops," 355–59; 355 (quote).

14. Wubben, *Civil War Iowa*, 62; Johnson, *Warriors into Workers*, 124.

15. *Roster and Record*, vols. 3–6.

16. Boman, *Balancing Freedom and Security*, 115–70; Geiger, *Financial Fraud and Guerrilla Violence*, 100–14; Joseph A. Mudd, *With Porter in North Missouri: A Chapter in the History of the War between the States* (Washington, D.C: National Publishing Co., 1909; reprinted 1992 by Press of the Camp Pope Bookstore, Iowa City).

17. Shea, *Prairie Grove Campaign*, 34–47; Mudd, *With Porter in North Missouri*.

18. Shea, *Prairie Grove Campaign*, 289–91.

19. Shea, *Prairie Grove Campaign*, 174–81; 134, 128 (quotes).

20. Larry Wood, *Civil War Springfield* (Charleston: History Press, 2011), 105–17.

21. *Roster and Record*, vol. 2; Ellis, "Letters of an Iowa Family," 562.

22. Peter Cozzens, *The Darkest Days of the War: The Battles of Iuka and Corinth* (Chapel Hill: University of North Carolina Press, 2006), 135–48.

23. Cozzens, *Darkest Days of the War*, 187; Albert Castel, *Decision in the West: The Atlanta Campaign of 1864* (Lawrence: University of Kansas Press, 1992), 400; Gary Ecelbarger, *The Day Dixie Died: The Battle of Atlanta* (New York: St. Martin's Press, 2010), 105.

24. Cozzens, *Darkest Days of the War*, 221–70; Bell, *Tramps and Triumphs*, 24.

25. Cozzens, *Darkest Days of the War*, 269. See also Albert Castel, *General Sterling Price and the Civil War in the West* (Baton Rouge: Louisiana State University Press, 1968), 108–27; David Nevin, *War on the Mississippi: Grant's Vicksburg Campaign* (Alexandria, Va.: Time-Life Books, 1985), 38–44; Johnson and Buel, *Battles and Leaders*, 737–60.

26. Cozzens, *Darkest Days of the War*, 32–33, 135–48; xii (quote).

27. Steve Meyer, *Iowa Valor: A Compilation of Civil War Combat Experiences from Soldiers of the State Distinguished as Most Patriotic of the Patriotic* (Garrison, Iowa: Meyer Publishing, 1994), 125–26; Throne, "Iowans and the Civil War," 98–102.

28. For a good description of the fight for Arkansas Post, see Mark K. Christ, *Civil War in Arkansas, 1863: The Battle for a State* (Norman: University of Oklahoma Press, 2010), 39–87.

29. Elder, *Love amid the Turmoil,* 85–86 (quote).

Chapter Eight

1. Annie Wittenmyer, *Under the Guns: A Woman's Reminiscences of the Civil War* (Boston: E. B. Stillings and Co., 1895), 106–14.

2. Giesberg, *Civil War Sisterhood*, 85–112.

3. Louis S. Gerteis, *Civil War St. Louis* (Lawrence: University of Kansas Press, 2001), 202–35.

4. Reverend A. J. Kynett quoted in Zaring, "Competition in Benevolence," 18.

5. Leonard, *Yankee Women*, 81 (quote).

6. Wittenmyer War Collection.

7. George A. Remley to James Remley, June 23, 1863, quoted in Julie Holcomb, ed., *Southern Sons, Northern Soldiers: The Civil War Letters of the Remley Brothers, 22nd Iowa Infantry* (Dekalb: University of Northern Illinois Press, 2004), 76.

8. The order of battle is derived from James R. Arnold, *Grant Wins the War: Decision at Vicksburg* (New York: John Wiley and Sons, 1997), 319–25.

9. Timothy B. Smith, *Champion Hill: The Decision Battle for Vicksburg* (New York: Savas Beatie, 2006), 266–85, 302–27; Arnold, *Grant Wins the War*, 170–99; Edwin C. Bearss, *The Vicksburg Campaign*, vol. 2 (Dayton: Morningside Press, 1985), 603–22.

10. George Crooke, *The Twenty-First Regiment of Iowa Infantry Volunteers* (Milwaukee: King, Fowle and Co., 1891), 73 (quote).

11. Crooke, *Twenty-First Regiment*, 110–14, 210–15; Bearss, *The Vicksburg Campaign*, vol. 3, 863–64.

12. Throne, ed., "Letters of Abner Dunham," 311–20.

13. Throne, ed., "Letters of Abner Dunham," 319 (quote).

14. Larimer, *Love and Valor*, 198–99 (quote).

15. Christ, *Civil War in Arkansas, 1863*, 88–115.

16. Christ, *Civil War in Arkansas, 1863*, 116–44.

17. A. F. Sperry, *History of the 33d Iowa Infantry Volunteer Regiment 1863–6* (Fayetteville: University of Arkansas Press, 1866; reprinted 1999, edited by Gregory J. W. Urwin and Cathy Kunzinger Urwin), 35–41, 38 (quote).

18. Popchock, *Soldier Boy*, 66 (quote).

19. Christ, *Civil War in Arkansas, 1863*, 116–44; Sperry, *History of the 33d Iowa*, 38; Johnson and Buel, *Battles and Leaders*, vol. 3, 460–61.

20. Popchock, *Soldier Boy*, 27, 28 (quotes).

21. Popchock, *Soldier Boy*, 25 (quote).

22. Popchock, *Soldier Boy*, 39, 58 (quotes).

23. Popchock, *Soldier Boy*, 65, 67 (quotes).

24. Popchock, *Soldier Boy*, 66, 65 (quotes).

25. Popchock, *Soldier Boy*, 54, 84 (quotes).

26. Popchock, *Soldier Boy*, 56, 57, 58 (quotes).

27. Throne, ed., "Letters of Abner Dunham," 314 (quote).

28. Carpenter quoted in Wubben, *Civil War Iowa*, 141; Elder, *Love amid the Turmoil*, 57; Throne, ed., *Diary of Cyrus F. Boyd*, 121 (quote).

29. Ellis, "Letters of an Iowa Family," 582 (quote).

30. Brodnax, "Iowa's African American Regiment in the Civil War," 266–92; Leslie A. Schwalm, *Emancipation's Diaspora: Race and Reconstruction in the Upper Midwest* (Chapel Hill: University of North Carolina Press, 2009), 111–23.

31. *Muscatine Daily Journal*, November 20, 1863, 2 (quote); *Muscatine Daily Journal*, November 26, 1863, 3 (quote).

32. *Roster and Record*, vol. 5, 1047–56; Popchock, *Soldier Boy*, 81–82.

33. Christ, *Civil War in Arkansas, 1863*, 145–96.

34. Sperry, *History of the 33d Iowa*, 55–60; Popchock, *Soldier Boy*, 82, 85; Elder, *Love amid the Turmoil*, 225, 238, 242, 249.

35. Christ, *Civil War in Arkansas, 1863*, 14, 103–4; Elder, *Love amid the Turmoil*, 240, 251.

36. Christ, *Civil War in Arkansas, 1863*, 158–59, 195, 249; Popchock, *Soldier Boy*, 56, 59, 85.

37. Urwin and Urwin quoted in Sperry, *History of the 33d Iowa*, xxix.

38. *Muscatine Daily Journal*, October 8, 1863, 3 (quotes).

39. *Proceedings of the Loyal Women's Convention, Held in Muscatine* (Muscatine, 1863), 6 (quote).

40. Fullbrook, "Relief Work," 218–26; *Muscatine Daily Journal*, November 21, 1863, 2 (quote).

41. Zaring, "Competition in Benevolence," 19; *Muscatine Daily Journal*, November 21, 1863; *Muscatine Daily Journal*, November 24, 1863, 2 (quote).

42. *Muscatine Daily Journal*, November 24, 1863, 2 (quotes).

43. Fullbrook, "Relief Work," 218–26; Zaring, "Competition in Benevolence," 20.

44. Fullbrook, "Relief Work," 227–35.

45. Popchock, *Soldier Boy*, 92 (quote).

46. Fairall, *Manual of Iowa Politics*, 67.

47. Wubben, *Civil War Iowa*, 141–45; 145 (quote).

Chapter Nine

1. Benton McAdams, *Rebels at Rock Island: The Story of the Civil War Prison* (DeKalb: Northern Illinois University Press, 2000).

2. Throne, ed., "A Commissary in the Union Army," 74 (quote).

3. Lieutenant Elias V. Miller, 13th Iowa Infantry, quoted in Meyer, *Iowa Valor*, 331.

4. Hood quoted in Meyer, *Iowa Valor*, 366.

5. Throne, ed., "Letters of Abner Dunham," 314 (quote).

6. Michael J. Forsyth, *The Red River Campaign of 1864 and the Loss by the Confederacy of the Civil War* (Jefferson, N.C.: McFarland and Co., 2002), 124–25; Edwin C. Bearss, *Steele's Retreat from Camden and the Battle of Jenkins' Ferry* (Little Rock, Ark.: Pioneer Press, 1990).

7. Popchock, *Soldier Boy*, 124 and 125 (quotes).

8. William L. Nicholson, "The Engagement at Jenkins' Ferry," *Annals of Iowa* 11 (1914): 510 (quote).

9. Nicholson, "Jenkins' Ferry," 511 (quote).

10. Popchock, *Soldier Boy*, 125 (quote).

11. Popchock, *Soldier Boy*, 125 (quote).

12. Forsyth, *The Red River Campaign*, 185 (quote).

13. Throne, ed., "Letters of Abner Dunham," 320 (quote); Badgley, ed., *Downing's Civil War Diary*, 163–64.

14. Johnson, *Warriors into Workers*, 88, 95.

15. Matthew Warshauer, *Connecticut in the American Civil War: Slavery, Sacrifice, and Survival* (Middletown, Conn.: Wesleyan University Press, 2011), 131; Donald Allendorf, *Long Road to Liberty: The Odyssey of a German Regiment in the Yankee Army: The 15th Missouri Volunteer Infantry* (Kent, Ohio: Kent State University Press, 2006), 238–39.

16. Nicole Etcheson, *A Generation at War: The Civil War Era in a Northern Community* (Lawrence: University of Kansas Press, 2011), 110–12; Robert M. Sandow, *Deserter Country: Civil War Opposition in the Pennsylvania Appalachians* (New York: Fordham University Press, 2009), 109–10. In one county in Indiana, mobs of armed farmers in several townships confronted the enrollment officers in their homes and seized the coveted enlistment books. In the poor hill country of north-central Pennsylvania, farmers opposed to the draft threatened to kill the enrollment officers as they made their rounds. With no one willing to step up and assume the duties of enrollment officer, Pennsylvania administrators gave up trying to canvass four townships in one antidraft county.

17. Michael J. Pfeifer, "Law, Society, and Violence in the Antebellum Midwest: The 1857 Eastern Iowa Vigilante Movement," *Annals of Iowa* 64, no. 2 (2005): 139–66.

18. Wubben, *Civil War Iowa*, 162; Mahaska County Militia Register, 1864; Gue, *History of Iowa*, vol. 2, 115; *Roster and Record*, vols. 2 and 5.

19. Johnson, *Warriors to Workers*, 59 (quote); Wubben, *Civil War Iowa*, 159–61.

20. Doris Kearns Goodwin, *Team of Rivals: The Political Genius of Abraham Lincoln* (New York: Simon and Schuster, 2005), 627–66.

21. Badgley, ed., *Downing's Civil War Diary*, 192 (quote).

22. Badgley, ed., *Downing's Civil War Diary*, 193 (quote).

23. Throne, ed., "A Commissary in the Union Army," 81–82 (quotes).

24. Throne, ed., "A Commissary in the Union Army," 84–85 (quotes).

25. Woodworth, *Nothing But Victory*, 559 and 568 (quotes).

26. Castel, *Decision in the West*, 387 (quote).

27. For the best detailed account of the day's battle, see Ecelbarger, *The Day Dixie Died*.

28. Woodworth, *Nothing But Victory*, 492–568; Henry Ankeny is the Iowa soldier quoted (517).

29. Ecelbarger, *The Day Dixie Died*, 70–84; Rice quoted in Meyer, *Iowa Valor*, 326.

30. Castel, *Decision in the West*, 400 (quote).

31. Ecelbarger, *The Day Dixie Died*, 119–26.

32. Ecelbarger, *The Day Dixie Died*, 119–28, 133–47; Woodworth, *Nothing But Victory*, 551–57.

33. Woodworth, *Nothing But Victory*, 559 and 568 (quotes).

34. Ecelbarger, *The Day Dixie Died*, 191–207.

35. Ecelbarger, *The Day Dixie Died*, 148–90.

36. Woodworth, *Nothing But Victory*, 557–59; Edward S. Cooper, *William Worth Belknap: An American Disgrace* (Cranbury, N.J.: Associated University Presses, 2003), 95.

37. Ecelbarger, *The Day Dixie Died*, 215 (quote), 223 (Strong quote).

38. Mildred Throne, ed., "An Iowa Doctor in Blue: The Letters of Seneca B. Thrall, 1862–64," *Iowa Journal of History* 58 (1960): 179 and 180 (quotes).

39. Throne, ed., "An Iowa Doctor in Blue," 180 (quote).

40. Throne, ed., "An Iowa Doctor in Blue," 180–81 (quote).

41. Carpenter quoted in Meyer, *Iowa Valor*, 317.

42. Noah Andre Trudeau, *Southern Storm: Sherman's March to the Sea* (New York: Harper Collins, 2008), 358–66.

43. Meyer, *Iowa Valor*, 424.

44. Larimer, *Love and Valor*, 391 (quote).

45. Larimer, *Love and Valor*, 415 (quote).

Chapter Ten

1. Wubben, *Civil War Iowa*, 145–74.

2. Cook, *Baptism of Fire*, 150–55.

3. Popchock, *Soldier Boy*, 148 and 150 (quotes).

4. Gue, *History of Iowa*, vol. 2, 112–13; 112 (quote).

5. Wubben, *Civil War Iowa*, 162–63; Gue, *History of Iowa*, vol. 2, 113 (quote).

6. Gue, *History of Iowa*, vol. 2, 112–13 (quote).

7. Wubben, *Civil War Iowa*, 162–63; Gue, *History of Iowa*, vol. 2, 112–13 (quote). In response to reports accusing two militia captains of disloyalty, Adjutant General Baker refused to grant their commissions. One decommissioned militia captain had apparently been dismissed from the regular army "for the utterance of treasonable sentiments," while the other had allegedly engaged in guerrilla activity in Missouri. Gue, *History of Iowa*, vol. 2, 113 (Baker quote).

8. Cook, *Baptism of Fire*, 151; Wubben, *Civil War Iowa*, 145–69.

9. Mahaska County Election Record No. 2, 147.

10. Wubben, *Civil War Iowa*, 174; George A. Remley (the 22nd Infantry soldier) quoted in Holcomb, ed., *Southern Sons, Northern Soldiers*, 160 (emphasis in original).

11. Cook, *Baptism of Fire*, 150–53; Dykstra, *Bright Radical Star*, 204; Goodwin, *Team of Rivals*, 487.

12. *Proceedings of the Loyal Women's Convention.*

13. Popchock, *Soldier Boy*, 127 (Musser quote); Blain quoted in Mark K. Christ, ed., *"All Cut to Pieces and Gone to Hell": The Civil War, Race Relations, and the Battle of Poison Springs* (Little Rock, Ark.: August House Publishers, 2003), 133.

14. Brodnax, "Iowa's African American Regiment in the Civil War," 281.

15. Captain S. S. Farwell quoted in Meyer, *Iowa Valor*, 432.

16. Lieutenant King quoted in Woodworth, *Nothing But Victory*, 624.

17. Captain Ritner quoted in Larimer, *Love and Valor*, 430; Lieutenant King quoted in Woodworth, *Nothing But Victory*, 614.

18. Woodworth, *Nothing But Victory*, 610 (quote).

19. Woodworth, *Nothing But Victory*, 607–31; 627 (quote).

20. Woodworth, *Nothing But Victory*, 616–18; Meyer, *Iowa Valor*, 424–37; Lee Miller, *Crocker's Brigade* (published privately, 2009), 387–88.

21. Corse report quoted in Meyer, *Iowa Valor*, 436.

22. Larimer, *Love and Valor*, 430 (quote).

23. Larimer, *Love and Valor*, 429 (quote).

24. Throne, ed., "A Commissary in the Union Army," 88 (quote).

25. Wubben, *Civil War Iowa*, 198–99; Peter Melendy quoted in Kenneth L. Lyftogt, *From Blue Mills to Columbia: Cedar Falls in the Civil War* (Iowa

City: University of Iowa Press, 1993), 158. Wubben counted no fewer than twenty-five towns and villages where an ordinary citizen who expressed delight in Lincoln's assassination was physically assaulted for his remarks; *Civil War Iowa*, 199.

26. Cook, *Baptism of Fire*, 159–65, 155 (*Gate City* editor quote); Dykstra, *Bright Radical Star*, 200–6.

27. Cook, *Baptism of Fire*, 159–65; Dykstra, *Bright Radical Star*, 200–6.

28. Cook, *Baptism of Fire*, 162–66; Dykstra, *Bright Radical Star*, 203–14.

29. *Proceedings of the Iowa State Colored Convention* (Muscatine, Iowa: Daily Journal, 1868), 1 (quote); Brodnax, "Breathing the Freedom's Air," 175 (quote).

30. Brodnax, "Breathing the Freedom's Air," 175–77 (quotes).

31. Dykstra, *Bright Radical Star*, 208–15; Fairall, *Manual of Iowa Politics*, 72; Wubben, *Civil War Iowa*, 200–5; Mahaska County Election Book No. 2, 165.

32. Cook, *Baptism of Fire*, 177–78, 188.

33. Throne, *Cyrus Clay Carpenter*, 81–86; 86 (quote).

34. Cook, *Baptism of Fire*, 168–73; Dykstra, *Bright Radical Star*, 223.

35. *Proceedings of the Iowa State Colored Convention*, 11, 12 (quotes).

36. Wubben, *Civil War Iowa*, 200–2; *Oskaloosa Herald*, November 5, 1868, 2 (quote).

37. Robert R. Dykstra, "Iowa: 'Bright Radical Star,'" in James C. Mohr, ed., *Radical Republicans in the North: State Politics during Reconstruction* (Baltimore: Johns Hopkins University Press, 1976), 167–93; Wubben, *Civil War Iowa*, 200–2; Robert R. Dykstra and Harlan Hahn, "Northern Voters and Negro Suffrage: The Case of Iowa, 1868," *Public Opinion Quarterly* 32 (1968): 205, 208. After examining election returns in 437 Iowa townships, Dykstra and Hahn calculated the margin of difference at 10 percent or less in 84 percent of the districts.

Epilogue

1. *1900 U.S. Census*, vol. 5: *Agriculture, Part I*, clxi, 692, 699, 703–11; vol. 6: *Agriculture, Part II*, 162–63.

2. Brian Edward Donovan, "'Like Monkeys at the Zoo': Politics and

the Performance of Disability at the Iowa Soldiers' Home, 1887–1910," *Annals of Iowa* 71 (Fall 2012): 338 (quote).

3. Donovan, "'Like Monkeys at the Zoo,'" 323–46.

4. *1883 History of Pottawattamie County*, 116; Popchock, *Soldier Boy*, 4–7.

5. *1883 History of Pottawattamie County*, 116; Popchock, *Soldier Boy*, 4–7.

6. 1880 U.S. Census Manuscript, St. Louis County, Missouri; 1900 U.S. Census Manuscript, St. Louis County, Missouri.

7. *History of Delaware County, Iowa* (Chicago: Western Historical Co., 1878), 418, 425, 574; *Biographical Souvenir of the Counties of Delaware and Buchanan County, Iowa* (Chicago: F. A. Battey and Co., 1890), 684–86; *History of Delaware County, Iowa, and Its People*, vol. 2 (Chicago: S. J. Clarke Publishing Co., 1914), 145–46.

8. *1890 Biographical Souvenir*, 684–86; *1914 Delaware County History*, vol. 2, 145–46; Timothy B. Smith, "The Politics of Battlefield Preservation: David B. Henderson and the National Military Parks," *Annals of Iowa* 66 (2007): 293–320.

9. Wittenmyer's quote is etched in stone on the campus of the University of Northern Iowa.

10. Glenda Riley, "Annie Turner Wittenmyer, Reformer," *Iowa Woman* (September 1986): 26–33.

11. Gallaher, "Annie Turner Wittenmyer," 562–63; Raymond E. Garrison, *Goodbye, My Keokuk Lady* (Hamilton, Ill.: Hamilton Press, 1962), 162.

12. Donovan, "'Like Monkeys at the Zoo,'" 323 (quote); William C. Lowe, "'A Grand and Patriotic Pilgrimage': The Iowa Civil War Monuments Dedication Tour of 1906," *Annals of Iowa* 69 (2010): 41.

13. Gallaher, "Annie Turner Wittenmyer," 561–62 (quote).

14. For a good summary of the historiography, see Tony Klein, "Memorializing Soldiers or Celebrating Westward Expansion: Civil War Commemoration in Sioux City and Keokuk, 1868–1938," *Annals of Iowa* 71 (2012): 291–322; Lowe, "'A Grand and Patriotic Pilgrimage,'" 1–50.

15. Brodnax, "Breathing the Freedom's Air," 223; *Clark v. Board of Directors*, 24 Iowa 266 (1868).

16. *Coger v. North Western Union Packet Company*, 37 Iowa 147–49 (1873).

17. Richard Acton and Patricia Nassif Acton, *To Go Free: A Treasury of Iowa's Legal Heritage* (Ames: Iowa State Press, 1995), 133–34; Petersen, *Story of Iowa*, vol. 2, 1047.

18. Brodnax, "Breathing the Freedom's Air," 255–58.

19. Brodnax, "Breathing the Freedom's Air," 277 (quote).

20. Lowe, "A Grand and Patriotic Pilgrimage," 6–20.

21. Throne, *Cyrus Clay Carpenter*, 104–99.

22. Throne, *Cyrus Clay Carpenter*, 215–29.

23. Brodnax, "Breathing the Freedom's Air," 202–5, 237–42, 279.

24. Bergmann, "The Negro in Iowa"; James W. Loewen, *Sundown Towns: A Hidden Dimension to American Racism* (New York: New Press, 2005); *Des Moines Sunday Register*, January 22, 2006, E1; *Des Moines Sunday Register*, June 16, 2005, 9A.

25. Christopher Waldrep, *Vicksburg's Long Shadow: The Civil War Legacy of Race and Remembrance* (New York: Rowman and Littlefield, 2005), 182–84, 222–23.

26. Waldrep, *Vicksburg's Long Shadow*, 182–84, 222–23; Lowe, "A Grand and Patriotic Pilgrimage," 24.

27. *Des Moines Register*, July 23, 2015; July 7, 2015.